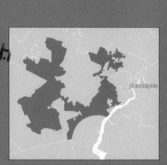

RATF**KED

RATF**KED

THE TRUE STORY BEHIND

THE SECRET PLAN TO STEAL

AMERICA'S DEMOCRACY

DAVID DALEY

LIVERIGHT PUBLISHING CORPORATION

A Division of W. W. Norton & Company

Independent Publishers Since 1923

New York | London

Original Collage of Gerrymandered Districts (top row, from left to right): Pennsylvania (07), Ohio (09), North Carolina (04), North Carolina (01), North Carolina (12), Michigan (14) *(Design Chris Welch)*

For information about permission to reproduce selections from this book,
write to Permissions, Liveright Publishing Corporation,
a division of W. W. Norton & Company, Inc.,
500 Fifth Avenue, New York, NY 10110

For information about special discounts for bulk purchases, please contact
W. W. Norton Special Sales at specialsales@wwnorton.com or 800-233-4830

Manufacturing by Quad Graphics Fairfield
Book design by Chris Welch
Production manager: Louise Mattarelliano

ISBN 978-1-63149-162-7

Liveright Publishing Corporation
500 Fifth Avenue, New York, N.Y. 10110
www.wwnorton.com

W. W. Norton & Company Ltd.
Castle House, 75/76 Wells Street, London W1T 3QT

1 2 3 4 5 6 7 8 9 0

For my dad, Donald H. Daley, whose passions and belief
inspired everything, with endless thanks, admiration, and love

The decayed condition of American democracy is difficult to grasp, not because the facts are secret, but because the facts are visible everywhere.

—William Greider, Who Will Tell the People

CONTENTS

INTRODUCTION

Wearing a resplendent red tie, the color of the Republican Party, Barack Obama delivered his victory speech on November 4, 2008. The nation's first African American first family joined him, celebrating together the historic evening. Watch Obama's Grant Park speech eight years later, and it's not only his youth and the jubilant throngs that make the moment so electrifying. It's that sense of post-partisan possibilities that matched Obama's carefully chosen metaphor. "If there is anyone out there," Obama told the nation, "who still wonders if the dream of our Founders is alive in our time, who still questions the power of our democracy, tonight is your answer."

As it turned out, Obama captured Republican stronghold after stronghold that early November evening. Down South, he picked off North Carolina and Virginia. In the Midwest, he grabbed Indiana. He won the two states where Democratic dreams had died hard in 2000 and 2004—Florida and Ohio—then added Colorado and Nevada for good measure, conjuring liberals' visions of a future western majority. As polls closed late in Oregon, Alaska and Minnesota, and Republican incumbents went down, pundits, professors and politicians marveled at the new Democratic supermajority in the Senate and spoke of emerging—even unbreakable—coalitions. On television and on the front pages of newspapers, they openly questioned how the GOP would survive to the next election.

"The question now becomes what is the future of the Republican party nationally," wondered one political science professor in the *New York Times*. The mood turned grim on *Fox News*, where Bill O'Reilly bemoaned, "Barack Obama is a star. . . . The Republicans have, who? Sarah Palin?" Conservative radio host Laura Ingraham bluntly called the Republican beatdown well deserved. "We've seen a lack of competence at every level of government, frankly, under Republican rule," she opined.

"It's a party adrift. It's a party lost," added longtime Republican communications adviser Torie Clarke on *ABC News*. Over on CNN, Wolf Blitzer and John King peered deeper into the blue map and found suburban Pennsylvania counties, like Bucks, Montgomery and Chester—previously reliable for George W. Bush—now tipping toward Obama by double digits. "If you are the Republicans looking at this map this morning," observed King, "you are very troubled."

One of those concerned conservatives, Rich Lowry, the editor of William F. Buckley's *National Review,* didn't like what he saw either in swing states such as Pennsylvania, Ohio, North Carolina, Wisconsin and Virginia. "It's a bad thing for the Republicans when you drill down into these states," he said. "It's like, where did all the Republicans go? Did they all move to Utah?"

The 2008 election looked like a transformative moment, a wave election that announced an ascendant new movement. Even the brightest conservative thinkers thought it signaled danger for the GOP. And it might have. What no one knew—not even despairing Republicans eyeing *Fox News* through a fuzzy third-cocktail haze—was that the truly transformative election was two years away. It would not be celebrated live around the world from a Grant Park awash in klieg lights, but in VFW halls and Holiday Inn ballrooms and strip-mall party headquarters as hundreds of new Republican state legislators claimed victories— in those very states Lowry feared were lost forever.

This is the story of the audacious Republican plan which not only penned in the Obama presidency but managed, in spite of jubilant 2008 Democratic expectations, to create supermajorities for conservative policies in otherwise blue and purple states. This is the story of the actual redrawing of the American political map and of our democracy itself. It's the story of how Republicans turned a looming demographic disaster into legislative majorities so unbreakable, so impregnable, that none of the outcomes are in doubt until after the 2020 census. It is the story of new mapping technologies so exact that they've re-sorted and resegregated Americans, while creating congressional districts where the only competition comes from someone more extreme.

It's legal, it's breathtaking, and much of it happened in plain sight. The Democratic majority was *ratfucked*.

In politics, a "ratfuck" is a dirty deed done dirt cheap. You can trace the term back as far as Edmund Wilson's *The Twenties*. It was used decades later in *All the President's Men,* the story of how *Washington Post* reporters Bob Woodward and Carl Bernstein uncovered the Watergate scandal and brought about the resignation of Richard Nixon. They quoted Donald Segretti, an operative tied to Nixon's reelection campaign, as using the colorful term to describe political sabotage and the early shenanigans of seamy strategists linked to the burglars who bungled the Watergate break-in. The operatives who quite legally changed the complexion of Congress worked in a far more sophisticated fashion.

This twenty-first-century version begins in 2009, when Chris Jankowski awoke on July 22 at his Richmond home still feeling kicked in the gut by the election results. He sat down with the morning *New York Times,* and buried inside a story about state legislatures and census projections he read something that snapped him back to action. After reading past a downcast first sentence whose truth he knew far too well—"Republicans in search of good news these days have had to rely on bad news for the White House"—Jankowski found this, by *Times* correspondent Adam Nagourney:

> 2010 is not just any election year: it is crucial given that this class
> of governors will be in charge as their states draw Congressional

and state legislative districts as part of the reapportionment process after the next census. And given historical trends in midterm elections and the lopsided majority Democrats enjoy in Congress, the possibility that Republicans could make gains in House races next year could give the party a psychological boost at the halfway point of Mr. Obama's term.

Jankowski immediately recognized the opportunity. As provided in the Constitution, every state redraws all of its district lines every ten years, that is, after the census. That means elections in "zero years" matter more than others. Jankowski realized it would be possible to target states where the legislature is in charge of redistricting, flip as many chambers as possible, take control of the process, and redraw the lines. Boom. Just like that—if Republicans could pull it off—the GOP would go from demographically challenged to the catbird seat for a decade. At least.

As one of the leading tacticians behind the Republican State Leadership Committee, Jankowski has few peers as a strategist, even if Karl Rove and Frank Luntz then vacuumed up all the TV airtime. State government has always been his passion. He had spent years trying to arm-twist GOP strategists and donors to spend more time and money on down-ballot races: state houses, state attorneys general, local judges. Those might not be the sexy elections to invest in—no wealthy player feels like a kingmaker or a Koch brother by writing a check to the Republican running for state representative in Pennsylvania's 130th— but he proved time and again that they often provided the best value. Donations that would be a mere drop in the bucket to a presidential or Senate candidate might make all the difference at the local level. And policy outcomes, he would readily discern, could actually be influenced in state capitals—unlike in gridlocked Washington, DC.

It's hard to believe, but the lightbulb moment that would reshape American politics came almost immediately over a breakfast with the supposedly liberal *New York Times:* Republicans should mount an aggressive campaign to flip state legislatures ahead of post-census redistricting, then press the advantage to both redraw congressional and state legislative lines in their favor and aggressively advance the conservative agenda. Presidents almost always lose seats in a midterm election. Democratic turnout always falls in non-presidential years. Smart money spent on the right races had the potential to make more of a difference than ever.

Republican operatives would use the oldest trick in the book—the gerrymander—but in a brilliant and totally modern way.

"I read it and I thought we could do this," Jankowski told me. "I know those state legislators. I know who's going to be the speaker in Pennsylvania if we get the majority. We should do this. This will make our guys happy. I can go to these guys in the legislature and say, hey, we've been struggling for years to try and help you guys compete. I think we can get millions—and you don't have to do anything other than what you were going to do anyway."

Jankowski was right, and the race was on. In short order, the RSLC would call the plan REDMAP—for Redistricting Majority Project— a name which also described its very elegant goal. These strategists would turn the electoral map bright red. Jankowski took the lead as executive director.

By the time election 2010 heated up, two big things had already changed since the swooning that marked Obama's victorious evening in Grant Park. First, that January, the Supreme Court issued its *Citizens United* verdict, tossing out the ban on independent political expenditures by corporations as an unconstitutional breach of free speech. In a 5-to-4 decision, rendered on January 21, 2010, the court's five conservatives ruled that corporations and unions had a permanent green light to spend essentially as much money as they wished. Super PACs and other tax-exempt nonprofit political groups could now raise and spend unlimited amounts, much of it "dark money" impossible to trace back to the donor.

President Obama found the ruling so antithetical to democracy that he took the rare step of criticizing it, harshly, during his State of the Union speech six days later, which was attended, awkwardly, by six of the nine justices. But *Citizens United* was just the continuation of Obama's political nightmare. A Republican, Scott Brown, improbably captured the late Ted Kennedy's Senate seat, erasing the Democratic supermajority in the Senate. Obama's push for universal health care descended into a debate over "death panels," creating a summer of ugly town hall meetings for Democrats nationwide, and thereby speeding the rise of the Tea Party.

Jankowski didn't see all of this coming that July morning, however. He just saw a way to get his side back into the game. Instantly, his post-election malaise began to fade.

"We were depressed as hell but we weren't going to quit," he confides.

In *All the President's Men,* Woodward and Bernstein investigated several longtime Nixon aides and kept hearing the term "ratfucking" used to describe sabotage by operatives in Nixon's inner circle, going all the way back to their days as students and young Republicans at the University of Southern California. As Woodward and Bernstein wrote: "'Ratfucking?' The word struck a raw nerve with a Justice Department attorney. 'You can go right to the top on that one.'"

Twenty years later, in the early 1990s, the phrase would reemerge, when the new Republican National Committee legal counsel was tasked with fixing the Republicans' redistricting problem. The solution Ben Ginsberg hit upon was to use the Voting Rights Act's provisions governing majority-minority districts to create African American seats in Southern states. Work closely with minority groups to encourage candidates to run. Then pack as many Democratic voters as possible inside the lines, bleaching the surrounding districts whiter and more Republican, thus resegregating congressional representation while increasing the number of African Americans in Congress. The strategy became known as the unholy alliance, because it benefited black leaders and Republicans at the expense of the Democratic Party. Ginsberg had another name for it when a reporter asked him to describe it: Project Ratfuck.

The REDMAP ratfuck was done in such plain sight that Karl Rove himself announced it on the op-ed page of the *Wall Street Journal*. "Some of the most important contests this fall will be way down the ballot in communities like Portsmouth, Ohio, and West Lafayette, Ind., and neighborhoods like Brushy Creek in Round Rock, Texas, and Murrysville Township in Westmoreland County, Pa.," Rove wrote in early March 2010, naming some of the specific towns where Republicans would come gunning for Democratic incumbents. "These are state legislative races that will determine who redraws congressional district lines after this year's census, a process that could determine which party controls upwards of 20 seats and whether many other seats will be competitive."

Control redistricting, Rove understood, and you could control Congress. A midterm rebuke of President Obama, coming in a census year like 2010, would have far-reaching implications stretching across the next decade, if not longer. Win big in 2010 and Republicans could redraw the maps and lock in electoral and financial advantages for the next ten years. Push just 20 districts from competitive to safely Republican, and the GOP could save $100 million or more over the next decade.

"There are 18 state legislative chambers that have four or fewer seats separating the two parties that are important for redistricting. Seven of these are controlled by Republicans and the other 11 are controlled by Democrats, including the lower houses in Ohio, Wisconsin, Indiana and Pennsylvania," Rove continued. "Republican strategists are focused on 107 seats in 16 states. Winning these seats would give them control of drawing district lines for nearly 190 congressional seats."

The assertion is so bold, yet so sensical, that one does not know whether to stand back and admire the audaciousness, indict the Democrats for gross negligence and lack of imagination, or simply howl over the undemocraticness of it all.

It is perhaps surprising that no one had tried such a daring move before. After all, politicians have gerrymandered since before there was a Congress, since before gerrymandering even had a name. As long ago as 1788, the anti-Federalist Patrick Henry used his powerful persuasive tools to force James Madison and James Monroe into competing for Virginia's very first 5th congressional district, hoping to sideline the hated Madison. Madison won anyway, and in an odd historic twist, his second vice president, years later, would be Elbridge Gerry. In 1812, as governor of Massachusetts, it was Gerry who signed into law a state senate map tilted dramatically to advantage his once-linked Democratic-Republican party. Accordingly, one district around Boston contorted wildly to the north and east to avoid large pockets of Federalist support. A cartoonist noted its similarity to a salamander, and Gerry's name entered political folklore to describe districts which twerk and gyrate jaggedly for no reason other than naked partisan gain. (It worked: the Federalists won 51,766 votes that year and elected 11 senators, while Gerry's party won 50,164 votes but 29 seats.)

"Partisan gerrymandering has always been a weapon of the parties. But it has become a much more lethal weapon," wrote political scientists Jacob Hacker of Yale and Paul Pierson of UC Berkeley in their 2005 book *Off Center*. "Due to the hardening of partisan allegiances, voters' leanings are more easily predicted than they once were. At the same time, the technology for drawing partisan districts has become vastly more sophisticated. These enabling factors have intersected with the growing influence of the GOP in state Houses and the federal capital to produce a series of concerted and mostly successful attempts by Republicans to redraw districts in their favor."

REDMAP's efforts, eclipsing the most ambitious dreams of Elbridge Gerry, were the most strategic, large-scale and well-funded campaign ever to redraw the political map coast to coast, with the express goal of locking in Republican control of the U.S. House of Representatives and state legislative chambers for the next decade or more. Until this point, gerrymandering had been a tool to enhance an incumbent's chances of reelection or shiv a political enemy—rascally politics as usual. REDMAP played out on an altogether new and impressive scale. Call it the gerrymandering's shock-and-awe campaign—or redistricting's Moneyball moment. ("Moneyball" is the writer Michael Lewis's term for the strategy of using advanced analytics to identify undervalued baseball players developed by Oakland A's general manager Billy Beane, who realized that the only way to compete with wealthier teams like the New York Yankees was to outsmart them on the numbers side.)

No one will ever confuse a small-market baseball team with the Republicans; a party blessed with billionaires and deep-pocketed corporations is not usually outspent by anyone. But both Jankowski and Beane recognized bang for the buck. The $30 million Jankowski raised for REDMAP seems, in retrospect, like a bargain—say, the cost of one U.S. Senate seat these days, or the amount some casino or energy magnate's Super PAC pours into a hopeless presidential campaign. Actual numbers demonstrate this far more urgently. Here's what the Republicans spent, according to REDMAP's 2010 annual report, and what these dollars bought:

- In New York, Republicans spent $1.4 million targeting four state senate seats. Democrats had held a slim 32–30 edge. Republicans won 2 of those seats and control of the chamber.
- In Pennsylvania, where Democrats held a 104–98 advantage, RED-MAP focused almost $1 million on three of the toughest races in the state and won them all, flipping the House to the GOP.
- REDMAP helped reverse a 53–46 Democratic advantage in Ohio, where Republicans zeroed in on 6 seats with almost $1 million, and won 5, again turning the chamber red.
- A commanding 65–42 Democratic advantage in Michigan's House was wiped out with REDMAP's help. Republicans spent another $1 million in alliance with the Michigan Republican Party and the Michigan House Republican Campaign Committee, which paid off with 20 seats and new GOP leadership.
- Another $1.2 million in North Carolina returned GOP majorities in the state House and senate. Alabama turned its state House red for the first time in 136 years with $1.5 million from REDMAP. In Wisconsin, $1.1 million helped flip both the senate and the lower

assembly, knocked out the powerful senate majority leader, and made governor-elect Scott Walker's move on public employee unions possible.

Those aren't, however, the only numbers that illustrate the dramatic GOP gains. On the state level, this was the biggest rout in modern history. Republicans gained almost 700 seats nationwide—that's more than the 628 Democrats grabbed in the penumbra of Watergate and Republican shame in 1974.

In fact, Republicans ended election day 2010 with majorities in 10 of the 15 states scheduled to gain or lose seats under reapportionment and where the legislature controlled the new lines. National Public Radio that year had deemed only 70 of the 435 congressional districts nationwide to be competitive—Republicans now controlled how 47 of those would be drawn, Democrats just 15 (the others were dictated by independent commissions). That would help them shrink the number of competitive districts and tilt things even more steeply in their direction.

"At the state level, election years ending in zero reverberate throughout the decade," said Tim Storey, a senior fellow at the National Conference of State Legislatures. "In 2010, Republicans were more successful on multiple fronts: legal strategy, national coordination, electoral strategy, mapping experts. It all paid off. If the Democrats ever want to break out of this, it's an uphill climb. The technology got better, the data got better. Once you're in the driver's seat, in some ways [elections become] academic. They really knew what they were doing."

Perhaps the most revealing statistic is this: during the 1991 redistricting, Democrats controlled the lines in 172 districts, 240 were under split control, and Republicans controlled merely 5. (The remaining seats were either delineated by commissions or were in states with only one U.S. representative.) By 2001, the Democrats' advantage was down to 135–98, with 161 seats under divided control.

After election day 2010, the transformation was complete. Commissions (88) controlled twice as many seats as the Democrats (44).

Another 103 seats were drawn by both parties. The Republicans could draw 193 on their own. A party needs only 218 seats to control Congress.

An election spending comparison puts the gambit on an impressive scale. In the state of Connecticut, Republican Linda McMahon would spend $100 million on two losing Senate bids in 2010 and 2012. For less than a third of what she would squander in defeat, REDMAP locked in control of half of Congress until at least 2020—or until Democrats can theoretically beat Republicans on the newly drawn maps.

What would that take? David Wasserman of the *Cook Political Report* is one of the smartest analysts of state races and redistricting. According to his study, the maps have become so tilted that to retake the House of Representatives, "Democrats would need to win the national popular vote by between six and seven points in order to win the barest possible House majority." As *Rolling Stone* observed, that would require "100 Democratic voters to turn out for every 94 Republicans."

Once newly elected legislatures with Republican majorities were in power in Florida, Wisconsin, North Carolina, Ohio, Michigan and several other states where Republicans controlled every aspect of redistricting, the political sleight-of-hand began. Many legislators and strategists spent weeks during 2011 behind closed doors. In Ohio, they holed up in a secret hotel suite nicknamed "the Bunker." In Wisconsin, legislative aides barricaded themselves in law offices to work on maps, hoping to claim confidentiality privileges, and forced legislators who wanted to see the new maps to sign nondisclosure agreements first. In Florida, where a constitutional amendment had just passed mandating the removal of partisan politics from redistricting, elected officials held public hearings as an apparent ruse while operatives conspired on the real maps behind the scenes. The Republican State Leadership Committee—now the second biggest 527 (a tax-exempt organization created to influence political process) on the right—provided legal help and their skilled mapmaking team to ensure that every advantage was maximized. In Virginia, years later, GOP lawmakers would admit in court filings that the "overarching priorities" in drawing maps after 2010 was "incumbency protection and preservation of cores to maintain the 8–3 partisan division established in the 2010 election."

Democrats got their first taste of the new maps in 2012, which was, in fact, a big Democratic year. Barack Obama won reelection, besting Mitt Romney in the Electoral College by a decisive 332–206 margin, and by some 3.5 million in the popular vote. One-third of the Senate was up for election, and Democrats handily won 23 of the 33 races. Nationwide, 1.4 million more Americans cast their votes for Democratic U.S. House candidates than Republican candidates—and yet Republicans still came away with a 33-seat advantage in the House. This lopsided spread allowed John Boehner and Republican leaders to claim a mandate along with President Obama, even without a majority of the voters. This was the first time since 1972—when Democrats withstood Richard Nixon's 49-state sweep of George McGovern and held the House—and only the second time since World War II that the party with the most votes did not also win the most seats. REDMAP built a firewall against the popular will. And it held strong.

"It means basically that the whole constitutional notion of the House as a mirror of popular views comes into jeopardy," says the veteran Congress-watcher Norman Ornstein, a resident scholar at the widely respected, conservative-leaning American Enterprise Institute. His office there is so covered in books we barely found two places to sit. Ornstein had been skeptical of gerrymandering's influence on partisanship for many years but has begun to change his mind. "Now, I don't believe the idea that a majority of the nationwide popular vote should automatically transfer to a majority of the seats. But the idea that almost nothing happens when you have a broad public expressing its disfavor with the party in power and it doesn't do anything? That's not good."

Some academics and political journalists discount the importance of gerrymandering and redistricting, even in the 2012 election. It is not trendy to suggest that redistricting matters; no one gets tenure or retweeted for making the case that the thing that put us all to sleep in high school civics is actually a chief cause of our democratic decay.

The most influential book shaping this discussion remains Bill Bishop's often brilliant and always provocative *The Big Sort: Why the Clustering of Like-Minded America Is Tearing Us Apart,* which redrew the way the smart set thought about redistricting. Bishop argued that we'd sorted ourselves into increasingly homogenous and "ideologically inbred" communities. Our polarized politics and congressional districts were not the fault of gerrymandering, he argued, but the result of a new American propensity to cluster around people who share our opinions on politics and religion, our taste for *Girls* or *Two Broke Girls,* Whole Foods or Hobby Lobby. Bishop is right: we have surrounded ourselves with people who agree with us. He was also right about gerrymandering in 2008, when his book was published. But the extent of the REDMAP effort—and the pure political will behind it—was something new to American politics, the map-making technology has improved dramatically, and *The Big Sort* can no longer be the only aperture through which we see our uncompetitive congressional races. We may well have sorted ourselves into cities, suburbs, or rural America. But 435 sets of lines, drawn by experts, informed by more data than ever before, have *sorted us* into congressional districts. Those districts, intended by the Founders to be directly responsive to the people's will, have now been insulated from it.

The Big Sort still has an outsize influence on how we think about gerrymandering, and it obscures the national debate over just how effective the GOP strategy has been. The Big Sort theory can be at once true and yet not enough to explain what has happened. In a 2014 *New York Times* "The Upshot" column Nate Cohn wrote that "Democrats often blame gerrymandering, but that's not the whole story. More than ever, the kind of place where Americans live—metropolitan or rural—dictates their political views," before going on to suggest that *Democrats* have made blue districts more blue by loading up on young, socially liberal and well-educated voters—and that Pennsylvania was perhaps the best example.

But consider these numbers from Pennsylvania: in House races in 2006, Democrats received 2,229,091 votes, and Republicans 1,732,163. That advantage in the aggregate vote was enough to defeat the Republican gerrymander of 2000 and flip the delegation from a 12–7 Republican advantage to an 11–8 Democratic edge. In 2012 Pennsylvania House races, however, Democratic candidates received 2,793,538 votes, and Republicans 2,710,070, yet Republicans took 13 of the seats and Democrats 5. Or look at it this way: Barack Obama carried Pennsylvania in 2008 and 2012 with a roughly similar margin. In 2008, that led to the election of 12 Democratic congressmen. In 2012, it generated 5.

Is it possible that between 2006 and 2012, hundreds of thousands of Democratic voters in Pennsylvania sorted themselves into Philadelphia and Pittsburgh, abandoning the rest of the state? Sure. Or perhaps the obvious explanation is the better one: the lines were changed. It's not the Big Sort but the Big *Sorting*. Republican mapmakers packed as many Democrats as possible into just five districts, some of the most artfully gerrymandered in the nation. All were won with a minimum

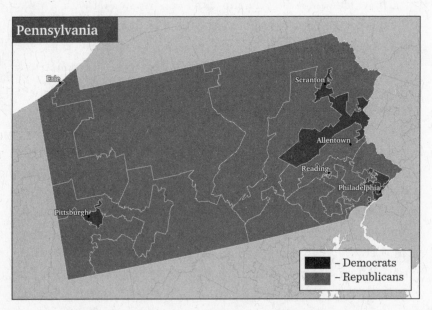

Pennsylvania's congressional map: "I'm not suggesting that we've never had bizarre districts before, but we never had so many."

of 60 percent of the vote; two of them, with more than 80 percent. That didn't leave many Democrats to vote in the remainder of the state. In the 2nd district, Chaka Fattah received 318,176 votes, more than any House candidate nationwide. Had some of his voters been sorted with different lines, the Philadelphia-area members might have a completely different look.

In Illinois, it was the Democrats who controlled redistricting after 2010. They did the opposite: their mapmakers attached pieces of urban, Democratic Chicago to the neighboring Republican suburbs, diluting the Republican vote. We can be sorted in any number of directions.

Mapmaking technology, like technology itself, gets more advanced every year. With computer programs like Maptitude, which allow cartographers to break down districts on a block-by-block basis, and the vast databases of information available individual consumers, it has never been easier for us to be sorted. "Everybody assumes that it's sorting, the Big Sort, and that demographics are driving this," said Chuck Todd, the host of NBC's Sunday morning tradition *Meet the Press* and a district-by-district student of American politics. "But the fact of the matter is they're not looking at the lines. Big Data has ruined American politics. Big Data could be used for good and is instead used for evil. Big Data has given you the tools to not have to coalition-build. We don't do political persuasion anymore. If you have competitive districts, you force political persuasion. The data is what has destroyed our political campaigns."

Nate Persily, a constitutional law professor at Stanford and non-partisan voice who was the court-appointed expert assigned to draw redistricting plans in Georgia, Maryland and New York, as well as the special master for Connecticut's congressional redistricting, sees something similar. "This is not just about technology. We've had sophisticated block-level analysis for quite some time," he says. "The information we have on voters and on those census blocks is what makes it better. We have more of it, and it is more reliable because we're more polarized. If everybody votes reliably Republican or reliably Democratic, then districting becomes everything. How you put the lines together is all that matters."

What Persily is saying has far-reaching implications. The same computer algorithms that recommend your next purchase on Amazon and know the exact Netflix show you want to binge-watch can also determine, in this time of hardened partisanship, how you are likely to vote. Part of that determination is smart guesswork based on census information. And part of it we surrender willingly every time we click on a website, order something online, or like a politician or news story on Facebook. Buy this information for pennies online, match it against zip codes and census blocks, and you can draw districts that may look competitive but are really reliable partisan performers.

Pennsylvania is not the only example of the REDMAP firewall. After the 2010 gains in Michigan, Republicans on the state legislative level redrew the state's 148 legislative and 14 congressional districts. Barack Obama carried the state, Gary Peters won election to the Senate by 20 points—and Republicans captured 9 of the 14 House seats.

In Ohio, Republicans had the power to draw 132 legislative and 16 congressional districts. Republicans then commandeered a supermajority in the state House despite losing the aggregate vote, and won 12 of the U.S. House seats—75 percent of them—with just 51 percent of the vote.

If drawing the lines does not matter, if the media elites are right, then the brilliant operatives and big donors were wasting their time and money. The proof that this matters is in the attention that the most astute and technologically savvy political minds gave it—and in the Democrats' recent desperation to catch up. The simple truth is this: America is the only major democracy in the world that allows politicians to pick their own voters. And since the 2010 election, the system has been gamed to create an artificial—but foolproof—Republican majority in the House and in state capitals nationwide.

Democrats and Republicans alike have the sense that something in our politics is broken, that Congress is not responsive to the will of the people. You see it in the approval ratings for the institution, which hit new all-time lows with each updated survey. When districts are uncompetitive and weighted to advantage one party, the only election that matters is the party primary, which means the only pressure on the majority of our elected representatives—the Republicans, in other words—comes from a sliver of the far right. This is why we have no action on gun control, despite the increasing carnage that has transformed our schools and colleges into crucibles of fear and occasionally bloody scenes of horror. It explains why we hold hearings concerned with the exact time when Obama administration officials called the Benghazi attacks an act of terrorism, but not on the administration's chaotic and uneven policies which helped push Libya into a hellscape. It explains the several dozen votes on repealing Obamacare, which majorities have now come to support. This is how an ultra-conservative, 40-member House Freedom Caucus was able to depose John Boehner as Speaker of the House. It's why we get more votes to defund Planned Parenthood than to help graduates with student loans. It's why Harvard political scientists have found that Congress has taken "the biggest leap to the far right" ever since 2011. It's why the government operates under the threat of shutdown and default over every vote on raising the debt ceiling. And it's why state capitals in blue and purple states such as Wisconsin, North Carolina and Ohio push harder right than the citizenry on controversial measures.

This book is not an argument for Democratic control of Congress. Nor is it an apologia for a mushy, split-the-difference centrism, nor a history of the Voting Rights Act or the various Supreme Court cases which have brought us here. Those important stories have been well told by brilliant reporters and scholars. Rather, this is the story of how one election tilted our democracy in unforeseen ways, for the unforeseeable future. It is the story of how, in Karl Rove's words, when you draw the lines, you make the rules. It is an argument that when our democratic institutions become separated from the popular will, they cease to be effective and democratic.

The outcome of the 2016 and 2018 elections for Congress are no longer in doubt. On the Sunday morning talk shows and cable news panels from now through these elections, we will endure dozens of conversations about "who will control the House" and "can Democrats take the House." They are all wasting your time. Let's answer those questions. One: the Republicans. Two: no, it's settled. There is no need to hold the vote.

This is how it happened.

*RATF**KED*

CHAPTER 1

THE MASTERMIND

"It Will Take Years to Recover"

Just two years removed from being written off as a national party, the Republicans swept to modern record gains in the midterm election of 2010. The GOP captured 63 seats in the House of Representatives, the biggest midterm swing since 1938, when the nation was still struggling to wrest itself from the grip of the worst economic depression in American history. Congress was only the beginning. The Republicans grabbed 680 new seats in state legislatures. President Obama, recognizing the historic nature of the defeat, stood before the nation the following day, chastened and newly chained to John Boehner and Mitch McConnell as his partners, and declared it a "shellacking."

Chris Jankowski realized it was about to become an even more historic election. Bleary-eyed and giddy, he told an Associated Press reporter before going to bed that "the Democrats will not soon recover from what happened to them on a state level on Tuesday. It was significant. It was devastating in some areas. It will take years to recover." When Jankowski's dad called to congratulate him the next day, he mocked his son's trash talk, which he'd read in the local paper.

"Even my old man was like, 'Come on,'" Jankowski remembers, as he tells me about it. "I told him, 'Yeah, Dad, it was an ass-kicking and they don't even know it. It can't historically be undone very easily.'

"I was tired and I hadn't slept when I said that, but I meant it—and I was right. I knew it at 4 A.M. This is my stuff. I live this stuff. For ten years we were playing a game between the 40-yard lines, and 4 A.M. we're down on their goal line. Well, I knew we *could* get the ball down this far, but I'd never seen it happen."

The game plan was elegant in its simplicity. As the census neared in 2010, Jankowski launched a plan to take or retain control of legislatures in states where politicians were in charge of drawing new lines. Every state handles this task a little differently. Arizona, Iowa, California, Washington, Idaho and New Jersey all use various commission models. But the vast majority of states leave redistricting up to some combination of the legislature and the governor, and that means political results matter; Loyola law professor Justin Levitt's redistricting website counts 37 of 50 states where state legislatures have "primary control" over their own lines, and 42 of 50 where the legislatures draw congressional districts.

Jankowski, armed with a modest war chest by twenty-first-century terms, had $30 million to spread around and had to prioritize the best places to invest. He looked for states that were likely to gain or lose seats after reapportionment, and would therefore be tearing up the old maps and starting from scratch with a different number of districts. Pennsylvania, Michigan, Texas and North Carolina made that list. He looked for states where control was tight, and swinging just a handful of districts might tip the chamber to the Republicans, such as Wisconsin, Ohio and Virginia, even New York. Then he checked for states where Republicans might control the legislature and the governor's office, and would therefore be able to lock the Democrats out of redistricting altogether. He didn't want a Democratic governor, for example, to be able to veto a plan, or have a Democrat at the table who might lessen the impact of a GOP map.

The 2010 annual report by Jankowski's organization, the Republican State Leadership Committee, laid out the mission for the world to see: "The rationale was straightforward: Controlling the redistricting process in these states would have the greatest impact on determining how both state legislative and congressional district boundaries would be drawn," they wrote. "Drawing new district lines in states with the most redistricting activity presented the opportunity to solidify conservative policymaking at the state level and maintain a Republican stronghold in the U.S. House of Representatives for the next decade."

What excited Jankowski was the opportunity to march into state capitals and create a conservative laboratory of ideas. "We had to sell it in terms of Congress," he says. We're in the conference room of his Richmond, Virginia, offices, a beautiful townhouse on a historic block which they've named the Ronald Reagan Building. Shelves are filled with elephant memorabilia and coffee mugs from Reagan's presidential library. Jankowski is a gracious, cerebral Southern gentleman, soft-spoken, charming, with a touch of an accent and a full head of chestnut-colored, side-parted hair.

"Our pitch document said, look, there are 25 true swing congressional districts. We pulled the numbers. We went back to those races from 2002 to 2008 and we found that $115 million had been spent on those 25 congressional races. All hard dollars. We had a graphic on the screen: $115 million hard dollars or $20 million in soft and we can fix it. We can take control of these 25 districts. We can take them off the table."

But never did he imagine it would work this well. "I have in my office the poster white easel with some of the polling we were doing in 2010. I've saved it because it's hilarious. Come on, I'll show you," he says, and we climb the stairs. The easel sits underneath a framed copy of a *Rolling Stone* hit piece on the RSLC. Jankowski just chuckles at the piece, and notes that Lou Reed's obituary was on the cover of the issue. "I love Lou Reed," he volunteers.

On the easel, there's a column labeled "Must Win": Indiana House, Ohio House, Pennsylvania House, North Carolina senate, Michigan House, Wisconsin senate, New York senate, Alabama House, New Hampshire senate. There are check marks next to each of them. Then there's a column labeled "Bubble": Colorado House/senate, Wisconsin House, Iowa House, North Carolina House, Maine senate, Iowa senate,

Oregon senate, Illinois House. Most of those have check marks from that exciting 2010 election night as well.

"It doesn't even have everything we got," he says, still in disbelief. "I was like, 'This is crazy,' but we just kept writing states."

By the fall of 2009, after his Eureka redistricting moment, it made sense for Jankowski and his boss Ed Gillespie to reposition the RSLC as a redistricting vehicle. They were not the only Republicans in Washington thinking ahead to the census, but they had an organization already up and running with a history of smart spending, donor confidence and solid results.

"There were people who had the idea that they were going to start a new 527 from scratch, put $20 million into it overnight and go into state capitals and win these races," he says, shaking his head. "I said, look, you're talking about building an aircraft carrier and driving it up the Chesapeake Bay and parking it off Annapolis. You don't do that in state races. You will become the issue. They were just going to run ads. They were going to go American Crossroads style, Super PAC style. No. You can't do that."

In early 2010, Gillespie and Jankowski took a PowerPoint presentation on the road. They met with Wall Street donors, oil magnates, hedgefunders, Washington lobbyists and trade associations—anyone open to an audacious, long-term play. "A lot of what we were selling internally to donors in a non-public way was stewardship," he says. "I knew that we had arrived when I was invited to the American Crossroads meetings and we were at the table. We talk to a lot of the same donors, and they would ask the Crossroads people, 'Are they trustworthy? Is this group worth investing in?' I could tell they were getting good feedback. We were going to put 100 percent of the money in. We already had our overhead covered." At one of those fundraising meetings, in Dallas, as *Politico*'s Ken Vogel reported, Karl Rove told the potential donors this: "People call us a vast right-wing conspiracy, but we're really a half-assed right-wing conspiracy. Now it's time to get serious."

That they did. By the end of 2010, their fundraising haul would make them the fourth wealthiest 527 in Washington, behind only their allies at the Republican Governors Association ($117 million), the Democratic Governors Association (a distant second with $55 million) and the American Federation of State, County and Municipal Employees ($47 million). The U.S. Chamber of Commerce kicked in just under $4 million. The American Justice Partnership—a conservative Michigan-based organization often aligned with the American Legislative Exchange Council (ALEC), a powerful right-leaning influence in state capitals nationwide—added another $2.5 million, followed by two tobacco companies—Reynolds American and Altria—and then Rove's American Crossroads. Other big donors included Walmart, Anthem, AT&T and, oddly, the Poarch Band of Creek Indians. (An internal RSLC memo would later allege, as reported by *Politico*, that that money was a "pass-through for controversial Indian tribe donations, essentially laundering 'toxic' money from the gaming industry by routing it out of state and then back into Alabama.")

As *ProPublica* reported, the "GOP relied on opaque nonprofits funded by dark money, supposedly nonpartisan campaign outfits, and millions in corporate donations to achieve Republican-friendly maps throughout the country. . . . Other donors, who gave to the nonprofits Republicans created, may never have to be disclosed."

The Republican Governors Association was active as well, as *ABC News* noted, raising a record $58.3 million to direct back into state races in the first half of 2010 alone. That far exceeded the $40.4 million raised by the Democratic Governors Association during the same period. Together with the 3-to-1 fundraising advantage that the RSLC held over the DLCC before Labor Day 2010, it shows how much more serious—and more effective—the Republicans were in planning and executing a state-by-state strategy in this essential election.

Jankowski had established networks in these states. He knew whom to talk to, who could be trusted with the money, how it would be spent. And after years of being in the trenches with them, he loved being able to write them the checks they needed. Gillespie and Rove tried to imagine what the Democrats' redistricting operation would look like. They decided they'd counter labor and any outside groups making a similar audacious play with Rove's American Crossroads Super PAC. The RSLC would handle Congress and the state races. At the time, they imagined they'd come close to a majority in Congress in 2010 but not quite achieve it. Donors were told they'd deliver Congress in 2012 after redistricting. But by late summer, as Tea Party fervor grew along with President Obama's negatives, they realized 2010 would be a GOP blowout and that the redistricting that followed would allow them to lock in their gains for a long time—a decade at least, perhaps even longer.

"There's an access model—which is always a certain amount of money—but what we transitioned into for 2010 was something bigger than that," Jankowski says. "We weren't selling access anymore. *We were selling an outcome and an impact on the political system.* That was the jump you have to make. That's what we do."

Jankowski had to take a big leap of his own to reach this point. His road to engineering Republican domination of the House actually began with life insurance. "This may be boring, but I want to tell you exactly how it all came about," says Jankowski. We've walked to Tarrant's for lunch, a classic Southern pub for a steamy June afternoon. He pushes his onions off to the side like a man who has had the Caesar salad and iced tea here before, and takes the story back to his law school days at the University of South Carolina. We'd talked of the two men who helped create modern South Carolina politics— strategist Lee Atwater and former congressman and governor Carroll Campbell—on the short walk to Tarrant's, and both men played interesting roles.

The presidential race turned to South Carolina after Iowa and New Hampshire, and Jankowski, president of the law school Republicans, caught campaign fever. Atwater built the South Carolina primary into a firewall for the GOP's conservative wing in 1980, after George Bush defeated Ronald Reagan in the Iowa caucus and thought the "big mo" would rocket him to the Republican nomination. Atwater, then Reagan's state chair, had other plans. As the *New Republic* reported in a story about Atwater's influence on South Carolina's dirty politics, "In one of his most infamous ploys, he got South Carolinian Reid Buckley to tape radio ads calling Bush a liberal, which, because Reid sounded so much like his brother, William F., made voters think they were listening to the conservative icon. These attacks, Atwater later gloated, pounded the pro-choice preppie from Connecticut 'into the dirt.'"

If Atwater ratfucked Bush in 1980, however, in 1988, he helped move him into the White House as his campaign manager. First, Atwater reframed Bush's religious beliefs to appeal to Southern evangelicals. "I believe in Jesus Christ as my personal savior and always will," the no-longer pro-choice preppie from Connecticut told an audience of about two dozen fundamentalist ministers in Greenville, South Carolina, under Atwater's direction. If talking about religion and Jesus helped transition Bush from an effete establishment wimp to the favorite in Southern primaries, however, it took one of the most brutal attack ads in modern presidential history to cement his victory that fall over Democrat Michael Dukakis. Dukakis, as governor of Massachusetts, had vetoed a bill which would have blocked furloughs for first-degree murderers. When a convicted killer named Willie Horton, on a weekend furlough from a Massachusetts prison, escaped and raped a woman multiple times, it became central to Atwater's case that, in this election, the out-of-touch New England liberal was Dukakis.

Atwater, named chairman of the Republican National Committee after Bush's victory, died of a fast-moving brain cancer in 1991—after setting a goal for Republicans to retake Southern legislative seats, and then Congress, through redistricting. The job Jankowski completed in 2010 through superior strategic smarts and a keen understanding of campaign finance laws had been begun by Atwater in 1989 with cunning and a similarly keen understanding of the Voting Rights Act.

It's hard to imagine that Bush would have been routed in quite the same way by Bill Clinton in 1992 had Atwater been around to steer the campaign. Nevertheless, Atwater had not only proven that a South

Carolina mastermind could put a Republican in the White House, he'd made the state's primary an important test for conservative presidential hopefuls. The year 1996 would be the first time since 1980 that the GOP field did not include an incumbent president or sitting vice president, and only the second occasion since 1968. Jankowski, as an undergraduate at the College of Charleston, had volunteered for the Bush–Quayle reelection campaign in 1992, then threw himself into gubernatorial and attorney general races as well. The buildup to the wide-open 1996 race was even more exciting. "I was never going to class and I was very much a C student," he says with a grin, and you can still hear his youthful enthusiasm, "but 1994 and 1995 were great. The show comes to town. It's bright lights, big city. This was pre-Internet so everything was more retail. You had to be there to be there."

Show up and work hard on a South Carolina race and the state's political culture is small and intense enough that you get noticed quickly. Jankowski was tapped as an assistant state attorney general out of law school in 1996, but that wasn't as much fun as politics. Carroll Campbell, the state's immensely popular former governor (and a longtime Atwater client), took over the American Council of Life Insurers association in Washington after running into the only opponent that could stop him: term limits. Jankowski knew Campbell's team well and they brought him in for an interview.

"They asked, 'What do you know about DC?'" he remembers. His reply: "I don't know anything other than I don't like it." That was the right answer. The association already had a full team of Democrats and Republicans to lobby lawmakers on Capitol Hill. But insurance, after all, is largely regulated on the state level. What the group needed was help coordinating efforts in state capitals. Jankowski came on board in January 1998 as counsel and director of state political affairs, but when he discovered the association also had a political action committee, he immediately realized how to multiply his efforts. His allies in state legislative, judicial and attorney general races needed the money more, could do a lot with a little, and if they won might do the industry a lot of good.

"I went to my boss and said, why don't we make this PAC bigger? We're wasting our time," he says. "This was during the soft-money period. Tom DeLay and Governor Campbell were friends. We were writing $100,000, $200,000, $250,000 checks like they were nothing to the RNC and other groups and leadership PACs. I was watching that, and then I was watching $500 checks—literally, $500 checks—go to candidates in Iowa. I told them that for a little more than you're spending now—but a fraction of what you're spending in DC—we could really have an impact in these states."

It was an early set of lessons Jankowski never forgot: money goes a lot farther in state races than national ones. You can push policy change more effectively off-the-radar on the state level too. But that means convincing donors that their money is better spent in Dover or Des Moines than DC, when donors like the "bright lights, big city" of national races and leadership PACs. Not everyone saw the same value in the off-off-Broadway races.

Then came a Supreme Court decision that looked good for insurers. In 1996, the Court—in a decision written, perhaps surprisingly, by liberal justice John Paul Stevens—threw out a $4 million punitive damages finding in *BMW v. Gore*. Dr. Ira Gore had sued BMW after discovering that the car he bought as new had been repainted prior to his purchase. Over the course of the case, BMW was forced to admit that it routinely sold damaged cars as new, so long as they could repair any problems without exceeding 3 percent of the sticker price. Gore received $4,000 in compensatory damages, but the jury also hit BMW with punitive damages for the years of misconduct. Stevens and a Supreme Court majority found that to be excessive and a violation of due process rights.

While the Supreme Court rejected the seven-figure damages as unconstitutional, the insurers nevertheless got very nervous over the original award by the Alabama jury. Their fears were exacerbated when the influential trial lawyers' lobby—traditionally a big donor to Democratic politicians—got involved in the subsequent tort reform fight, trying to ensure they could preserve the biggest paydays possible for themselves, with the help of their liberal allies in elected office. "The right to a jury trial is as important as the right to vote. My side doesn't say that very often," he says. "But this isn't about a trial. These cases never go trial. They're extortion. They're rackets. When you have juries that would return the BMW case, that's not rational. And when you have judges who let it go, that's when companies start settling. Anyway, the insurance industry was like, 'All right, we've got to change these courts.'"

Jankowski was so passionate and determined that Campbell agreed to put him before top insurance industry CEOs to make his case. They agreed, and soon afterward the U.S. Chamber of Commerce signed on as well. At the age of twenty-seven, he found himself working alongside other rising GOP masterminds who also recognized the value, both political and economic, of winning state races. It was the mid-1990s, and while other Republicans were obsessed with blue dresses and the impeachment of President Clinton, Jankowski and a young Karl Rove, the brilliant next generation of Republican strategists, were experimenting way off the grid with a state-based plan that would pay tremendous dividends many years later. Rove, of course, would go on to mastermind George W. Bush's two White House victories, before founding one of the biggest conservative Super PACs, American Crossroads.

"The first time I ever met Karl Rove was in Alabama, in a meeting of funders and operatives working on state Supreme Court races," Jankowski says. "Karl had spotted this in the nineties and would go into each state and set up the machine that was needed. To get the judges, you had to recruit good lawyers. It's a really soft-touch process. You're not recruiting guys who want to run for Congress. You've got to do it subtly, you've got to move the money in the right way, you've got to fight the trial lawyers.

"I got to work with the best people in the business. We all knew that Governor Bush was likely our nominee and we knew who Karl was, but no one really knew him yet. Mike Murphy was involved and he ended up with McCain. I got to see how millions of dollars are spent, how polling works, how the big races are run—but we started running them in a real junior-varsity environment."

Two other big settlements had Republican legal circles feeling frustrated. In late 1998, the four major American tobacco companies reached a $206-billion deal with forty-six state attorneys general over Medicaid payments for smoking-related illnesses. A later deal with Microsoft over pricing and abuse of monopoly power was settled for a smaller amount, just under $2 billion, but nevertheless it put trial lawyers and activist state attorneys general on the move. "We were seeing the tobacco case start to fund all the other stuff," Jankowski said. Many states, facing budget deficits and an antipathy to tax increases, used the tobacco money to expand new programs, and corporations naturally feared that they'd be targeted again.

Believing that the activist trial lawyers had taken over the national state attorneys general organization, nine Republican state attorneys general formed their own group, RAGA, for the Republican Attorneys General Association. Jankowski's old boss in South Carolina, attorney general Charlie Condon, became its first chairman; Jankowski signed on as a founding member of its finance committee.

RAGA and Jankowski had great success in increasing the ranks of Republican attorneys general nationwide. (By 2014, RAGA would become an electoral and fundraising juggernaut all its own.) But the McCain–Feingold campaign finance reform law was about to make a new organization necessary, and Jankowski felt ready for a bigger challenge. RAGA had gotten a little too easy. "There was a standing donor base," he says. "They don't care, they don't ask for anything. They just like that they're suing the Obama administration, and say, 'Yeah, here's another $100,000. Keep it up.'"

Jankowski was impressed with the idea behind a "moderately successful" Democratic group called the Democratic Legislative Campaign Committee, which worked with state legislatures. He thought the GOP needed one of their own. They went to ten companies, laid out the plan and asked for $25,000 from each. They called it the Republican

State Leadership Committee. "I made up the name to make it as broad as possible," Jankowski says with a laugh. "Mission accomplished."

The Republicans' plans for 2010 were already coming together when the Supreme Court issued its *Citizens United* decision in January, ruling that corporations have the same free-speech rights as citizens, and as a result, removing almost all restrictions on corporate contributions to political campaigns. The era of Super PACs and unlimited, anonymous "dark money" was on, ending decades of reforms, from Watergate through McCain–Feingold, which were aimed at making political donations more limited and transparent. The RSLC had its plans locked in already. "Did it make everything easier? Yeah," Jankowski says. "But it didn't change anything. We were still going to run the same play." Nevertheless, big donors were no longer limited to capped donations to the party or a candidate. They could go big, and Gillespie and Jankowski had the perfect plan. The Republicans would mount a comeback from the states.

Jankowski walks me through the questions he asked then. What would the Republicans need to control the entire redistricting process? Did the legislature hold the strings, or did the governor also play a role? What would it take to capture the chamber, and what kind of conservative policy changes might be likely? Which seats looked the most vulnerable? How could REDMAP work most surgically and efficiently? He zeroed in on a few dozen seats in states like Ohio and Pennsylvania, then did extensive polling to further determine which Democrats looked vulnerable, and which issues and approaches might help defeat them.

Almost every Democrat looked vulnerable during the summer of 2010. As the *Christian Science Monitor* noted, the headlines were apocalyptic for the party. "Fewer Young Voters See Themselves as Democrats," shouted one. "Dems in Power Could Be in Peril," warned another. "Dangerous Numbers for House Democrats." "Americans Most Likely to Favor GOP Newcomers for Congress." "Generic Ballot Continues to Suggest Major Losses for Dems." Polls went from bad to worse for Barack Obama and his party. "It appears that the best type of candidate to be this fall is a Republican challenger," wrote the Gallup Poll's Jeffrey Jones. In a column that summer, the respected political scientist Larry Sabato, a CNN regular and the director of the University of Virginia's Center for Politics, noted, "Conditions have deteriorated badly for Democrats over the summer. The economy appears rotten, with little chance of a substantial comeback by November 2."

If the Democrats had any redistricting play of their own, it got buried by discouraged Democratic voters—who had turned out in record force for Barack Obama only two years earlier—and by fired-up Republicans. I asked Carolyn Fiddler of the Democratic Legislative Campaign Committee whether redistricting had been at the forefront of the party's plans that fall. "From my perspective, it was not," she says. "Everyone's house was kind of on fire that summer, with death panels and things like that. After 2008 and all those successes, it was such a jarring shift that everyone went into reactive mode."

Jankowski, meanwhile, went in for the kill. Suddenly the states that had looked like long shots and fantasies when he first whiteboarded REDMAP were all in play. It was house money—and they had lots of it. It just kept flooding in. "The amazing thing was money came in late—it always does—and we got it right back out the door where it needed to be." Upward of $18 million arrived after Labor Day and was directed to races in Ohio, Michigan, North Carolina, Wisconsin, Pennsylvania, Indiana and other states—an avalanche of campaign cash in races where a candidate's entire budget might be less than six figures. "In Michigan, in the first week of August, I was able to [tell] our allies on the ground we were in for a million dollars. And they were like, 'A million?' Yes. Start spending like you have a million dollars. A million extra. Put these races in play—we're going to have mail budgets for you, we'll do cable in these spots. And we picked up 20 seats. I never did another thing in Michigan. I just sent the checks and they still have the senate."

Just as amazing: there was no sign of the Democrats. It was a crucial year, and in football terms, Jankowski had his opponents gasping for air at midfield while he sprinted untouched to the end zone. "October. October, I was like, why aren't they out here? We were pummeling them. I could see they were shoring up and playing defense in September. But overall they were nonexistent. Labor was there in Wisconsin, and the teachers' unions. In the Midwest they invested some. . . . I just don't know. The environmental groups, the trial lawyers—we didn't see them much."

Tom Reynolds, a now-former congressman from upstate New York who chaired REDMAP, later observed to *Politico* that "The Obama team has done some amazing things, those guys are really something, but the Democrats plain got skunked on the state houses." Jankowski, meanwhile, could expand his playbook. In Ohio, the RSLC began by targeting 10 to 12 House districts, spent in all of them, then realized the most essential 5, and doubled down on cable TV and more mail. In Pennsylvania, they eyed 20 of 203 districts, and kept polling for the issue that would work. They wanted to take down the chairman of the influential state House Finance Committee, a veteran, liberal Democrat named David Levdansky, and couldn't find the silver bullet. Despite the anemic economy and the apathetic Democratic base, all of the RSLC's polls found Levdansky running above 50 percent and his challenger still basically unknown.

When you're playing with house money, however, you can keep polling and probing, and finally the polls revealed an issue that really angered voters. Earlier that year, the legislature had appropriated money from the $600 million capital budget for a university library they planned to name after Arlen Specter. Specter had once been the state's favorite son. The moderate Republican began his nearly five-decade career in politics as a lawyer for the Warren Commission, investigating the assassination of President Kennedy. Over five terms and thirty years in the U.S. Senate, Specter helped defeat the Supreme Court nomination of conservative jurist Robert Bork, but cleared Clarence Thomas's path to the high court with his aggressive questioning of Anita Hill, a law professor whose sexual harassment claims had placed Thomas's nomination in jeopardy.

After Barack Obama's election, and facing a likely Republican primary challenge, Specter switched sides and ran as a Democrat in 2010. He'd been a Republican so long, however, that he lost the Democratic primary, despite his incumbency and name recognition. Republicans and Democrats alike had rejected Arlen Specter; in a tough economy, it was not the best year to be budgeting millions to honor him. Jankowski pounced. "When you vote to spend $10 million for the Arlen Specter library, which is what we hit him with"—though some of the mailers would also call it a $600 million library, conflating the Specter piece with the capital budget for the entire state—"it apparently really pissed people off. The numbers collapsed in the poll on him like *pffftt*." Air going out of a balloon has never sounded so giddy. "We thought, let's just do it. So we sent it, and it worked."

With even more money remaining to be spent, the RSLC went after a longtime opponent in Wisconsin, the powerful majority leader and former labor negotiator Russ Decker. All of the Wisconsin races seemed equally close, so Jankowski took the chance that they might be able to take down a long-desired target and create the potential for real conservative change in Wisconsin. The RSLC helped coordinate the spending. Other groups hoping for Republican victories moved their money to other candidates, and Jankowski decided, "We'll drop a bomb on Decker. He came back hard with money attacking us for our insurance donors, tobacco, all that stuff." That made it personal. "So I paid extra and flew a camera crew out to his home town and we filmed people in the street saying, 'Decker's gotta go, Decker's gotta go, Decker's gotta go.' They were locals! That's how we finished." Decker lost, Republicans took over both chambers, and Wisconsin would become a laboratory for conservative governance in a purple state.

"Low Democrat turnout and the right wave and you just wipe those people out. Redraw the districts. Boom. So. Arlen Specter library. Done. Everything is context, but you've got it." Jankowski grins. "It was a good year."

That's how it was set up: a cohesive conservative strategy, years in the making, thought out district by district, dollar by dollar, nationwide, in just the right year. Winning in 2010, however, was only the first part of the strategy, and perhaps the easiest. Delivering an enduring Republican majority in Congress—the "outcome model" the RSLC promised donors—and ensuring lasting conservative policies in state Houses would require another set of victories. District by district, and state by state, again, new maps had to be drawn. These maps were the true spoils of the 2010 victories. The Republicans were determined to claim them.

CHAPTER 2

PENNSYLVANIA

"So This Wasn't a Personal Attack"

D avid Levdansky wants to meet outside the Dollar General store. His pickup arrives not three minutes after I do, and I follow him through the exhausted downtown of Elizabeth, Pennsylvania. The Grand Theatre now only opens for special events. A café so all-American-sounding that it's called the Lemon Grill claims victory for the area's top ethnic eats. As we corkscrew up a steep hill, the Monongahela River and the nearby blue-collar, industrial town-ships come into view. We pass the Catholic school where a nine-year-old Levdansky cried at the news of President Kennedy's assassination and began to think of a political career of his own.

His roots here run deep. This district, Pennsylvania's 39th, has been home for almost all of his sixty-one years. Levdansky credits his early name recognition to his uncle's TV repair business; in the 1950s and 1960s, long before cable, you needed a Levdansky to get your antenna working and cathode ray tubes replaced.

If the family business brought entertainment to steelworkers and their families on evenings and weekends, Levdansky was determined to make a difference in their paychecks and in the safety of their work-days. U.S. Steel plants had lined the Monongahela for decades; after nine steelworkers were killed during the Homestead Strike of 1892, the anarchist Emma Goldman wrote of how "words had lost their meaning in the face of the innocent blood spilled on the banks of the Monongahela." Levdansky returned from Penn State with degrees in labor studies and political science, then began to organize local steelworkers and worked with an airline pilots' union, all while studying for a masters in economics at Notre Dame. In 1984 he won his first term as a state representative, deposing an incumbent and taking a seat in the legislature despite Ronald Reagan's national Republican landslide.

By the fall of 2010, Levdansky was a thirteen-term state representative and had won some twenty straight primaries and general elections. He'd risen to chair the powerful state finance committee in the capital of Harrisburg. He was responsible for setting state tax policy, and was a strong voice for corporate accountability. If he'd wanted, he could spend every night on the capital's North Second Street restaurant row as the guest of one lobbyist or another. Instead, he hauled his truck, the same one he picked me up in that morning outside the dollar store, the three-plus hours west along the deserted Pennsylvania Turnpike, back to Elizabeth.

That fall was a brutal time to be a Democrat seeking reelection. The Tea Party fervor that swamped 2009 town halls with outrage over Obamacare and supposed "death panels" still lingered. Deflated Democrats knew they'd be playing defense approaching midterms with an unpopular president and surging GOP passion. But Levdansky's long ties to the hardworking but economically challenged towns of the 39th district had enabled him to beat back challengers from both parties in the past, even as these largely white Reagan Democrats edged conservative and were consistently targeted by the National Rifle Association.

He had not a clue that Elizabeth, Pennsylvania, already sat squarely in the crosshairs of the RSLC's ratfucking plan. The blood spilled on the banks of the Monongahela would be his own.

David Levdansky's seat mattered because Democrats held the slenderest possible majority in Pennsylvania's House: 102–101. Republicans controlled the state senate. The conservative attorney general,

Tom Corbett, seemed certain to take the governor's office, replacing term-limited Democrat Ed Rendell. In Pennsylvania, congressional lines are drawn by the state legislature and are subject to a veto by the governor. The state looked likely to lose a seat in Congress, which meant the post-census map could be a blank canvas. Republicans only needed to flip one district to control the entire process.

In Washington, DC, the RSLC's Jankowski, sensing the opportunity, eyed 20 possible state House districts as possible targets. As Labor Day neared, he narrowed those down when his polling revealed a silver-bullet issue: the Arlen Specter library.

"The fucking Arlen Specter library," Levdansky says now, still seething.

The day we talk, it has been five years since the brutish negative ads that drove David Levdansky out of office in 2010. But the old fury comes back, just as it did every evening that fall when for three weeks straight he pulled his pickup to the mailbox and found yet another attack mailer waiting for him.

"Shame on you, David Levdansky!" screamed big block letters—and this was supposed to be one of the positive ads, playing up the military record of Republican opponent Rick Saccone, an Iraq War veteran and former Air Force counterintelligence officer. The photos were always a little blurry. Some used nefarious black-and-white, suggesting a mugshot or a school photo. "Big government at its worst: Pounding Pennsylvania with reckless tax abuses and inexcusable spending." It all made Levdansky look like his hand was caught in the cookie jar; his little mustache became almost sinister.

"I wouldn't vote for me either, if any of this was true," Levdansky says, shaking his head angrily after all this time, his head a boiling teakettle. We are on his quiet screened-in porch on a Sunday morning; it's coffee for us, while a hummingbird sips sugar water from a feeder in the yard. The RSLC put about $150,000 into the race, Jankowski estimates, most of it on the late mail, and some of it on a cable spot. As Levdansky's neck goes eggplant-colored, I feel grateful that Levdansky did not record the even tougher radio and cable TV ads.

"Three weeks out, that all started hitting." It was a new piece every day for the last twenty days of the campaign. Stop the truck at the end of the driveway, reach in the mailbox, pull out yet another full-color, four-page mailer with quivering hands. "No amount of door-knocking or one-on-one could do anything about this," he says. "I've had primaries where I was outspent two-to-one. I've had challengers who were well-funded and came after me with everything. But to see such an avalanche of money come in during the last two to three weeks? My campaign plan just didn't assume there would be at least twenty-one pieces of predominantly negative mail."

He still remembers the first piece: On Saturday, October 9, just three weeks before the election, Levdansky found a glossy four-page color mailer waiting for him. It urged voters to "Stop David Levdansky from increasing taxes by a billion dollars again," next to a photo of a worried young white couple staring forlornly at a bill. It was paid for by something called the Republican State Leadership Committee and mailed from Alexandria, Virginia, right across the Potomac River from DC. Appropriately for something so slanted, the address read "Diagonal Road."

From that moment, the race changed—and Levdansky was cooked. Like clockwork, a new mailer arrived every day through the election, some paid for by the state Republican Party but the rest bearing the RSLC's out-of-state postmark. The negativity piled up. So did Levdansky's rage.

The ads were devastating and brilliant. In one of the funniest, the library was depicted as a marble book, cracked open at a Corinthian spine, with Arlen Specter's image chiseled on the front and back covers. Capital letters screamed, "State representative David Levdansky voted to waste $600 million to build an Arlen Specter library." Another classic featured three senior citizens chatting on a park bench.

"Did you hear about the $600 million wasted to build a library in honor of Arlen Specter?" asked the first man.

"Yeah, who in their right mind voted to waste such an obscene amount of money during the recession?" replied a woman.

Luckily, her friend knows the answer: "Well, David Levdansky voted for it. $600 million down the toilet just to honor Arlen Specter."

Levdansky picks up the story from here. "It was all anyone wanted to talk about after that. I'd go out knocking on doors, people I'd talked to for years. And suddenly it was, 'Dave, you're wasting all this money in Harrisburg.' You'd tell them no, that we actually cut taxes. We didn't raise them. And they'd just say, "No, no, no. All of you guys have been there too long.' I would say, 'Well, could you tell me what I'm doing that you don't like?'

"And it's the fucking Arlen Specter library," Levdansky says with a sigh, again. "It ended up being $2 million in the end. The capital budget might have been $690 million for the whole state. Look, we always authorize it at a higher number, and then the governor's office negotiates with whoever is going to receive the money. How much are they raising locally, how much are they raising privately. What the economic development numbers will be. I've got to be able to explain that to people, right? Have them understand how it works? But, you know, you don't have to tell the truth during campaigns. You can flat-out lie, right? I've had nasty campaigns, but this . . ." His voice trails into silence.

Jankowski claims not to remember Levdansky's name, but he knows every detail of what happened: "People had known him all their life. They always voted for him. They saw him at church. So this wasn't a personal attack. It was 'Here's his vote on the budget. Here's what was in the budget.' And they decided, 'We can't send him back, he's changed.'"

In the end, Levdansky lost his seat representing the 39th district, in a massive GOP avalanche year, by only 151 votes. Rick Saccone, 10,761; David Levdansky, 10,610. The Pennsylvania House went to the Republicans, who now controlled all three legs of the redistricting stool at exactly the right time. A big check mark went up on Jankowski's whiteboard.

In the small rural community of Oley Township, 260 miles away, two-term state representative David Kessler started seeing simi-

lar mailers, also postmarked Alexandria, Virginia. Oley is a farm-
ing community about 11 miles northeast of Reading. To get here you
drive through small towns with just one stoplight but two miniature
golf courses, and sometimes three soft-serve ice cream stands. One of
those towns is called Virginville.

Kessler works on alternative fuel sources now. Combating global
warming has become a passion; he was that rare state representative with
a global vision and brought grant money into the district for cutting-edge
research. He owns a small building off the road with a pizza restaurant
out front, where we sit and talk on a spring afternoon.

"I could have been running against that salt shaker and I would
have lost," he says, "because it all came down to those mailers. The last
two weeks, it was every day. They said I wanted to ban guns in Oley
Township because when I was a local supervisor, the police chief came
to us and asked us to adopt an ordinance that said you couldn't have a
concealed weapon in a police station."

Then they hit him with the Arlen Specter library. A John Deere
tractor slowly rumbles by, and it's so quiet here that the exhaust makes
it momentarily hard to hear, but the frustration comes through. "You
can live someplace for thirty years," he says, "but a name and a reputation can get washed away under that much money."

"He voted for a $600 million library! The Taj Mahal library to Arlen
Specter. I think it was a few hundred thousand going to a college to
help expand a library. You know what, it was funny." His laugh is rue-
ful. "I'm knocking on doors, and I knock on a Republican family door
and they said, 'Dave, we voted for you in 2006, in 2008, but can we talk
to you? Can you come in for a second?' I said sure, and there on the coffee table, there's the Taj Mahal flier."

Kessler had thoughts of Congress. He won recognition from conservatives for the effective way he worked across the aisle. He thought he
could make Republicans see that combating global warming could be
big business. Now he's the landlord of a pizza place. "I couldn't knock
on every Republican door, of course," he says, shaking his head. After
winning by 4,000-plus votes in 2008, Kessler got swamped in 2010,

losing by more than 3,000 votes. He tried again in 2014 with the new district lines, and the result was even worse.

The Republicans made their new majorities matter. "The gerrymander of the decade?," asked *Real Clear Politics*.

"The most gerrymandered map I've seen in the modern history of our state," Franklin & Marshall College political scientist Terry Madonna told the Harrisburg newspaper. "I'm not suggesting that we've never had bizarre-looking districts before, but we never had so many."

The GOP ingeniously managed to carve itself a lasting domination of the congressional delegation, despite Pennsylvania's longtime status as a blue state. In November 2010, there were almost 1.2 million more registered Democrats than Republicans. (That number is now just under 1 million.) The state last gave its Electoral College votes to a Republican in 1988. More votes are cast for Democratic congressional candidates than Republican ones. But the makeup of the congressional delegation was competitive and tended to reflect national trends. In the 2008 Obama wave, Democrats took a 12–7 advantage.

Republicans reversed it to 12–7 the other way in the 2010 GOP wave—and then they locked in such advantageous new lines that their majority grew to 13–5 in 2012, even as President Obama crushed Mitt Romney by some 310,000 votes in Pennsylvania, and despite 2.7 million votes for Democratic House candidates compared to only 2.6 million for Republican nominees. Put another way, Obama won 52 percent of the vote, Democratic House candidates won 51 percent of the vote, and Democratic House candidates won 28 percent of the seats.

How can that math possibly add up? When you craft the lines just right, you control every last detail of a state's politics. You can even create 12 of 18 districts that are more Republican *than the country as a whole* in a state that would naturally lean blue. That's how powerful the lines can be. "Pennsylvania is arguably the most distorted map in the country in terms of comparing the vote share and the seats won," Nicholas Goedert, a researcher at Washington University in St. Louis, told the *Pittsburgh Post-Gazette*.

All of this starts by packing as many Democrats as possible into the urban seats of Philadelphia and Pittsburgh. You want Democrats to win a small number of seats with a high percentage of the votes, and Republicans to win more seats with safe but not excessive majorities. It worked: Republicans captured 9 of their 13 seats with less than 60 percent of the vote. But 3 of the 5 Democratic seats were won with landslide majorities above 75 percent.

Or consider it this way: The five Democrats who won in 2012 averaged 76 percent of the vote. The thirteen victorious Republicans won with an average of 54 percent.

"The basic idea that guided Republicans was this: Take the five extremely vulnerable Republicans, and push them all into Democratic-leaning districts," wrote *Real Clear Politics*. Then, crack the Democratic-leaning suburbs of Philadelphia and attach them to areas that are trending Republican. "This limits the potential for a 'dummymander,' where redistricting backfires as districts shift over the course of the decade. . . . It maintains solid Republican majorities in all but the worst Republican years, while maintaining the potential for further Republican gains. It's probably the most effective gerrymander we've seen so far."

Preventing another dummymander was the goal. By 2006, the gains Republican mapmakers thought they'd locked in back in 2001 had melted away, as people moved, George W. Bush and the Iraq War turned unpopular, and Democrats retook their natural advantage. Republicans spun this properly: they used their failings to argue that no gerrymander could last forever, then went back to the computers to figure out how to do better next time.

"They were so greedy and did it in such a way that when the worm turned, they couldn't stop it," Democratic congressman Mike Doyle told the *Pittsburgh Post-Gazette*. "They learned from that, unfortunately, and didn't make that mistake this time."

That meant fortifying the lines around three Republican-leaning seats in the Philadelphia area, especially the 7th district, represented by Republican Pat Meehan and considered one of the most contorted districts in the country, as it stretches across parts of five rural counties. Meehan added almost 40,000 rural, Republican-leaning voters to his district.

Pennsylvania lost one seat to reapportionment, so Republicans forced two Democratic incumbents, representatives Mark Critz and Jason Altmire, to battle one another in a difficult 12th district of GOP-leaning Pittsburgh suburbs. Critz won the primary then lost in 2012 to Republican Keith Rothfus. Just like that, two Democrats were knocked out.

After that, the Republicans' focus shifted to locking in the 2010 gains. Take the 11th district around Scranton as a perfect example. A Democrat, Paul Kanjorski, had represented the region for thirteen terms, and many considered it as likely a Democratic district in the state as any that did not include Philadelphia or Pittsburgh. But when Lou Barletta, a conservative with a hardline immigration policy, toppled Kanjorski in the 2010 GOP tsunami after several attempts to beat him, the party moved quickly to give Barletta a safer district. Scranton was knocked out of the district as was Wilkes-Barre, two Democratic-dominated cities which were attached to a mega-Democratic 17th district. Some rural Republican areas were tacked on from neighboring counties, and suddenly Barletta had a new district that was considered 10 points more Republican than it had been before. It also looked a lot like a horned antelope barreling down a hill on a sled. Naturally, he won reelection in 2014 much more comfortably, with 66 percent. The district, once viewed as one of the swing districts nationwide, is now reliably red.

"It's a pretty amazing redraw to go from one of the top races in the country to not even on the list," Nathan Gonzales, deputy editor of *Rothenberg Political Report*, told *Bloomberg Political Report*.

A Philadelphia firm called Azavea, which works with data and map analysis, decided to put the new districts through their own set of tests. The conclusion: ratfuckery. They gauged the compactness of the districts with a standard statistical tool called the Polsby–Popper Index, which compares the actual lines against what the district would look like if it was a perfect circle. By that standard, often used in redistricting court battles, Pennsylvania's districts were actually the least compact of any state's. Its 7th district tied North Carolina's famously contorted 1st district, which looks something like a snowball splattered against a car windshield, then melting, as the eighth most gerrymandered district in the country, and among the top five most gerrymandered districts drawn after 2010.

One of Azavea's maps caught my eye. It showed just how carefully the Philadelphia-area districts had been divided. Drive the Pennsylvania Turnpike north of the city, toward King of Prussia, and if you get off the highway close to Main Street in Norristown, you're in the 13th congressional district. Drive a couple of miles and you hit a small slice of the 7th, before crossing into the 6th. In a mile, you can travel through three districts—the 6th and 7th held by Republicans, the 13th by a Democrat.

Norristown is poor; help wanted signs are in Spanish. People walk along Main Street in branded short-sleeve shirts from chain-store jobs. You drive past the Premier Barber Institute, bail bondsmen and wig shops. There is still a 99-cent store. But as you drive away from Norristown, head around a corner and up a hill, things get momentarily leafy and green. Suburban-looking dads walk large dogs with flowing tresses. The houses are lovely and set back from the road. I check the map: This is, bizarrely, the three-quarter-mile stretch of the 7th. Signs warn drivers not to tailgate. I cross into the 6th and the demographic downscales ever so slightly: strip malls contain a farmers' market, a gun store and a beer depot.

A couple of turns deeper into the 6th, looping back toward the highway where Azavea tells me I can cover these three districts in less than 800 feet, the roads are named after presidents: Monroe, Van Buren, Madison. A gas station uses the Mobil font and red, white and blue colors, but is called Liberty. I check the map again and realize this is Valley Forge. This is where George Washington's ravaged, undernourished Continental Army sheltered for the winter during one of the lowest moments of the Revolutionary War. This is where the army persevered through its most desperate moments in a fight for freedom and liberty. This is where we have now carved up our democracy beyond recognition.

Actually, the 7th has not been carved beyond all recognition to Mary Ellen Balchunis. She knows exactly what she sees when she stares at the district lines.

"I see Donald Duck kicking Goofy!" she says gleefully.

Balchunis knows this wackadoodle map as intimately as anyone. The La Salle University political science professor ran unsuccessfully against Republican congressman Patrick Meehan in 2014, losing 62 percent to 38, or by more than 55,000 votes. "When I teach gerrymandering to my students, I think of the salamander," she says. "This is much worse than the salamander."

I want to know what it is like to run for office in a district that really does look like two Disney characters out for a rumble. So, well before

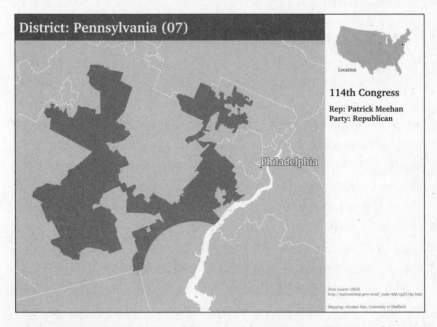

Pennsylvania's 7th: "I see Donald Duck kicking Goofy! . . . This is much worse than the salamander."

noon on a Sunday, with Balchunis's political director Bill Thomas at the wheel, we head out for three local Democratic picnics.

"You're exhausted in a district like this," she says. "It's dealing with five different county chairs. Five different committee meetings and dinners and picnics and candidates' nights. You need them all to help you because it is so overwhelmingly Republican. But when you make your fundraising calls, people will say, 'I'm sorry, you're in *that* district. You're not going to win. It's gerrymandered for Republicans to win.'"

Balchunis is sixty-two and still resonant of the 1960s; with her bangs and long blond hair she looks like she could have stepped off a Mary Travers or Joni Mitchell album cover. Thomas is her Tip O'Neill: long face, white straw hair, street-by-street knowledge of every block along the way. That comes in handy here: these towns and counties are divided with such specificity that Balchunis often finds herself talking with voters who have no idea what district they're in anymore. She has to tell them to enter their address and zip code into the house.gov website.

"Even last night, at a Democratic dinner, I was pulling out my phone doing it for people to show them," she says. "People have had their front yards in one district and their backyards in another. It's totally bizarre."

Our first stop on this 100-degree July afternoon is in Du Pont horse country, beautiful Delaware County, home to the gentleman farmer set. I meet George Badey, a local attorney who sought and lost this seat in 2012, the first year it looked like Donald Duck kicking Goofy. "This used to be a Democratic seat," he says. "I worked hard, had events every day, raised a lot of money." In the end, he got kicked even harder than Goofy, losing by some 66,000 votes in an otherwise solid Democratic year. "It's forcing all representatives regardless of party to lean to the extremes," he says, the frustration still palpable. "It's obscene. It's an abomination of democracy. It's bad for everybody."

The drive out here took about seventy-five minutes from Balchunis's house. Balchunis says a few words, grabs a hot dog for the car, and after no more than twenty minutes visiting we are on our way to Lancaster County and picnic number two. "Now this is God-fearing country," Thomas says, about forty-five minutes into our drive. "God, guns and gravy make America great out here. These people do not work for DuPont." Balchunis gives a quick hello, runs to the bathroom and we're on our way to the next picnic. "That's another part of the gerrymander problem," she says, "you can't get to know any of your constituents because you're running from one place to another all the time."

By the time we arrive at picnic number three, they are packing up the pineapple upside-down cake, the 50–50 raffle winner has claimed his loot and the signs are being taken down. "You're finally here and we're closing!" Balchunis's finance director says. Thomas and I try to find a cold soda and I ask about the campaign's strategy. "Meehan will have three million dollars," he says. And you'll raise? "Us? Oh, $20,000?" He laughs. "It's not like I'm above putting it all on a high-priced hooker. I'm really not. But we'll do our best."

The high-priced hooker plan doesn't seem any more dishonest than the Arlen Specter library, the devious ad which set all of this in motion. Those mailers tilted the districts that flipped the House and handed Republicans a redistricting monopoly which they used to exquisite perfection. Jankowski will admit now that the ads took a little bit of "artistic license," and told a public radio reporter that they "did not state that was the actual price of the library." They definitely cost a thoughtful legislator his life's purpose and identity. He's sixty-one, and unemployed.

David Levdansky gets offers to be a lobbyist, but always turns them down. "I think there's a role I could play in Harrisburg. But it has to be for the right people for the right reasons. I'm not gonna go do what a typical finance committee chairman would do. Can't do that. So I took my retirement. After taxes I live on $2,600 a month, which in these parts, you know, I'm able to make my mortgage payment and pay my taxes.

"If the worst thing is I can't find anything to do, well, you know, I could just live out my days working in my garden and fixing up the house, picking black raspberries the third week of every June and making spaghetti sauce. In October and November, get my bow and go archery hunting for deer, right on that hill over there."

But a caring guy, left to hunt and refill sugar water and build a shed for his guns, has a lot of hours to think. Levdansky earned a rematch with Saccone in 2012, running in a harder district redrawn by the GOP. Levdansky went to bed ahead and thought he had recaptured his seat. When he woke, provisional and absentee ballots had been counted, and he lost by 112 votes, a tighter margin than 2010. He was pretty much done after that. Sitting on his porch, our coffee gone cold, I half-expect Linda Loman to burst into the room and deliver an "attention must be paid" speech. But Levdansky's marriage collapsed in divorce around the same time as his defeat; there is no one to mourn the death of a politician, but perhaps we can listen for a moment to the kind of voice we have cast aside.

"For me, politics was about understanding people and communicating to them about their issues and problems, and showing that I had a background that would enable me to put solutions together and work with coalitions. But that has nothing to do with politics today, does it? That's not what government's about. It's not about figuring out a way amongst competing divergent interests. How to try and do the right thing.

"Now, democracy is one man, one vote. We should just say, you know what, it's one dollar, one vote. Because that's really what it is. It's all about the money. That's what democracy is in America. It's the best government money can buy—and money's bought it. It either rents it, it leases it, or it owns it." Levdansky reaches into his pocket and pulls out his money clip, waving it so close to my face that I can read all the bills. They are singles. His Mr. Smith outrage builds with such fervor that if this was an email, he'd be typing in capital letters.

"I don't mean this as a partisan Democrat; this is democracy with a little 'd.' Is this good, what politics has become—with money being the number one criteria for being elected? It's not about your individual qualities as a candidate, your ability to communicate, your ability to empathize with ordinary voters, your ability to craft solutions, be a policy wonk, work on compromises. Those skills are practically irrelevant in today's political world. Even now down to the statehouse floor." He practically spits that with bitterness, but then his tone softens and saddens. "I mean, I know in Washington, but . . . even now down to the statehouse legislature?"

As I head back to the Turnpike along Highway 53 and drive past two different sets of homemade, Burmashave-esque signs deriding President Obama as a monkey and a Communist and a Jesus-hating secret Muslim, it becomes all the more impressive that Levdansky won so many elections in these towns. The Republicans who have run the state in his absence have engaged in ratfucking tactics of their own. In 2011, Dominic Pileggi, the state Senate majority leader, introduced a plan to distribute Pennsylvania's Electoral College votes based on the number of congressional districts a candidate won. That would have awarded Mitt Romney 13 of the state's 20 votes, despite Obama's 5.4 percent victory.

When that failed, shot down by Republicans who worried it would make Democrats fight harder to win gerrymandered congressional seats, he tried something else: awarding Electoral College votes based on the proportion of the popular vote. Under that plan, Obama would have earned 12 votes and Romney 8, based on Obama's 52–47 win. Think of its impact this way: if Romney had earned those votes, it would have had a bigger influence on the race than if he'd carried Oregon (7), Iowa or Nevada (6) or New Mexico (5).

Pileggi was then removed from Senate leadership by his fellow Republicans for being too moderate.

The majority leader in the House, meanwhile, talked honestly and openly about the purpose of new state voter ID laws which he promised Republicans would pass in 2012. "Voter ID," he said, "is gonna allow Governor Romney to win the state of Pennsylvania." The law they enacted, which required voters show a state-issued ID at the polls, was ultimately struck down in 2014 by a judge who ruled that the state's reason for the law—fighting voter fraud—was full of holes and misinformation. "Voting laws are designed to assure a free and fair election," he wrote. "The voter ID law does not further this goal."

Outcomes like this would be very different in North Carolina, however, where the gerrymanders went beyond the state legislature and congressional districts, and into the judiciary itself.

CHAPTER 3

NORTH CAROLINA

Truly Space-Age
Software

In Pennsylvania, careful mapmaking in the regions surrounding Philadelphia and Pittsburgh helped pack Democratic voters into five big-city districts while maximizing Republican support in the other thirteen. In North Carolina, race—along with equally savvy cartography—has played an even more explicit role in changing the makeup of the state's congressional delegation.

The Capitol dome casts a long shadow across Independence Avenue and fills the window overlooking David Price's desk. But my eye is caught instead by one of the many photos that span Price's career as a North Carolina congressman. This one in particular looks to show much of the state delegation from not long after Price arrived in Washington back in 1987. That's based on the presence of Senator Jesse Helms—perhaps the most conservative senator of the 1970s, '80s and '90s, and a man who used race so aggressively in his campaigns that a columnist as down-the-middle as David Broder called him out upon his 2001 retirement as the "last prominent unabashed white racist politician in this country."

When Price was first elected, representing the university communities of the Raleigh–Durham–Chapel Hill triangle at the tail end of the Reagan era, North Carolina's eleven congressmen—and they were all men—included eight Democrats and three Republicans. Over the next two decades, population growth and reapportionment grew the delegation to thirteen seats, and redistricting flipped the partisan balance. In 2014, North Carolina elected ten Republicans and three Democrats from some of the most fancifully spirographed districts anywhere in the country.

Price had a front-row seat as Republicans took control of North Carolina over three redistricting cycles, with the help of several influential and divisive Supreme Court cases, and with the cover of the Voting Rights Act. In the 1990s, under a strategy inspired by Lee Atwater and executed by the brilliant Republican attorney Ben Ginsberg, Republicans savvily partnered with black Democrats to create new districts that would almost certainly elect a minority candidate. African Americans made historic and necessary gains in congressional representation. Republicans claimed the rest for themselves. Now, a closely divided, purplish-red state which has only elected three GOP governors in the last century, which went for Barack Obama in 2008, and which recently sent Kay Hagan and John Edwards to the U.S. Senate, has a congressional delegation that's 77 percent Republican. (This pattern has repeated itself across the South. When Georgia Representative John Barrow lost in 2014, he was the last white Democrat representing any of the deep Southern states of Alabama, Georgia, Louisiana, Mississippi and South Carolina.)

You can see the impact of redistricting by looking at the Cook Partisan Voting Index for each seat. The nonpartisan *Cook Political Report* created the statistic to judge the competitiveness of particular districts. In North Carolina, the three Democratic districts are packed overwhelmingly blue, with CPVIs between 19 and 26. The ten Republican seats are weighted with just enough Republicans to be essentially out of reach, all of them carefully balanced between CPVIs of 8 and 13.

As a politician and a political scientist—Price taught public policy at Duke University for thirteen years before his election to Congress, and returned to teach when he briefly lost his seat for one term in the 1994 GOP wave—he has watched with a mixture of admiration and disgust. "I don't have the evidence to prove it, but there's just too much uniformity across the country in what these legislatures did," Price says. "The intricacy and the expertise involved is really something. The closest we came"—referring to Democratic gerrymanders—"were a couple of states, Maryland and Illinois. I don't think we even measured up technically. In any case, it was so lopsided the other way that where they did act on it . . ." Price rattles off the REDMAP roll call: Michigan, Pennsylvania, Ohio, North Carolina, Virginia, Wisconsin, Florida. "Well, that's pretty much control of the House right there."

It's always uncomfortable to suggest to one of the 435 Americans elected to serve in Congress that the institution has been poisoned against democracy. They believe passionately in the institution. But when I ask Price if this all adds up to a strategy designed to subvert the popular will, he doesn't flinch. Indeed, he takes it a step further. "I think you're putting it very mildly," he replies. "It's a concerted effort, I think, in North Carolina. When you can win over half the votes for Congress and be 35 seats down? At least half of that is redistricting."

The 1990 redistricting battle began in 1982, with amendments to the reauthorized Voting Rights Act as interpreted by the Supreme Court in the 1986 case *Thornburg v. Gingles*, which mandated the opportunity for minorities to "elect representatives of their choice" in states with a pattern of racial-bloc voting, after the next census, where there was sufficient population to do so. Ari Berman narrates the story brilliantly in his book *Give Us the Ballot*. Lee Atwater, who became chairman of the Republican National Committee after directing George H. W. Bush's 1988 presidential campaign, had the foresight to understand that majority-minority seats would help make every surrounding seat more Republican. With the help of the Voting Rights Act, ironically, Atwater would crack the decades-long Democratic hold of the House. Atwater told Ben Ginsberg, the RNC's new counsel, exactly how to do it as soon as he walked in the door.

"I began working at the RNC in 1989 and Lee Atwater's first words to me were, 'Do something about redistricting,'" Ginsberg told the *New*

Yorker in 1995. "We began looking at the data, and we saw that white Southern Democrats had dominated the redistricting process literally since the Civil War, and that had created underrepresentation for two groups, Republicans and minority voters. It was evident, especially to blacks and Republicans, that there was an alliance to build in the state legislatures that were going to be handling redistrictings."

The alliances formed by Ginsberg changed the face of the South and the Democratic Party, and set the Republicans on a course to control the House for a generation or more. "I guess you could call it an unholy alliance," Frank R. Parker, the head of the voting rights project of the Lawyers' Committee for Civil Rights Under Law, told the *Washington Post* in 1990. "We're looking forward to whatever help we can get from them."

As Southern states considered redistricting plans based on the 1990 census, black Democrats and Republicans worked together to shape them, carving seats that ultimately benefited both sides. African Americans increased representation, while Republican seats grew rapidly in numbers. Sometimes they brought redistricting into the courts, as the Reagan years had already tilted many courts to be more friendly to conservative arguments. Other times, they shared resources, such as the "truly space-age" software Ginsberg boasted of in a 1990 interview with the *Washington Post*.

"Anyone with a PC"—and it was so early in the technology revolution that the *Post* felt the need to explain that the abbreviation stood for personal computer—"is going to be able to draw a redistricting plan, not just the Democratic-controlled legislatures," Ginsberg presciently boasted. "You will be able to hit a button and see what effect it will have if you move the lines one block in one direction or another."

Ginsberg saw nothing unholy about it; it was a "natural" alliance born of the gerrymander. Still, when he presented his audacious plan to the Congressional Black Caucus Foundation, he admitted to the *New York Times* in 1991, he feared he'd "get the living hell beat out of me." Rereading his remarks twenty-five years later, it's remarkable how perfectly every last step was executed.

"The fact is that minorities remain grossly underrepresented in

Congress, state legislatures and local boards and commissions," he said, rattling off the stats: minorities made up 20 percent of the population but held just 10 percent of House seats. "The culprit is the gerrymander," he told the CBCF, "the drawing of representatational districts by a majority that ignores established communities so it can lock in the status quo (i.e. incumbents) and lock out emerging groups. . . . It has been done to Republicans (who now get about 48 percent of the congressional vote but hold only 40 percent of the seats) and to racial minority groups. . . . The bottom line is that if the minority community is not packed, cracked, stacked or fractured, minority representation should be dramatically increased."

Ginsberg knew he'd be received with suspicion by black leaders. He was offering a Machiavellian deal which would increase the number of African American legislators, potentially at the expense of the Democratic Party. Jeffrey Wice, counsel to the Democratic State Legislative Leaders Association, argued with the CBCF for patience, coalition building, and trusting that African Americans had more in common with the Democratic Party than the GOP. Under the Voting Rights Act, the number of elected black officials had multiplied from 500 to 7,200, he noted. Ginsberg, however, recognized that many African Americans wanted to see faster progress and greater representation, especially in Congress. So he made an aggressive appeal to divide black Democrats from white leaders who wanted them to wait their turn while continuing to support white Democrats for these seats. "Tour the minority's neighborhoods and compare them with the majority's neighborhoods. Are the roads as good? The schools? Police protection? If the answers are yes, the current representational system is working," Ginsberg said. "But if the answer is no, then that is why the Voting Rights Act was passed and why every community deserves . . . elected officials whose only priority is being sure his or her community gets its fair share."

Ginsberg's fear of getting "the living hell" beat out of him was unwarranted. His plan paid immediate dividends for both sides. In 1992, redistricting helped elect thirteen new African Americans to

Congress. That was the largest black caucus in Congress since the days of Reconstruction. Twelve of those sixteen were from the South. That same year, twelve white Democrats lost their seats. In 1994, another sixteen white Democrats were defeated—and Republicans took control of the House of Representatives for the first time since the 1946 midterm election. Racial gerrymandering, wrote conservative columnist George Will, "is one reason that Newt Gingrich is Speaker."

The North Carolina redistricting fights continued throughout the 1990s, where the delegation flipped from 8–4 Democratic in the 1993–94 Congress to 8–4 Republican in Gingrich's first term as Speaker. How that happened, as Berman and others help explain, is a complicated story.

Under state statutes, the legislature was in charge of congressional redistricting, which meant that state House Speaker Dan Blue—the first African American Speaker in the South since the days after the Civil War—played an important role. Blue and his redistricting coordinator, Toby Fitch, were both on to the Republicans' game and interested in majority-minority seats. They proposed one majority-minority seat. Republicans countered with two (and considered a third, which would stretch narrowly across the state from Charlotte to Wilmington, saved on a computer file as the "Just Dreamin' A Bit Too Much Plan."). But the Justice Department was likely to smile upon a plan with two minority districts rather than one. "If you can draw a majority-minority district, even if it's bizarre in shape, you're going to have to justify your failure not to draw that district," said Gerry Hebert, the longtime Democratic redistricting lawyer who was then deputy chief of the Justice Department's voting section. "We were not concerned about the political ramifications. If it helped Republicans, so be it. Our job was to help blacks and Latinos get elected."

That knowledge—that two districts would be better than one, and that strange shapes would not be immediately discarded—is why two Democrats, state representative Thomas Hardaway and John Men-

nitt, an aide to the longtime incumbent Charlie Rose—found themselves in a Howard Johnson's off I-95 one day.

That's where they drew the district that has been considered one of
the most gerrymandered in the country ever since, North Carolina's
12th, with a perimeter of some 907 miles, essentially with the goal of
tying together minority populations in four North Carolina cities. It
hugs I-85 so closely in some places that the northbound lanes are in
one district and the southbound lanes in another. The *Washington
Monthly* once wrote that the "district respects no county lines, no city
limits, no test of common sense."

The district, which would be represented by Mel Watt, would wind
up before the Supreme Court in a case called *Shaw v. Reno*. Writing
for a 5–4 majority, Sandra Day O'Connor wrote that the district's lines
were "alleged to be so bizarre on its face that it is 'unexplainable on
grounds other than race.' . . . We believe reapportionment is one area
in which appearances do matter," she wrote, finding that redistricting

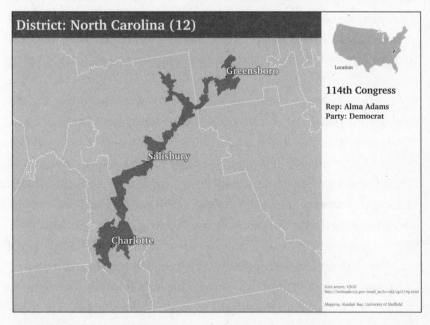

District: North Carolina (12)

Greensboro

Location

114th Congress

Rep: Alma Adams
Party: Democrat

Salisbury

Charlotte

Data source: USGS
http://nationalmap.gov/small_scale/mld/cgd114p.html

Mapping: Alasdair Rae, University of Sheffield

*North Carolina's 12th, it has been said, "respects no county lines, no city lim-
its, no test of common sense."*

based on race could be ruled constitutional if it did not meet a compelling government interest, if it was not narrowly tailored, and if was not the least restrictive method for reaching that goal.

The 12th, she said, "bears an uncomfortable resemblance to political apartheid." Watt's response was outrage: by this standard, he argued, a district 53–47 black was apartheid, but several 80–20 white districts were integrated. It was a statement that would be echoed twenty years later—as would the alliance of Southern Republicans and black Democrats—by Florida representative Corrine Brown, when her similarly twisty district joining African American strongholds in the central part of the Sunshine State would be rejected by a judge.

"It's hard not to be deeply cynical. There's a version of this cynicism that says, 'Oh, they've always done this to each other,'" David Price says to me. "But I don't agree with that. This is different."

Price is a Democrat, of course, but he is also a political scientist who has spent parts of four decades in Congress, so his sense of history is worth hearing out. He readily admits that Democrats added a "tilt here and there" when they controlled redistricting, but suggests that in previous decades there was a sense of honor among petty thieves.

"There was also a sense that they did not want to go too far," he says, pointing to evenly divided delegations throughout the 1990s and 2000s, and plenty of seats within North Carolina that both parties could target, compete in strongly and hope to come away victorious. When there was a partisan wave, he says, such as the one that swept him out of office in 1994, seats flipped parties. "We had four seats in the crosshairs that could go either way. We don't have a single one in that category now."

When districts are competitive, Price readily admits, members of Congress pay more attention to the middle, to independents and even to the other side. They can't afford to vote a strict party line or close their mind off to arguments from the opposing party. "Until this last time, I had a district that could flip, and it made a difference in the way

I operated. This is not same-old, same-old. This has been taken to an extreme. These guys are absolutely audacious."

The reality, however, is that it's hard to make redistricting a winning political issue, especially in districts drawn to lock in one side or the other. "Do you know of any instance where a legislative majority got in trouble, politically, because of redistricting excesses? I don't. Maybe they just figured out they could've gotten away with this all along." Price knows he can't lose now. His district is packed with Democrats, most of them of the progressive, college-town variety. The only threat would come from someone more liberal than he is. His fourth district is long and thin, like a horse up on its front legs, joined at the barest point between Lee and Harnett counties. The nearby Republican districts, meanwhile, are not as concentrated. Price's district is surrounded almost completely, both east and west, by Republican Renee Ellmers's larger 2nd district. (Imagine Wile E. Coyote on a hoverboard behind Peppa Pig.) "The result, in my case, is to make all the

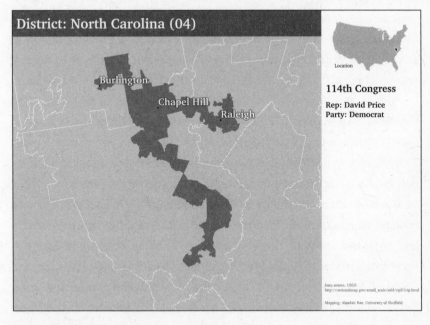

North Carolina's seahorse-shaped 4th district is designed to make all surrounding districts safely Republican.

districts around me safely Republican," he says. "There's not much question what this is all about."

Or how it happened. It was REDMAP and lots of cash. In October 2010, just as David Levdansky in Pennsylvania found himself buried under an avalanche of last-minute ads paid for by hard-to-trace dollars, Democratic candidates in North Carolina woke to nasty radio ads and found similar negative mailers waiting for them. The RSLC's fingerprints were on them, but only indirectly: Some $1.25 million was shoveled to Real Jobs NC, which claims to be a nonpartisan effort in support of the free market system but is actually part of the constellation of dark money groups funded by Art Pope, the state's would-be Koch brother and GOP power player.

Some twenty Democrats in the state legislature found themselves on the receiving end of ads like this one: "Steve Goss . . . nice guy. Too bad he's voting with the Raleigh liberals over hometown conservatives." Goss lost.

John Snow had dozens of mailers sent into his state senate district, including one which some believed played the race card as virulently as the 1988 Willie Horton ad. The ad suggested that Snow would be soft on a brutal killer named Henry Lee McCollum, who had raped and murdered an eleven-year-old, saying that "Thanks to arrogant State Senator John Snow, McCollum could soon be let off of death row." It wasn't true, but that didn't matter. Snow lost.

In Fayetteville, Margaret Dickson faced similar attacks, including one she called "the hooker ad." Dickson described it to the *New Yorker* as starring "an actress with dark hair who was fair, like me. She was putting on mascara and red lipstick. She had on a big ring and bracelet." In the ad, the *New Yorker* explained, "A narrator intoned 'Busted!' and the actress's hand grabbed what appeared to be a wad of hundred-dollar bills." Dickson told the magazine that "The thrust of it was that I am somehow prostituting myself." She lost, too. Republicans took over both chambers of the state legislature—and, conveniently enough, redistricting—for the first time in more than a century.

The RSLC moved quickly to consolidate its gains. Jankowski followed up the victories with a letter to state legislative officials and other redistricting players. "We know the ongoing redistricting process will impact the legislative lines that we will have to defend in 2012 and beyond. Therefore, we have taken the initiative to retain a team of seasoned redistricting experts that we will make available to you at no cost to your caucus for assistance. We urge you to use them as a key resource for technical advice as you undergo this process," he wrote.

"Our team would be happy to assist in drawing proposed maps, interpreting data, or providing advice. Their practical solutions have been used through many decades of redistricting and their best practices help ensure that lines drawn take Voting Rights Act issues and statutory mandates into consideration. Our team can also provide strategic advice in cases of litigation as well. . . .

"The entirety of this effort will be paid for using non-federal dollars through our 501c4 organization, the State Government Leadership Foundation. . . . None of these resources will take away from our ability to help fund future state elections through the RSLC.

"We appreciate the complexities of redistricting and hope that you will consider using our veteran team when crafting new legislative and Congressional boundaries during this critical time."

The top resource mentioned by name in Jankowski's letter is the RNC's master mapmaker, Tom Hofeller. Jankowski wasn't kidding about his availability or about expense being no object. Some $166,000 found its way to Hofeller and his colleagues from the State Government Leadership Foundation; the Republican National Committee billed the state for additional tens of thousands for his services. He does not give many interviews, sometimes citing pending litigation that he can't discuss. But in a fascinating profile in the *Atlantic*, he vividly remembered election night 2010 with the same joy as Chris Jankowski.

"I'm sitting and watching, less interested than many in the congressional races," Hofeller recalled to Robert Draper. "I'm the one saying, 'Okay, so we won Congress. The question is, are we going to keep it?' he said. And then what I see is that we gained 700 state legislative seats. The night just kept getting better and better. Things happened in some states that we never expected. Alabama! North Carolina!'"

The job of keeping those gains would, of course, fall to him. Hofeller's skill is in creating maps that return huge partisan dividends while otherwise looking seemingly reasonable and fair. He knows the law, he does not overreach, and he does not leave a paper trail for judges and opposing counsel to hang him with.

In North Carolina, redistricting proceeded along two paths: one very public and the other behind closed doors, often headquartered at the state Republican Party, with Tom Hofeller in charge of drawing the lines and Art Pope not too far away. Hofeller tends to talk about redistricting only when deposed. But on a corner of the National Conference of State Legislatures' website, you can find the PowerPoint presentation he delivered for their 2011 national redistricting seminar. It's called "What I've Learned About Redistricting—The Hard Way!"—and much of that revolves around keeping your mouth shut. It's as if mapmakers are involved in some sort of risky espionage work, rather than designing the basic contours of our democracy.

"NEVER travel without counsel," he advised. "Loose Lips, Sink Ships." "Remember—A journey to legal HELL starts with but a single misstatement OR a stupid email!" "Emails are the tools of the devil." Use personal meetings, he advises, or a "safe phone." "Treat every statement and document as if it was going to appear on the FRONT PAGE of your local newspaper," then emphasized that point by suggesting that mapmakers print out the *Washington Post*'s logo and paste it at the top of their computer for a permanent reminder.

There's a section of personnel advice involving both salaries and when to fire people. "Pay your technical people well," he suggested, and also, "Don't 'can' the staff until you're sure redistricting is really over." His security paranoia did not end there. "Make sure your security is real." "Remember recent email disasters!!!" "Make sure your computer is in a PRIVATE location." "Don't walk away from it and leave your work exposed."

And then there was a reminder to look to the future—"Identify areas of future residential development"—and advice on misdirection: "Decide what types of plans you, or others, may wish to put out in public to make specific points." Lastly, a little joke: when practicing and getting to know the state, "Draw a 'good government' plan."

Dale Oldham, one of Hofeller's associates in North Carolina, appeared to be running this exact playbook in a deposition in a suit challenging North Carolina's post-2010 census districts, which was filed by former state senator Margaret Dickson, one of the Democratic politicians defeated in 2010. A suit by Dickson and one filed by the North Carolina NAACP were the key challenges to the new maps—and helped unearth a treasure trove of documents and depositions relating to how they were drawn. "Mr. Oldham," the attorney questioning him asked, "I have put in front of you a map that is labeled 'NC Without Odd Minority Districts.' Do you recognize that map?" Later, "Mr. Oldham, [exhibit] 396 is in front of you. It is a map entitled 'NC House Less Convoluted.' Do you recognize that as a map drawn by the map drawers in North Carolina in the 2010 redistricting cycle?" You can almost imagine the masterful Hofeller adding a line to the next version of his Power-Point presentation. "Don't get cute with titles when you save the plans."

Hofeller did leave at least one indecorous email, which surfaced in the Dickson lawsuit. He explained how the post-2010 North Carolina plan would "incorporate all the significant concentrations of minority voters in the northeast into the first district." If Republicans had pushed for two majority-minority seats in 1991, in 2010 they really would go for three—what, twenty years before, they'd deemed going a little too crazy.

These new districts followed a national pattern and were designed to "segregate African American voters in three districts and concede those districts to the Democrats," Bob Hall of Democracy North Carolina told *ProPublica*. Hall's group also joined the Dickson lawsuit challenging Hofeller's artistry.

ProPublica discovered an email trail which lays out the subterfuge: Republicans created districts that looked as if they would be competitive based on voter registration statistics. Hofeller's team, in a nod to the idea of a blue state, even mockingly titled the plan "Blue Horizon 3." But using statistical analysis of their own and some brilliant Maptitude work, they created indexes based around John McCain's performance in 2008. They used McCain's numbers precisely because he lost; the Republicans wanted to create reliably winning districts even in years when Democratic presidential candidates won. In the seven districts Republicans claimed in public would be competitive, McCain would have won big in 2008, despite actually losing North Carolina to Barack Obama. In one email, Brent Woodcox, the state general assembly's redistricting counsel, wrote to Hofeller and other influential Republican politicos and operatives, under the subject line "attorney client communication," suggesting this was smart misdirection and spin: "When Nathan and I counted earlier, I thought we counted 11 of 13 districts with a Democratic registration advantage. I could be wrong but it's worth double checking. I do think the registration advantage is the best aspect to focus on to emphasize competitiveness." The Republicans knew from their statistical analysis, of course, that the registration advantage was not a statistic which affected the actual performance of the district. They also knew, as Woodcox put it, that it "provides the best evidence of pure partisan comparison and serves in my estimation as a strong legal argument and easily comprehensible political talking point."

To knock out Representative Heath Shuler, a moderate-to-conservative Democrat and a former college football star, in the 11th district, they simply wiped away Asheville, the artsy-liberal college town, and handed it to Patrick McHenry. McHenry, a young conservative wunderkind, could handle the extra Democrats as he already had what the *Atlantic* labeled "the state's most Republican district over the previous 60 years." One by one, white, moderate Southern Democrats were pushed aside and replaced by much more conservative Republicans. National names including Brad Miller, Heath Shuler, Mike McIntyre, Larry Kissell: by 2014, all of them either decided not to run again or went down to defeat. The era of the moderate North Carolina Democrat came to an end; the delegation would consist of partisans with little reason to reach out to the other side, either at home or in Washington. Indeed, reaching out, working together, finding honest compromise—the process of governing—became the only thing that might make them vulnerable, to a primary challenge from someone calling them not partisan enough.

It is hard to see blue on the horizon in North Carolina. It is also hard to challenge the artistry or the reality of election day 2012. Democrats entered the day with 7 of the 13 seats. Democratic House candidates won 50.6 percent of the votes. Republican candidates won 9 of the 13 seats. Democrats won the 3 districts designed to pack in minority candidates with totals exceeding 70 percent. Mike McIntyre took their fourth seat by a few hundred votes, despite the fact that, as press reports noted, it "skewed heavily Republican and that his own home had been drawn out of it." That seat would flip in 2014, making the state 10–3 Republican.

McHenry, the Republican congressman, would celebrate success in 2012 beyond his wildest dreams. As he told *Politico*: "That is huge. No other states in the nation would gain as many Republican seats. This

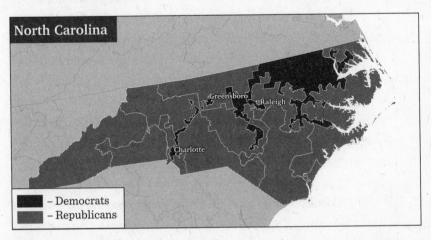

North Carolina's congressional map: "No other states in the nation would gain as many Republican seats."

would be in a state that Barack Obama won in 2008 and where we have had a Democratic governor since 1992—the longest such period in the nation. A 9–4 delegation is pretty good and would attempt to avoid the risk of a bad year for Republicans."

Finally, in February 2016, a three-judge panel in federal court agreed with the NAACP and ruled that two North Carolina districts—the 1st and 12th—had been racially gerrymandered. The judges ordered them redrawn within the next two weeks. "The record is replete with statements indicating that race was the legislature's paramount concern," the judges wrote in a stern ruling. The NAACP celebrated an end to "racially biased 'apartheid' districts [that] disenfranchise the power of the African-American vote" by packing it into the 1st and 12th districts.

Nevertheless, the odds remain stacked against the restoration of competitive districts across North Carolina. As the *Washington Spectator* found:

> One month before election day 2012, Justice Paul Newby was badly trailing Democrat Sam Ervin IV (grandson of Sam Ervin Jr., the Democrat who chaired the Senate Watergate Committee).
>
> Then the RSLC entered the race, contributing $1.65 million to Justice for All NC. Between October 11 and November 5, Justice for All spent $1.95 million on TV ads, turning the race around and reelecting Newby. Some of that money was provided by Pope and Americans for Prosperity, a frequent recipient of Pope family money.
>
> Newby outspent his Democratic rival by 10-to-1, with most of the money spent in October, and was reelected by a narrow margin.

The North Carolina Supreme Court was then asked to rule twice on the constitutionality of the state and legislative maps, and approved them both times, each on a 4–3 party line vote. Judge Newby was

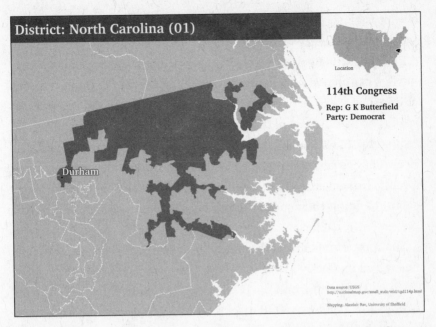

District: North Carolina (01)

Location

114th Congress

Rep: G K Butterfield
Party: Democrat

Durham

Data source: USGS
http://nationalmap.gov/small_scale/mld/cgd114p.html

Mapping: Alasdair Rae, University of Sheffield

North Carolina's 1st: The NAACP called it a "racially biased 'apartheid' district."

asked to recuse himself by critics who pointed to the role played in his campaign, and in the mapmaking, by the RSLC. He declined to do so.

That's right: The courts which hear these cases can be ratfucked, too.

The view of the Capitol through David Price's window is obscured by scaffolding, which somehow feels appropriate. His analysis is grim. His service here has covered parts of four decades, spanning Reagan, Bush, Clinton, Bush's son and then Obama. It has included three redistricting cycles and the demographic and partisan makeover of the South. He has watched the institution change and come to believe not all of that change has been organic. And he has watched the pressure it all exerts on fellow congressmen.

"It really affects the way members behave once they come here. I've heard some guys say they might be more moderate, but they just can't be," Price says. "The rule of thumb becomes don't let any opposition develop to the right. It all adds up to pretty extreme behavior. The gerrymandering really exacerbated that."

Price says his Republican colleagues will sometimes admit, openly, that fear of a challenge from the right affects the way they vote and how willing they are to compromise. It's part of what has made Congress so frozen and dysfunctional throughout the Obama years. "They'll say in their state, this Tea Partier rules the roost and everyone else runs for cover. They're really threatened by that." I ask him if Democrats ever have the same worry, that a challenge from the left might make them fearful of doing their job. His answer is immediate and dismissive. "Never."

The congressman runs through a litany of reform ideas, and rejects them all as ineffective. Wait until the next census? Not easy, because it still means winning on the GOP maps. The courts? Only if the partisan balance changes. Full disclosure and better regulation of dark money? Would never pass a GOP Congress, he says.

"It is scary. The voter suppression matters. The extraordinary interference in drawing local district lines. The big finance." Taken together, he says, and as demographics turn against the Republicans, it's a savvy but dangerous play. "I guess the idea is to stave off for some decades the kind of decline that they would otherwise have. People say it's a last-ditch strategy. Well, it's a *long* last ditch. It could last for decades."

In North Carolina, the strategy actually took three decades to implement. It started in 1990 with what Ginsberg amusingly described as "truly space-age" software, and twenty years later had advanced to something even more powerful and exact, a program called Maptitude.

CHAPTER 4

MAPTITUDE

"Donald Duck Kicking Goofy"

The debate over how you draw lines can feel a little theoretical— the usual cable-news partisan food fight—until you see exactly how it is done these days. The days of mapmakers with fancy pencils and parchment sheets and desks covered with papers have given way over the last two redistricting cycles to very powerful computer programs.

As the technology has grown more sophisticated, so too has the kind of demographic and personal information that we leave simply by traveling across the Internet on any given day. Mapmakers have access not only to the massive amount of demographic data collected by the U.S. Census, but they can also purchase any number of other databases or public records. Anything you like on social media, anything you purchase online, any license or registration or magazine subscription: in the same eerie way that you are tracked across the Web by an ad, you are likely landing in some direct marketer's database as well.

All that statistical data might have been too much information before computers became so fast, but the tools available to the mapmaker in 2010 have improved so rapidly since 2000 it's as if they had been using those old America Online discs included with the Sunday newspaper. The mapmaker has become all-knowing.

William Desmond greets me at his Scottsdale, Arizona, home looking more pumpkin-cheeked than omnipotent. Desmond's living room is filled with vinyl records, lots of indie rock and alt-country. Jason Isbell's *Something More Than Free* sits atop the stereo system. The technology is more state-of-the-art in his office, where he's agreed to show me how easy and powerful the Maptitude program is while the perfect desert sunset unfurls through the window over McDowell Mountain. Desmond works as a senior microtargeting analyst for a company called Strategic Telemetry, and served as the lead map-drawing consultant to the Arizona Independent Redistricting Commission on their legislative and congressional districts.

He joined the firm after being one of the young stats wunderkinds who helped elect Barack Obama, as the project manager for modeling on the 2008 Obama for America campaign. There's Obama inauguration memorabilia on the walls; Strategic Telemetry was viewed as a center-left firm when the Arizona commission hired them, and suspicious conservatives used the firm's political history in an attempt to discredit the independence of the commission.

"My very first day in Arizona was August of 2011. I show up at the airport. I've never been to the state before, and three hours later I'm at the very first public hearing after we were selected—and there was two and a half hours of public testimony just yelling at me and accusing me of the most awful things. Eric Holder [Obama's attorney general, an African American viewed with suspicion and hostility by the Tea Party right] had sent us here, and how I'm from New York and I'm a cockroach. Just tearing me to shreds. I took diligent notes, like 'unhappy with selection of the mapping consultant.'"

We start Maptitude on Desmond's desktop. He still has the laptop he did all the Arizona mapping on, but he's stopped using it because of all the legal challenges. It's been forensically examined at least twice, and lawyers have perfect copies, but just to be safe, he doesn't want to use it to show me how to draw maps only to find those demonstrations later entered into evidence in court. That's how contentious the post-2010 census has become in Arizona. As the computer loads the system, Desmond explains how he became so fascinated by maps. He was a political communication major at George Washington University with a minor in fine arts when he started working at the firm, and he found he had a knack for numbers along with an eye for design. "I took on a project at work and it became my life," he says. "Maps are a really powerful way to look at data; they let you understand things in a different way. Suddenly I was working eighty hours a week on this for months on end. I was just totally consumed with these maps. You can get really lost in trying to build the perfect map, I will admit."

It's easy to see how. This might be the best political video game ever. It starts simply enough. Open plan manager. Select the type of map you want to build. We select an Arizona legislative grid, which is how the law dictates that redistricting should begin. You choose the number of districts, and the map divides the state's population by that number to give us the exact number of people we'll need in each one to pass constitutional muster. Maptitude comes preloaded with all the census data you could ever imagine, and some that you had no idea was even collected. A census block is the most granular level and corresponds to a city block. Put census blocks together to form census tracts, then cities and counties.

Within each census block, the statistics get even more granular: total population, male population, female population, white population, multirace, mixed race, "every other race," Desmond says, scrolling past hundreds of different backgrounds and ethnicities. As you highlight a census block for your district, it gives you a running tally of every imaginable breakdown. The more information you add—political, economic, demographic—the more exact a picture you have, street by street. Make a change, move a line in any direction, and you can see what it does to all of the neighboring districts.

"That's how you start weighing in different things," he says. "When we actually did this for the commission, we added a ton of other data to those kind of background files—things like election results going back through the last decade, some population estimates, prisoner populations, other things that the commission deemed important to consider when trying to draw the maps."

Layer on election results and you can almost immediately understand how these districts will perform for either party, in a good year or in a bad year. You've got party registration and voter turnout, sure. But cross-tab those numbers with precinct results and you can pretty much figure out how particular census blocks voted in every election going back a decade.

"This particular block has a voting-age population of 91 people. So 91 people live in this block, and then so you can see in 2008, 12 of those people voted for the Republican candidate in the state senate race and 7 of them voted for the Democrat. None of them voted for a third party. You can do this for anything. You could load up the Democratic mine inspector percentage of 2006 and look for areas where the Republican candidate did really well."

If your goal, of course, is to create districts that will reliably perform for a specific party, you want to consider all of these voting results carefully. They tell you where your base is, how the party performs up and down the ballot in good years and in bad. And if you use them correctly, you can create an index that bounds enough of the right people, in the right way, to guarantee a result throughout the decade, no matter the overall direction of the electorate. In states such as Florida, Ohio, Wisconsin and North Carolina, partisan mapmakers used complicated indexes like this with the intention of drawing not only as many Republican seats as they could, but seats that would *remain* reliably Republican even in an off-year for the party.

This level of technological sophistication—combined with hardened partisanship among voters who define themselves as red and blue—makes our voting preferences almost shamefully easy to predict. Add census details and public records to the formula—say, household income, ethnicity, and the elections in which a vote was cast—and the picture becomes even clearer. Then add all that online surfing and purchasing information. When a district line zigs oddly to scoop up or exclude a handful of voters, or a district contains 135 different edges, or narrows to the length of a bridge or a highway lane, there is nothing random or accidental about it. You can be sure that very smart people with detailed information and powerful mapmaking tools drew it that way for a reason.

Every ten years, a magazine or website will show the strangest-looking new districts as if they were Rorschach ink blots, and ask people to tell them what they see. The answers can be amusing: a praying mantis (Maryland's 3rd), an upside-down elephant (Texas's 35th). Or, as Mary Ellen Balchunis described Pennsylvania's 7th, Donald Duck kicking Goofy. The politicians and mapmakers see something very different: a sure thing.

"Obviously you can average all those things together if you think there's some certain combination of election results and partisan registration and ethnicity" that leads to a desired result, Desmond says. "In Maptitude, you can take as many fields as you want and build formulas and then shade it by that. If you wanted to quickly look at, say, areas that are very Caucasian and also very Democratic, and then

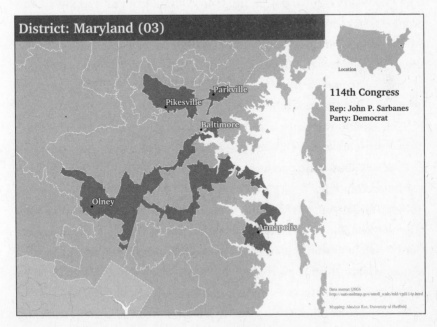

Maryland's 3rd, a praying mantis that favors Democrats.

commute times or average incomes or the number of people working in a blue-collar job. What percentage of the population has a master's degree? All that information's available at the block level. It's a little bit bigger, but just like you can desegregate election results from the precincts to the blocks, you can desegregate all that, too."

He shows me one of the indexes the commission developed for Arizona's 8th congressional district, which weighed 2000–08 election results. Under this index, the district tilted 51.3 percent Republican. With the redrawn lines, the GOP number dropped to 49.5. "It made the district closer to 50–50, more competitive," he says.

Desmond clicks through 254 different fields of information, and says it only gets better from there. "It's fairly simple once you get the hang of it. It's powerful when you add in all the data on the back end— there's just tons of things to look at."

Maptitude for Redistricting is made by the Caliper Corporation of Newton, Massachusetts, which was founded in 1983 to consult on transportation issues, producing traffic simulation and highway and public transportation planning models. It had detailed maps and terrific software, and recognized that standard redistricting software, then priced between $500,000 and $1 million, was beyond the reach of most state legislatures. In 2015, they were licensing Maptitude for between $5,000 and $10,000.

"You can be productive and it doesn't require you to be an expert user of the software," Caliper president Howard Slavin once told *Roll Call*. "You have a good product when you know it's simple enough for a politician to use it."

Many of Caliper's early clients included social causes and Democratic-aligned groups: the NAACP and the Southern Christian Leadership Conference, for example, wanted to double-check the lines drawn by white legislators for racial bias. But Slavin insisted to *Roll Call* that the software is nonpartisan. Whether it is used to lock in partisan control or to enhance competitiveness is in the hands of the person wielding the mouse.

"The complexity in redistricting comes not from the operation of the software," Slavin said, "but for whoever is doing it, figuring out what their objective is and how to achieve it."

I ask Willie Desmond if we could pretend to be right-leaning partisan mapmakers. Could we design districts in what's essentially a 50–50 red–blue state in such a way as to ensure a 10–3 ratio of Republican congressmen, as was achieved in North Carolina in 2014?

"You could."

How easy is it?

"Very easy."

Desmond grabs his mouse and starts drawing. "I mean, assuming that future elections look like past elections—looking at this block, for example, and then cross-referencing with election results, you can see a lot of things. Looking at voter files, you know who turned out to vote. I could load up the latitude and longitude of every single person in the entire state, and know that they live at this house, and know they voted in these three elections but they didn't vote in these two primaries."

So the mapmakers could know all of the voting patterns block by block, and even house by house? I ask. Desmond says that they're able to get pretty close to that. "You know who cast a ballot, and then along with that, you know how this neighborhood voted by precinct. So you take the blocks that make up this precinct and you desegregate that election result to the individual blocks." This does not sound like desegregation to me; it sounds like the mapmakers have the power to resegregate us. "I would know that this block, for example, gave 9.7 votes to John McCain and 5.8 votes to Barack Obama in the 2008 election. That's the level of information you're dealing with. That's the level of geography where you know things. That's the level of geography where you draw."

That the mapmakers have information this granular, and can use it so immediately, shouldn't be shocking. Yet it is. It puts the three-district swirl that fills in around the fighting Disney characters of Pennsylvania's 7th district in sharp context. You don't imagine that they could simply be sitting in a Starbucks carving precise, unbeatable lines, that this could be as easy as selecting a fantasy football lineup.

Before I can ask how much time something so complicated and intrusive would take, Desmond has the overlay complete. One more click and he can shade the partisan strength block by block in any color of his choosing. These lines look complex, and the thinking behind them is. However, the data and the technology make ratfucking almost as easy as one-click ordering on Amazon. It has made rewiring our democracy as simple as outbidding a rival on eBay, with the additional similarity that the side with the most money wins the prize. The data, the technology and the ease and certainty with which they can be manipulated if either side has the political will to do so are what made the post-2010 redistricting cycle fundamentally different from any other in the modern era.

Technology only gets more exact. Remember how you texted on your massive cell phone in 2000, with each number on the keypad standing in for three letters, and compare that to the sleek iPhone you had in 2010. Data analysis came a similar distance in that decade. I'm curious to know what Desmond thinks will be different in the next cycle, which begins in 2020.

"At this point the computer power is so good that you could do a kind of genetic algorithm, where you give it the parameters you're looking for and it basically just tries combination of things." I'm not sure if he's letting me in on a secret or a fear. A genetic algorithm? In the same way that Amazon and Netflix know exactly what I want to buy based on other purchases, the computer will figure out how I like to vote?

"Well," he says, "you say, 'I want the most compact district that's as close to a 50–50 split of this election result, without breaking many of these county lines'—and just let it go off and think. It can compute infinite numbers of combinations and find what would be the best combination."

Desmond seems like a nice guy, and he has enough faith in the technology that he isn't completely terrified as to where this could go. On the other hand, I spy the Obama inauguration souvenirs in his office and don't particularly want anyone's thumb on the scale. The partisans are right: there's no way to remove politics from something as human as redistricting. But putting it in the hands of brilliant algorithms opens the possibility that redistricting becomes nothing but politics.

"It's kind of almost reassuring, though"—and any time someone says something is kind of almost reassuring, that seems like a cue to make the face of Edvard Munch's *The Scream*—"to know that if you can be specific about what criteria you think are important, you can tell a computer to go off and work toward those criteria.

"If a commission wanted to build the most compact map and that was the only criteria they cared about, they could let a computer try every combination of every block with every other block and it would build you the most compact map. If you said all we care about is perimeter, we want the lowest total perimeter, all the districts have to be contiguous, and they all have to have equal population, a computer could find that combination."

Of course, compactness and contiguity and Polsby–Popper scores aren't really what partisan mapmakers are looking for. If the goal is actually to lock in an enduring majority, however, that's never been easier. So if a partisan wanted to ensure a decade's worth of dominance, how would this program help? Desmond doesn't even pause.

"The key thing is coming up with an index that I think locks it in." He quickly insists that this is not what his firm did here in Arizona. "You'd need algorithms that predict how districts would evolve over the next ten years, and all of that is fairly easy now to do. If you really wanted to get aggressive, what would happen and what's possible?" he asks. "The firm I work for was founded as a microtargeting firm. We do predictive analytics for campaigns—that's harnessing the hundreds of data points we have on every single person and trying to predict people's attitudes and behaviors. You could not only look for past behaviors"—and this is where it gets both interesting and scary—"but if you could build predictive models to think? Say, this is the age at which a person with this income and education and ethnicity might transition from

Democratic to Republican. Or this area is likely to become more African American and hence more Democratic, or this area is going to be gentrified and changing."

These predictive models, he suggested, aren't much different in the end than what Chipotle or Trader Joe's or Starbucks uses to figure out where they should put their next stores. With every click and every purchase, we give marketers more information about us, and that data provides a snapshot not only of what a neighborhood looks like, but what a neighborhood will become. The savvy mapmaker, Desmond says, would be thinking about what the map will look like mid-decade. Let the other side think the map is fair in 2022, for example, while you use predictive powers to understand how the partisan makeup is likely to shift over the rest of the decade. Now that's crafty.

"You would build districts that the other side could tolerate now, because they don't know what you know about what it's going to look like in the future. You set the table for future gains, knowing the way that populations are changing, the way people are moving, the way their opinions are changing. That's really how you could game the system going forward.

"Once people get really serious about trying to win state legislatures, it's going to be somebody building predictive models to tell you what that area is going to look like at some point in the future. Knowing the technology, that's where it easily could be. Now, it would take a huge investment in resources to do all that . . ."

What a smart investment that would be. That's the next political Moneyball. Now that the *Citizens United* decision has unleashed limitless dark money, it only takes one billionaire to write an eight-figure check and bet that his or her side could fine-tune a model so smart and intuitive that it locks in control of the House for another decade. An upfront investment like that would probably save money merely by taking potentially competitive races off the table for ten years. How simple would it be to devise that algorithm, given a big check and the resources?

Desmond turns back to the computer, clicks the mouse, and shrugs with his eyebrows. That easy.

CHAPTER 5

MICHIGAN

A Garbage Dump
Is the Cherry
on Top

Maptitude may be easy, but it is not usually pretty. A toddler too young for tangrams could not have created an odder collage of geometric shapes than the randomly aligned rectangles and triangles crowning Michigan's 14th congressional district. This is one of the most wildly engineered districts anywhere in America, and not only because of the Euclidian contortions at its northern tip.

If every gerrymandered congressional district is its own Rorschach test, Michigan's 14th resembles a snake—a very curious snake, coiled, perhaps asleep, then rising to stretch the top of its long body to the left, before craning its large head around.

It makes sense to see a snake within these lines. The 14th was drawn to shoehorn the African American-dominated cities of Pontiac and Detroit, 31 miles apart, into one district, packing in as many Democratic voters as possible. It worked beautifully. Democrat Brenda Lawrence, a longtime African American mayor and councilwoman from Southfield, carried it in 2014 with a resounding 78 percent of the vote. Meanwhile, Republicans swept the carefully carved surrounding seats and established a 9–5 delegation majority.

Well, "beautiful" might not be the word for the 14th. Artful, certainly.

After all, Pontiac and Detroit are surrounded by wealthier voters in whiter suburbs, which mapmakers wanted to spread across several new Republican districts. Hence the coiled snake beginning in the poorest neighborhoods of Detroit, the head that's the city of Pontiac, and that long, thin neck connecting the poor, black cities while surrendering as few white votes as possible. At its very top is that small knot—maybe a growth, or just a bump where our snake banged its head—of those strewn tangrams.

These lines look random or strange on a map; they don't reveal their reasons for being. The only way to appreciate their artistry—and understand their very real impact—is to trace them by car. That's how I found myself one August day as deep within that knot as you can get, making turn after turn within this bizarre formulation, and finding the answer to what's actually within that collection of shapes.

I had found the Pontiac region's garbage dump.

Yes, a garbage dump is the cherry on top of a district drawn to collect the most forgotten neighborhoods of America's most woeful city. It is almost funny, mapmaking as Dadaist performance art, Marcel Duchamp signing a urinal. Except the joke is on us.

But let's begin those 31 miles to the south. There was once a town in the heart of America that invented the Mustang and the assembly line, a town that gave birth to the modern labor movement and Motown, a town where Martin Luther King Jr. first delivered his "I Have A Dream" speech two months before enshrining it in history at the March on Washington in 1963.

The corner of West Jefferson Avenue and Zug Island Road is no longer that Detroit. This is the hellscape of Delray, one of the most polluted neighborhoods in Michigan, one of the poorest and one of the most abandoned. A century ago, Henry Ford built many of the houses in this once-thriving and largely Hungarian neighborhood so his autoworkers could walk to the nearby plants. Those who live here now suffer from some of the highest rates of asthma, lung cancer and emphysema in the state. Only 2,783 residents remain, according to the

2010 census, about 12 percent of the population at its peak. In Detroit overall, a third of the people live below the poverty line; here in Delray it's more severe than that. Almost half fall below the poverty line.

This corner is also at the southeast border of the 14th congressional district, commonly referred to as a "true monstrosity" or the "Eight Mile Mess," as its axis is Eight Mile Road, the traditional boundary between metro Detroit and its suburbs, immortalized by the Eminem biopic. ("You gotta live it to feel it, you didn't you wouldn't get it or see what the big deal is," he rapped. "To be walking this borderline of Detroit city limits is different; it's a certain significance.")

The district's borderlines are bizarre. Eight Mile Road is the long stretch of that coiled snake's body. Above the eastern edge of Eight Mile, the snake rises toward Pontiac. Underneath the western boundary of Eight Mile, the coils encircle the roughest neighborhoods of Detroit and the tony lakeside mansions of Grosse Pointe. Once you near Grosse

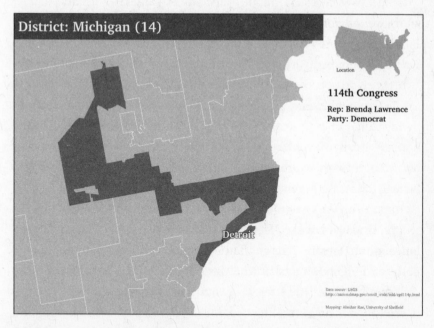

Michigan's 14th, drawn to link the African American voters of Pontiac and Detroit while leaving as many white suburban voters as possible for surrounding GOP districts.

Pointe, Eight Mile's strip clubs and dollar stores give way to Vernier Road, which dead-ends neatly at the Grosse Pointe Yacht Club.

The mapmakers who drew these complicated lines had one goal: to link the poorest parts of Detroit with the large African American population in Pontiac. A district that could pack that many blacks and Democrats within its lines would naturally color adjoining districts bright red. Indeed, not only did Lawrence sweep to victory here, but Democrat John Conyers retained the neighboring 13th with a majority only a shade below 80 percent. That's how reliably blue Michigan—which hasn't gone for a Republican presidential candidate since George H. W. Bush in 1988—sends a 14-member Congressional district to Washington that's weighted red with 9 Republicans and 5 Democrats. The winning Democrats in 2014 racked up huge margins, an average of 69.9 percent of the vote. The Republicans won more narrowly and strategically, with an average of 57.7 percent.

That's why the exact lines are key. The 8th and 11th districts candy-swirl around Pontiac like a summer camp sand art project. Attach the Pontiac region to either the 8th (won by Representative Mike Bishop with 54.8 percent in 2014) or the 11th (captured by Representative Dave Trott with 56 percent) and Michigan's delegation would come closer to the 7–7 split which more accurately reflects its citizens. The odd lines delineating the 14th district are the key to Republican control of the entire state. But if you want to know what was left in and what was left out (to borrow the words of Bob Seger, another Detroit rock icon), you have to follow the precise borders.

I start in Delray one sweltering summer morning, staring at the words "God has forsaken Detroit" scrawled on the side of an abandoned building on West Jefferson. The three boarded-up churches I pass between I-75 and the industrial waterfront seem to confirm that bleak observation. It's a little after 10 A.M. and, armed with a turn-by-turn map of the 14th district, I'm going to drive all 170 miles of its borders. I want to understand why the lines were placed where they were, to understand those juts, notches and tangrams and to see what, if anything, is different from one side of the street to the other. I want to get into the mind of the mapmaker, to see the district the way it looks at street view, after being carved with a mouse and the Maptitude program.

If you wanted to draw all of the poorest corners of the city into one district, you'd certainly start here. West Jefferson is desperate and desolate and forlorn. There are homes overgrown by weeds higher than the house itself. Vacant lots filled with tires make it look like Detroit's dumping ground. A block away on South Street, a shattered white Pontiac sports car sits abandoned in the middle of the road, spun to face the wrong way, glass coating the street.

I turn back toward West Jefferson, where historic Fort Wayne, home to the Museum of the Tuskegee Airmen and a national park, is completely closed. The park in front is a mess. A lone guard barely nods as I turn around and drive toward a Michigan Department of Human Services office that is ringed by barbed wire. There are no people to be seen. Deeper into the district along South Waterman, there are so many boarded-up houses that someone sees it as an advertising opportunity. "This boarding up donated by Danto Furniture," boasts a sign. The few houses that are still trying here sit behind high, locked gates.

Michigan Avenue forms the district's boundary as it turns toward downtown. A Nietzsche-inspired graffiti artist has scrawled "pointless" on the side of a long-abandoned gas station on Michigan and Williams. Across the street, a more literal-minded comic graffitist has added "evil wears a suit" to a burned-out bank drive-through.

The mapmaker draws his first joke farther down Michigan Avenue. Tiger Stadium used to sit at the corner of Michigan and Trumbull; the site is now a park. It would have been in the 14th. The baseball team's new home, Comerica Park, is just a mile away, as is Ford Field, where the NFL's Detroit Lions play. Both are outside the lines. This may be the mapmaker's favorite dig: time and again, whenever the 14th might include a local landmark—Faygo soda's headquarters, the Detroit Zoo, a major General Motors plant—it contorts itself in another direction. There will be no easy campaign cash and no famous constituency for the member of Congress from the 14th. It is as if the mapmaker found the very line between hope and despair, and etched it onto these streets.

Along Mack Avenue, a coffee shop warns that "in order to keep our visitors safe, this bakery is under 24 hour protection." But turn along one of the side streets—leaving the 14th—and after just a block things turn leafier. Five houses sport signs on their lawns for a MACC youth soccer league. Annsbury Avenue is one of the odder dividing lines, one of the two borders which make up the bent knee of the district's underside. The blocks to my left are not in the district. Drive down Evanston and Camden and there are well-manicured lawns, fluttering flags, flowers. Take a right and you're driving an obstacle course of trash cans. A smashed kitchen table holds open a front door of a house with no windows; gutters bisect at the same cockeyed angles of the district's lines, minus the careful planning. Keep moving along Grinnell Avenue and the district reaches out for just one block, to grab Traverse between Raymond and McClellan, scooping up a dozen houses and the world's saddest playground. This reaches nearly to the town of Hamtramck, which attempted to declare bankruptcy in 2010, only to be denied by the state. There's one steady thing here in Hamtramck, the General Motors Detroit–Hamtramck Assembly Center, where GM makes the Cadillac CT6 and the Chevrolet Volt. The unforgiving district line cuts off right in front of it.

A big loop around Highland Park and straight north to Eight Mile and I find one of the strangest cutouts of any district in the country. Eight Mile provides the 14th's axis for the almost 35 miles from I-275 to Lake Shore Road in Grosse Pointe—except for the block and a half from north of Whitlock Street to Farmington Road. Imagine a pointed index finger balancing the state of Oklahoma and you've got the town of Farmington—some 10,200 people and 71 percent white according to the 2010 census, with a median household income over $56,000. As recently as 2013, *Money* magazine ranked this tiny 2.66-square-mile town the 27th best place to live in America. These voters have been siphoned off for the 11th district. Farmington and Farmington Hills actually share a state representative, but not their member of Congress. It's a toss-up over what looks stranger: the map of the 14th with Farmington vacuumed out, or the map of the 11th, where it balances bizarrely over a corner of the district that would otherwise be contiguous.

I follow the convoluted top of Farmington, zigzagging along a couple of dead ends along Grand River and then West 10 Mile all the way to Orchard Lake Road. This is the northern spine of the district, the one road which stretches from Eight Mile all the way to Pontiac, except for the cutout in Farmington and another still to come. The further north you go through Farmington Hills and through West Bloomfield Township, the narrower the district becomes and the wealthier the stores get. The 14th gets the fancy shopping along this narrow bridge, but not the wealthy residents living on either side. At the south end, you drive past chains which must have excited people in the 1990s: The Gap, California Pizza Kitchen, Bed Bath & Beyond, Einstein Brothers Bagels. Orchard Lake Middle School is a gleaming campus. West Bloomfield High looks like a spaceship.

The road bends to the right, and this is the neck of the snake, a series of beautiful lakes which at times narrow the width of the district on land to mere tenths of a mile. Orchard Lake and Pine Lake feature some of the most beautiful homes imaginable; there are homes worth $3–5 million along the aptly named Commerce Drive. We are a long way from Hamtramck, even though we're not. We are also not far from Pontiac. Back on Orchard Lake Road, there's a tiny sliver where we leave the district for several hundred feet before merging onto Highway 24. I know I'm back in the 14th when I hit the stoplight and there's a homeless man approaching cars for change. A little farther along 24, a man in a wheelchair is trying to cross a five-lane highway, a flag hanging off the back of his chair.

I am now more curious than ever to see what lies inside—and outside— the growth atop the snake's head. Imagine a triangle at the bottom, and then three rectangles placed alongside each other. As far as I can tell, Collier Road—the diagonal boundary of the triangle—is the only actual street within this notch, which appears to be otherwise unpopulated and almost entirely surrounded by the 11th district. The map shows a creek near the top, but no people. Collier Road, meanwhile, cuts in and out of two districts. From Baldwin Avenue southeast, it is in the 11th district. Then it crosses the 14th, making that pointy edge at the top left. Perhaps a half mile later you're briefly back in the 11th for less than a half mile before Collier intersects with Joslyn Road and then runs as a straight line across the rest of the 14th's northern edge. So you're out, in, out, in, all in a little over a mile.

Collier Road appears bucolic, quiet and lovely, but at the very spot where the 11th gives way to the 14th there's a set of railroad tracks. We are now literally on the other side of the tracks. Things turn industrial. There's a plant to my right with a sign so small I have to get out of the car to read it. This is the ferrous scrap metal recycling plant. A dump truck rumbles at me. Immediately to my left, once the district encompasses both sides of the road again, is the Pontiac transfer station— that giant notch, literally, a dump.

The Collier Road insults, however, don't stop there. When Collier passes back into the 11th, a beautiful row of pine trees appears, guarding a small handful of houses far off to the right. There are stone fences, long driveways and college flags flying. Yellow center lines are suddenly paved in. From the top of the first driveway, you'd never know the dump sits across the street. Just in case, a sign warns trucks they'd better not come this way. Figure an average of two voting-age people in each house, and this particular boundary slips perhaps 15 voters from one district to another. Given the specificity and the purpose behind every quirky line so far, who wouldn't believe the mapmaker wants them there for a reason?

The next quirk I want to see is the bump which forms the snake's nose. Take a look at the eastern border of Pontiac and Auburn Hills, a straight line except for one acute triangle which nicks out at the corner of N. Opdyke Road and Featherstone Road. North of Featherstone, Opdyke sits in beautiful Auburn Hills and leads to the glittering Palace at Auburn Hills where the NBA's Detroit Pistons play . . . in the 11th congressional district. South of Featherstone, the 14th begins. So what is this corner all about?

Drive toward that notch, and it's like the spacecraft from *Close Encounters* crash-landed. A massive vacant lot is ringed by a chain-link fence and covered in signs hoping for "mixed use/redevelopment." Of course: it's the abandoned Pontiac Silverdome, where the Detroit Lions played until Ford Field opened in 2002. It once hosted a Super Bowl and an NBA All-Star game. Pope John Paul II delivered Mass here before almost 100,000 people in 1987. Led Zeppelin set what was then a world record way back in 1977 when they played before more than 76,000 fans, besting the 75,962 drawn by the Who less than eighteen months earlier. Now it's just one more mapmaker's indignity. Let's rehash: Ford Field, the Palace at Auburn Hills, Comerica Park, all short walks outside the 14th. The old Tiger Stadium and the dilapidated Silverdome, tucked inside the lines. "How complex are these boundaries?" asked political scientists Michael K. Romano, Todd A. Curry and John A. Clark. "One could drive along I-75 from the Pontiac Silverdome to Ford Field—a distance of about 30 miles—and change congressional districts six times." The district line hugs Opdyke all the way south to I-75. It's now almost 6:30 P.M. and I've been driving these boundaries for eight hours, so there's not much surprise when, after the highway interchange, Opdyke slims down from a four-lane fast-food stretch to a pastoral two lanes. Bloomfield Hills announces itself with antique-looking street signs and a country club. This is the 9th district. The 14th careens oddly a few blocks to my right, but I stop zigzagging to see how the other half lives. As I follow Woodward Avenue south toward Eight Mile, I pass an Audi, a Range Rover, a Fiat and a Porsche dealership in succession, and cross over Oxford, Harvard, Cambridge, and Columbia streets.

Just south of 10 Mile, in Pleasant Ridge, I notice another Oxford on the map, followed, naturally, by Cambridge Boulevard. The two streets connect at a horseshoe, or an NCAA tournament bracket, before Cambridge continues on—the name on the bracket's next line—before dead-ending at Maplefield. Take a left on Maplefield and travel a half-block south and you are back in the 14th. I smile at the beauty of Oxford and Cambridge boulevards being just out of reach of the 14th, and turn off to check it out. Neither street disappoints; these gorgeous homes have porticos and long columns, classical pediments and gabled roofs.

There's radar set up in front of a bucolic elementary school to warn drivers to watch their speed.

Pleasant Ridge becomes Oak Park as you turn onto Oak Park Boulevard, and the houses immediately return to normal, lovely middle-classville. I straddle the 14th's boundary down Forest Street, cross Nine Mile for two blocks and head down Central Street, curious about a quirk on the map ahead. Central Street is in the 9th district, but after about half a mile the road curves to the right and is renamed Northend Avenue. You guessed it: after the curve, it's back in the 14th.

I have seen this all day long but still find it hard to believe. I come around the corner, take the first, fast left onto Mitchelldale, and the houses collapse in size. Just blocks behind me, white neighbors on Cambridge Boulevard parked Lexus SUVs in the street and chatted while watering their majestic lawns. I note some random addresses, then later check the map, and the real estate sites Zillow and Homes.com. In the course of 1.4 miles, with three left turns, I have come in and out of the 14th district four times. Homes.com tells me the value of the grand houses on Oxford and Cambridge sits in the $500,000-to-$600,000 range. Cross the line into Oak Park, and the homes average in the $300,000s for the first block, then settle into the $200,000s.

The random address on Mitchelldale I took down? Zillow reports that it last sold in 2014 for $8,750.

Back on Eight Mile, a mall movie theater makes the limited promise of "only digital projection" and "new releases." The only glitter comes from the strip club palaces, one boasting a helicopter landing pad—I imagine, so that the executive clients and the high-priced talent don't have to drive this way.

Daylight is slipping away, but I want to make it back to the waterfront and to Grosse Pointe. Naturally, as Eight Mile heads east into Harper Woods then leafier Grosse Pointe Woods, the road becomes Vernier. The change is immediate; it's dusk, but there's a white family on bikes with kid cars attached. Vernier hits the waterfront at Lake Shore Road. Take a right and keep going, only a dozen miles or so, and Lake Shore becomes Jefferson, and soon you return to the waterfront horror show of Delray. But this is an altogether more glorious view, Canada and waterfront magnificence from the Grosse Pointe Yacht Club.

In 2012, Barack Obama captured 54.2 percent of the vote in Michigan, easily besting Mitt Romney's 44.7 percent. But in Grosse Pointe Shores, hometown hero Romney carried 75 percent of the vote. So the zillionaire owners of these stunning waterfront mansions really do share something in common with the residents of Mitchelldale Avenue. When it comes to voting for a member of Congress, their vote doesn't really count either.

One person could best answer my questions about Michigan's 14th district: the man who drew the lines. Jeff Timmer is waiting for me at Biggby Coffee, across from Michigan's state capitol building in Lansing. Whoever named this place wasn't exaggerating; a large coffee is the size of a Big Gulp. Timmer is in summer casual wear, a short-sleeve golf shirt with a company logo. We grab two coffees and settle by a window.

He's surprised that anyone is interested in redistricting, and eager to talk about the craft he has mastered and seen changed over three different cycles. "I liken it to the Halley's Comet of politics. It comes around on a recurring, predictable basis. It's great to be a Halley's Comet expert when it comes around. But in between times, no one really has any use for it. You know, one of the inside secrets of politics is how critical redistricting is."

I tell Timmer that I've spent the previous day taking the 14th turn by turn and congratulate him on his handiwork. By the end of the day, I say, it felt like I'd noticed so many inside jokes and little details that I imagined myself almost as his ideal reader and biggest fan. I mention the Silverdome, the zigzags by Oak Park above Nine Mile, and the crowning moment: the Pontiac garbage dump at the district's very peak.

"Oh really?" he says indifferently. "I'm just dealing with geography on a map."

I show him pictures from Collier Road: the landfill in one direction, the tree-lined homes in the other, two different districts.

"That's something I haven't done much, going in and inspecting."

It seemed to me, I tell Timmer, that a mapmaker had had a very good time drawing these lines. He gets very modest.

"Well, you know, even that district, there were two forces at work. There's the Voting Rights Act. Then when you look at the geography of Oakland County, there are these municipal boundaries. It's not the mapmaker's fault, or even the evil partisan politician. The city boundaries are what they are." He reaches for his laptop and a map of the district and points out the Pine Lake area, that wealthy, slender top of the snake's neck as it reaches toward Pontiac. "It looks like somebody had to go out of their way to do that, but that's the way the city plans work. They are connected, right here"—he points out the tissue tying the district together—"but you could probably hit a golf ball across it."

The crazy boundaries, he suggests, are just crazy county lines. And the mapmaker's first goal by Michigan statute is to try to keep counties together. "Those criteria haven't changed and they really do tie the hands. It's a puzzle to see who can get the fewest number of county breaks," he says, of the redistricters' art. That's an artful answer itself, reducing mapmaking to fitting counties together, suggesting there really aren't that many possibilities, and that the resulting partisan impact is out of his hands entirely. The mapmaker becomes just an assembler of jigsaw puzzles, the highly-paid technician with the cutting-edge computer tools just a blind monkey with a Sharpie. "The level of discretion you have as a map drawer might be, okay, if you have to split the city of Sterling Heights, do you do it at this road or that road. By that point there really is very little in the way of partisan calculation that can go into these. Surprisingly. I mean, everyone likes to think that there are a lot more Machiavellian smoke-filled rooms. 'Ha, ha! We can do this.' But it's just not the case."

Of course, if there weren't Machiavellian smoke-filled rooms, state politics wouldn't need so many Machiavellis. Lansing might not be Oz, but Timmer is one of Michigan's GOP wizards. When Halley's Comet is out of town, he does not lack for work: Timmer is a master strategist and communicator and wired deep into state politics through years as an adviser, operative and state Republican Party official.

He fell into the headlines not long after redistricting, when in 2012 Republican governor Rick Snyder gained authority to take over the finances of Michigan municipalities, break public union contracts and privatize local land. Critics started a petition drive to end that, which was promptly challenged by a group called the Citizens for Fiscal Responsibility. Media reports linked that association to a strategist named Bob LaBrant, who worked with Timmer at the Sterling Corporation, a GOP consulting firm. Citizens for Fiscal Responsibility tried to get the petitions thrown out on a technicality, arguing that the font on them was too small. The Michigan Board of State Canvassers had to rule on this, and the four-member bipartisan commission deadlocked at two apiece, putting the petition drive on hold. One of the two Republicans on that committee? Jeff Timmer.

Timmer never intended to become an expert mapmaker. In 1991, when the redistricting process got underway, he'd just started a job with the Republican leader of the legislature. The office shared a single computer, and a colleague spent the day at it, surrounded by maps and markers. Timmer was quickly interested. When the GOP set up an official redistricting HQ, he got a job there. Times were very different then. They worked on old 386 computers—"I remember when we got the 486's!" he says, still delighted—that were so clunky and cumbersome that it would take ten or twelve hours to open a set of maps. They had to stagger working hours so that one team worked days and another worked nights. Each team would leave instructions for the other, so that what they'd be working on next could be opened for them in advance. Still, this was an improvement: "Before '91," says Timmer, "things were done with flat maps, the county records, county assessors, registrars of deeds, the official plot maps, big paper in these giant vaults."

Bob LaBrant saw the technological and legal challenges coming even back then. He is an unsung genius of the Super PAC age, a visionary who saw where politics, the courts, technology and campaign contributions were headed decades before others did. After Michigan

Republicans found themselves stymied by Democratic judges during the 1980 redistricting cycle, and underfunded for legal challenges, he began raising money to pay for lawyers, new computers and then-primitive mapping software. He was miles ahead of the Democrats. LaBrant and Timmer brilliantly expanded that head start over the next twenty-plus years.

It is the curse of the operative and the political genius ahead of his time that he can't take credit for what he has done without risking the entire victory. Before Republicans took complete control of redistricting in 2000, there was always the concern that, when Democrats controlled a legislative chamber, they would come up with a plan that split fewer counties. If no legislative compromise could be reached, the competing plans would come before a judge, whose first step would be to find the plan with the fewest fractured counties.

"There were times where if I could have moved the line here to help so-and-so I would have, but I can't," Timmer says. "The congressional districts, there's a little more play there, I guess, because you end up having to split so many communities. But there again, we're somewhat controlled by different constraints. . . . It's not like the Upper Peninsula can be connected to Cheboygan County. That's just the geography. There's nowhere else to go."

Does anybody come to him looking for a map that yields a certain kind of delegation, one which sends a 9–5 or 10–4 group to DC?

"I'm sure lots of people think that. I didn't get any more gold stars on the refrigerator," he says. "At the end of the day, it's can you produce a map that will pass. I guess with all else being equal, once you've gone through the hierarchy of county, municipal, then it's, 'Okay, we can do this or we can do this.' What has always seemed to matter the most is the personalities involved. What does it take to get the votes?

"Democrats in Michigan tend to live very closely together in urban areas and this whole notion of the competitiveness or fairness of districts in a partisan sense—that we should strive to have a partisan balance in as many districts as possible—to me it's foolish. People live where they live, and if there aren't many Democrats in Grand Traverse County or Midland County, what should we do? Somehow draw a thin ribbon across northern Michigan so we can balance out the partisan fairness of this?" The thin ribbon connecting Pontiac and Detroit goes unmentioned.

Timmer tries to downplay the work he has done, and uses the example of the state House maps from 2001. Those maps held through most of the Bush years, but by 2008, Democrats recovered the majority. "In 2001 the moans from the Democrats were that the Republicans had gerrymandered themselves a majority forever. . . . 2008 was like a bloodletting. It was our lowest point in decades, on a map on which we couldn't lose, supposedly."

"Nice job," I tease, and we laugh.

"Let's just say for the sake of argument that I had drawn a very gerrymandered plan in 2001. By 2006, we're looking like fools. By 2008, we're downright stupid. I think the manipulation of the maps aspect is somewhat overblown. Elections are won in a given year, under certain circumstances, by certain people. Candidates still matter. It's an imperfect process done by imperfect people and there's no way you can see the future. Nostradamus maybe could have drawn a better plan."

There's little a state mapmaker can do in the face of an election like 2006, when Republicans were swamped by the national frustration over the state of the Iraq and Afghanistan wars, then faced voters in 2008 mere weeks after a stock market crash and bank cataclysm. It would have taken the Great Wall of China to hold back those waves.

The power behind the throne in Michigan is waiting at the neighboring Grand Traverse Pie Company. Actually, Bob LaBrant might be the genius who first recognized—and fought for—every element of the modern Republican redistricting strategy. LaBrant retired as senior vice president of political affairs for the Michigan Chamber of Commerce in 2014. His hair is now more salt than pepper, but this prescient political thinker is still looking ahead.

"If you have the right talent working, you could almost game-theory a lot of this stuff out and figure out what's this going to mean not only in, let's say, 2021, but what it's going to look like in 2028 as you get toward the end of the cycle," he muses.

Karl Rove and Frank Luntz might be the Republican strategists and thinkers everyone recognizes, but LaBrant quietly and effectively ran this playbook starting in the 1970s. As a twenty-five-year-old junior executive at the Chamber of Commerce in Appleton, Wisconsin, LaBrant read the Powell Memorandum, penned by future Supreme Court justice Lewis Powell in 1971. Powell wanted the business community to offer a counternarrative to that of Ralph Nader's consumer coalition and to speak up against what he saw as an anti-capitalist attitude on college campuses and in the media. "Business must learn the lesson . . . that political power is necessary; that such power must be assiduously cultivated; and that when necessary, it must be used aggressively and with determination—without embarrassment and without the reluctance which has been so characteristic of American business." A new generation of conservative media and pro-business think tanks emerged and laid the intellectual framework for the Reagan revolution. But despite LaBrant's pleadings, the Chamber of Commerce largely resisted becoming an overt political actor until Tom Donohue took over the national organization in 1997 and made it a serious force. That the national Chamber became one of the most reliable financial supporters of the Republican State Leadership Committee is no accident. LaBrant had spent the previous two decades showing how important an investment in redistricting could be.

The redistricting of the early 1980s was disastrous for Republicans, who found themselves cash-strapped and reliant on whatever legal advice they could get for free, while Democrats got help from the powerful United Auto Workers union. In the wake of this, LaBrant talked his business friends into launching a million-dollar-plus Michigan Reapportionment Fund for the next cycle.

"They had a pro bono lawyer and no money for expert witnesses and they just got their clock cleaned," he says. "At the time we had 18 members in the delegation and I think it went 12–6 Democrats."

LaBrant and a Republican colleague, later a judge, sat in a diner and sketched out a plan for raising just over a million dollars. Starting in 1991, "We did have money, we did have lawyers, we did have expert witnesses, we did have computer support. That cycle and then every cycle since that time. That was really important—to plan for redistricting in advance."

Seven figures for redistricting was a lot of money, especially in 1991. It helped purchase those early 386 computers Timmer and his colleagues used, as well as serious legal firepower.

LaBrant cemented his role as the conservative Zelig of redistricting by directing the challenge that would become *Austin v. Michigan Chamber of Commerce,* a key Supreme Court case on the road to Super PACs and *Citizens United.* LaBrant wanted to take on a state law banning corporations from endorsing political candidates, so he pushed the Michigan Chamber to take out a newspaper ad in the *Grand Rapids Press* backing a local state senate candidate. The ad was never placed; a judge refused the Chamber's request to grant an injunction that would have barred any enforcement of the felony provisions for publishing the ad, then upheld the provision a year later, in 1986. But the state Chamber kept pushing, and while they lost before the Supreme Court in 1990—with a howling Justice Antonin Scalia bemoaning an "Orwellian announcement" and an "erroneous injunction"—the last laugh was LaBrant's. Twenty years later, the Supreme Court, led by Scalia's long memory, delayed the *Citizens United* decision to collect briefs on the Austin case, then swept the precedent aside when it issued the eventful *Citizens United* ruling.

Perhaps no individual has done more than LaBrant to shape Michigan politics, let alone one who has never held office. LaBrant's memoir, aptly and hilariously titled *PAC Man*—self-published in 2014—does more to explain the GOP blueprint for, and domination of, the last forty-five years of campaign finance, redistricting and judicial election battles than any other book. It should be required reading, mostly because there's no real reason why a lawyer and Chamber of Commerce official should have such outsize influence. But LaBrant recognized Karl Rove's dictum early—you draw the lines, you make the rules—and figured out how to use the Chamber's PAC to not just grab a seat at the table, but to help pay to rent the room. And as the rules changed, so did LaBrant. As campaign finance law evolved and his reapportionment fund needed to become a 501(c)4, they just threw the word "institute" on it and called themselves the Michigan Redistricting Resource Institute. "It sounded academic," he says.

"When you add up all the money you're going to be spending every two years in legislative races," he adds, "better to have some input at the beginning."

"You just needed to get a core group of people that understood what was at stake and be relentless about it," he says. "Then at times you had to figure out, 'Okay, what's the best way to approach this.' It's nice to have Bob LaBrant walk through the door, but if you've got the Senate Majority Leader to walk through the door with you, that makes it a lot easier to get somebody to decide to write out a check. That's nothing new. That's how power works all of the time."

In Michigan, lines are drawn by the legislature and are subject to veto by the governor. By 2008, Democrats had beaten back the post-2000 gerrymander and established a bigger House majority on Barack Obama's coattails. REDMAP had its work cut out, but as their report states: "The effectiveness of REDMAP is perhaps most clear in the state of Michigan. In 2010, the RSLC put $1 million into state legislative races, contributing to a GOP pick-up of 20 seats in the House and Republican majorities in both the House and Senate."

When Rick Snyder was sworn in as governor in 2011, Republicans controlled the redrawing of all 148 legislative and 14 congressional districts. The firewall they built withstood Obama's reelection. Obama won by just under 10 points in Michigan, and Democrat Gary Peters rode a 20-point landslide into the U.S. Senate, but with the new legislative lines, the GOP retained both state chambers, and Republicans took a 9–5 majority in the congressional delegation.

"We thought we'd have divided control" after 2010, LaBrant says. "We had no idea we could pick up 20 seats in the House. That's why it was also very important to be involved in the [Michigan] Supreme Court races in 2010"—in case judges needed to be called in to break a legislative deadlock. So they raised a lot of money and coordinated with GOP groups in DC. "It was almost embarrassing, the amount of money that we were able to ship off to the Republican Governors Association," he says.

Then they got out the Maptitude and had some fun. First, they needed to connect Detroit and Pontiac in the 14th. That done, it was time to fortify the friendly Republicans and exact a little revenge on Justin Amash, a brash newcomer who was more the style of the Tea Party than the Chamber. Representative Tim Walberg, another Republican, had been defeated in 2008, then recaptured the seat in 2010. "The other goal in redistricting in 2011 was to take the Walberg seat, which had been flipping back and forth with Mark Schauer and Walberg. To solve that you just take Calhoun [County] out of that district and put it in the 3rd district, which was at the time the second most Republican district."

LaBrant is clear, direct and unapologetic. This is the way the game is played. "This is the most important political decision to be made in the state each decade," he says, "and to somehow say, 'We're going to ignore the politics in this and do something that isolates the process from any political input?' The only state that has had any success doing that is Iowa."

Or, as he wrote in his memoir: When you have power, "you exercise it." When you don't, you try and remove the other side's advantage "under the cloak of good government."

It is at once invigorating and terrifying to go from coffee with savvy operatives to a meeting across Capitol Avenue with state representatives Jon Hoadley and Jeremy Moss. Your eyes have to adjust from the dark, smoke-filled room to being blinded by sun-kissed earnestness. Hoadley is thirty-two, Moss just twenty-nine. Together they bring the kind of enthusiasm to redistricting that might get it trending on Twitter, that could rip down that cigar-stenched velvet curtain and show people once and for all that district lines are at the heart of hyperpartisan gridlock.

More likely, they'll be a very tasty snack for the political wolverines. Hoadley and Moss have introduced legislation to remove redistricting power from the consultants and operatives and give it to a truly nonpartisan commission. They are, as one might imagine, not having a lot of luck getting the legislature's leadership to give them a vote.

For Moss, redistricting isn't just theoretical. He was the youngest ever member of the Southfield City Council, in the northern suburbs of Detroit, when first elected in 2011, just as all the congressional lines in the neighborhood shifted and swirled. Suddenly, neighboring communities trying to deal with the same problems would have three different members of Congress. You didn't have to be a longtime politico to understand that West Bloomfield Township, Bloomfield Township and Bloomfield Hills might want to be in the same district.

"Those communities are in one state House district, but three different Congressional districts!" Moss says in disbelief. "If you look at the map of Oakland County and put your finger right on the center of the map, your finger will be on Pontiac. Now spiral your finger in three different districts, and those are our congressional districts. It makes no sense. This is all so one party can get a partisan advantage in an election cycle, but this is a complete disservice to those residents."

We pull out a laptop and study the 14th, which includes Southfield, and Moss's finger goes straight to the Farmington cutout off Eight Mile Road. "They have the same school district. They do everything together. Every community group is the "Greater Farmington this or that." They have the same state senator, the same state representative—and two different congressmen.

"For that carve-out, the purpose was to put the little-bit-more conservative Farmington into the 11th district to tilt it more Republican and to keep the more Democratic Farmington Hills in the 14th. The partisan problem we could talk about. But the practical problem is if you're an education leader, a school board member, you have to dupli-cate your efforts to advocate for anything on the federal level."

Moss sounds genuinely disappointed when he hears I drove the district turn by turn the day before. "I would have taken the drive with you! I should have," he says, calling out some of his favorite oddities.

"Even crazier than all the twists and turns you take to stay in the 14th—if you drive a straight line it's even more ridiculous. You could be in the corner of Square Lake Road and Opdyke. On one side of the road, you are in the 14th. One the other side of the road, driving south, you will be in the 9th. Drive a half mile further and you will be in the 11th. Keep going and you are back in the 14th."

What Hoadley and Moss propose contains elements of the nonpartisan, bureaucracy-driven process that has worked so well in Iowa, as well as the citizens' panel which has helped make redistricting somewhat more fair in California. A nonpartisan state auditor would lead the process and work with citizens who have not run for office, given money to candidates, or worked with candidates. It's not perfect, they know, but the goal, as Hoadley says, is to avoid the "activists who have a partisan mission to dismantle our state when drawing these lines."

When they talk about redistricting, Hoadley elevates it to theory and policy and details, and Moss nails the gut-level punch.

"So at some level," Moss says, "the legislature gets to influence the first portion of it, and then the second step is this double-arm's-length transaction where there is a bit of randomness. We are trying to minimize partisanship while recognizing that some is going to exist. So how do we make it fair and really put people back in charge? There are going to be places in west Michigan that are very Republican and places in central Detroit that are very Democratic. But you are not going to see this situation here where a straight line zigzags through districts and divides communities of interest."

Moss remains outraged that Pete Lund, the chairman of the state House's redistricting and elections committee during the 2011 cycle, took a job as director of the Michigan office of Americans for Prosperity, one of the Koch brothers' conservative lobbying arms. Oddly, however, Moss and Hoadley have struggled to convince even fellow Democrats that this is an important issue. Democrats win the majority of votes in state House races, if you aggregate the totals statewide, but still sit at the short end of a 63–47 partisan divide, yet they still don't get excited about redistricting reform, or perhaps even understand the way Republicans have organized around line-drawing for decades.

"People say, 'No, no, no—2020 is going to be our year. It's going to be a presidential election, more of our voters will turn out. We are going to be the majority,'" he says, sighing at the shortsightedness. "Enough is enough. Our citizens should be drawing the lines, not the legislators who will benefit from those lines. The idea that this will be fixed in 2020 is foolhardy."

Maybe worse than that, it's the kind of naiveté that lands most of your voters in a single district crowned by a garbage dump.

CHAPTER 6

OHIO

"A Small Carve Out Down 77 in Canton"

From a garbage dump to the crown jewel: Ohio is traditionally the most contested prize in presidential politics. The ultimate American swing state is so evenly divided between Democrats and Republicans that Wolf Blitzer and Tom Brokaw have been forced to stay on the air until midnight or later to call it, and Bruce Springsteen fans can usually count on acoustic shows from the Boss every four years, as he tries to excite Democratic turnout in cities and venues that his big tours would not otherwise play.

This national bellwether, however, also has a congressional map where the most likely result is that Republicans win 12 or 13 of the 16 seats even in years when Democrats collect more votes statewide. The maps were drawn by some of Ohio's smartest political strategists, in active consultation with national Republicans in Washington, DC, and top political aides to then House Speaker John Boehner, himself an Ohio congressman. Their secrets might have stayed completely private had a handful of revealing emails not been discovered under a public records request from the Ohio Campaign for Accountable Redistricting. Those emails are enough to show exactly how the Buckeye State was ratfucked.

The process started in summer 2011, behind closed doors and away from the state capitol. But perhaps the most telling email is from the evening of September 12 that year. The following morning, Ohio legislators would be introducing a bill laying out the state's new congressional map. Two veteran Republican political hands, Heather Mann and Ray DiRossi, had been focused on the new lines for many months, and had to finalize the bill and distribute it to officials right away. Tom Whatman, commander of Team Boehner, the House Speaker's political machine, emailed Mann, DiRossi and a redistricting coordinator at the National Republican Campaign Committee with a last-second special request.

"Guys: really really sorry to ask but can we do a small carve out down 77 in Canton and put Timken hq in the 16th. I should have thought about this earlier," he wrote at 9:28 P.M.

"Yeah, sure, no problem," replied the NRCC's Adam Kincaid eight minutes later. His email signature identifies him as the NRCC's Redistricting Coordinator. "Ray/Heather, do you want me to do it and send the file over, or will y'all do it?"

"You do and get equivalence file to use asap," answered DiRossi just moments later.

"Thanks guys," Whatman wrote back at 9:41 P.M. "Very important to someone important to us all. I relly [sic] should have thought of this."

At 10:55 P.M., Kincaid circulated the new maps, as he wrote, "virtually unchanged from before."

The "someone important to us all" is easy to decode. That's the House Speaker himself, who launched Team Boehner in 2011 focused on "one goal: maintaining and expanding our new House majority." Boehner had tapped Whatman, a veteran Ohio GOP operative, to lead those efforts, which naturally included a close eye on redistricting.

By "virtually unchanged," Kincaid meant that he'd added a peculiar peninsula jutting out of the northeast corner of Republican incumbent Jim Renacci's new district. It's the only part of Canton, Ohio, that sits in the 16th district and not the 7th. The census shows that the population of this puppet-shaped peninsula is zero. It contains something more valuable than voters: campaign contributions. The lines were hastily redrawn in order to add the Timken Company and two of its industrial manufacturing plants to the 16th. Perhaps coincidentally, Renacci had been the recipient of almost $210,000 in political donations from Timken executives, family members and the company's PAC—baldly named the Timken Co. Good Government Fund—over the previous three years, according to the *Cleveland Plain Dealer*. (A report by the Ohio Campaign for Accountable Redistricting titled "Elephant in the Room" notes other last-minute changes to the 15th district, creating two odd peninsulas, one to include Congressman Steve Stivers's new house in Upper Arlington, the other sneaking into a Democratic district in Columbus to steal for Stivers—a former banking lobbyist—the headquarters of Nationwide Insurance and other deep-pocketed banking and insurance interests.)

The mapmakers and national Republicans didn't blink at the last-minute redraw. They didn't ask any questions. They didn't even loop in the Ohio legislative leaders ostensibly responsible for the bill, such as the state House Speaker or senate president, even though they had signed off earlier that day on what they believed was the final version. DiRossi, Kincaid and Mann knew they were calling the shots.

"I am still committed to ending up with a map that Speaker Boehner fully supports, with or without votes from two members of leadership," state senate president Tom Niehaus wrote to Whatman after requesting changes to the congressional map desired by those two members. Final maps arrived in Niehaus's inbox the next day. Niehaus's first emailed question to an aide was, "Did Whatman sign off?"

The Speaker of the U.S. House of Representatives and his political team don't have an official role to play in Ohio redistricting. By law, Ohio's congressional districts are drawn by the state legislature, with veto power to the governor. State legislative districts are mapped by an Apportionment Board consisting of five officials: the governor, the state auditor, the secretary of state and one representative of each party chosen by the state legislative leaders.

They didn't need an official role: Republicans controlled the entire process, from a 4–1 majority on the Apportionment Board to domination of the legislature and governor's office. They held those advantages because of REDMAP. In 2008, Barack Obama had helped Democrats capture a decisive 53–46 majority in the state House. To turn that around, REDMAP allocated nearly $1 million to a mere six state house races in 2010. They won five of the six, and Republicans rode the anti-Obama wave all the way to an even more decisive 59–40 cushion. The GOP added two seats to their majority in the state senate, grabbing a commanding 23–10 advantage.

That's the rhythm of a swing state, after all, and how Ohio politics has traditionally worked. A statewide swing toward the Democrats elects Democrats to the legislature. A big year for Republicans nationally puts the GOP in charge. What happened in 2012, however, broke the usual rules. It was a solid victory by Barack Obama, yet Republican dominance of the state legislature and the congressional delegation continued. Whatman, Mann and DiRossi maximized the GOP's strength, creating district lines that functioned as sandbags against the Democratic wave.

In 2012, helped by the improving economy and an effective bailout of the Midwest auto industry, Obama defeated Mitt Romney by three percentage points in Ohio. U.S. Senator Sherrod Brown, one of the most liberal members of the Senate, was reelected by 6 points and a 325,000-vote margin over the Republican state treasurer. Democrats got more votes than Republicans in races for the state House—but Republicans commanded a 60–39 supermajority of seats, *despite getting less support at the ballot box*. The aggregate statewide vote for U.S. House races did narrowly favor Republicans, but that slim edge earned them a staggering 75 percent of the seats. That result, said longtime Ohio politics writer Steve Hoffman, was "a margin so huge as to overwhelm other explanations, among them ticket-splitting and population patterns that show a concentration of poor and minority voters in urban areas." It had to be the gerrymander, he concluded.

Republicans agreed, and even boasted of their success. REDMAP's 2012 summary report concluded this about Ohio: "The GOP controlled the redrawing of 132 state legislative and 16 congressional districts.

Ohio: A swing-state with congressional maps so lopsided it looks entirely red.

Republican redistricting resulted in a net gain for the GOP state house caucus in 2012 and allowed a 12–4 Republican majority to return to the U.S. House of Representatives—despite voters casting only 52 percent of their vote for Republican congressional candidates."

A bare majority, in other words, elected a congressional delegation that was 75 percent Republican. The GOP retained the U.S. House with a 234–201 margin. Had 17 more seats changed hands, so would have the House. Now you know why John Boehner's political team was so interested in redistricting: the 8-seat Ohio advantage alone provided 25 percent of his cushion.

"All restraints went by the boards after the 2010 census," wrote Hoffman. "It is hard to imagine Obama coattails long enough to have dragged Democrats to winning a majority of U.S. House seats from Ohio. Republicans drew oddly shaped districts that made little sense in terms of communities of interest. The overriding goal was to pack Democrats into as few safe seats as possible, opening up advantages for Republicans everywhere else."

The secret emails uncovered by the Ohio Campaign for Accountable Redistricting tell of near-comic efforts to keep all the proceedings behind closed doors. "Keep it simple, keep it safe" was the theme of Republican National Committee redistricting training materials, which were provided to Mann and DiRossi. (Indeed, a review of internal emails shows that the only time the GOP operatives snapped at one another was when Mann forwarded a map to Mark Braden, a national GOP attorney and redistricting expert whose official bio boasts that he "can rightly claim to be the father of 'soft money' as now used in national political campaigns." Braden wanted to see a map in color for a September 2011 meeting in Washington, at which the lines would be reviewed by national officials. DiRossi responded angrily, writing, "this is exactly what i said I didnt want to do. not the content. but external maps.")

A private PowerPoint presentation used to train Mann and DiRossi suggested a redistricting headquarters with "control access to location," "machine security, plan security, personnel security" and "away from distractions." Mann's initial idea was the capitol's sergeant at arms's office, across from the House clerk. But when she learned in an email that there would be rare instances when others might have access to the room in order to use the autopen, she began looking into other options. Ultimately the redistricting team rented a room at the Columbus Doubletree hotel from July 17 through October 15 (cost to taxpayers: $9,614.89), moved out the furniture and dubbed it "the Bunker." Even the Doubletree staff was confused. "What is the purpose of the room," the hotel's sales manager asked in an email. "Why is it being used for 3 months, privately? This is just a security issue for both parties involved."

"The Bunker" stuck as a nickname for the office, showing that Republicans had a sense of humor about how seriously they took security. The Republican team paid such careful attention to their privacy that when they discussed the location of their meetings, or where they'd be working from that day, they'd refer to the Doubletree as the Bunker. "Im [sic] free all day today at the Bunker," DiRossi wrote Matt Schuler, the Senate Republicans' chief of staff, in an August 16 email with the subject line "Tuesday at redistricting office" sent to Schuler's personal account. "Let me know when you are coming over—Troy is here now and most of the day too." Troy, it seems likely, is Troy Judy, the chief of staff for GOP House Speaker William Batchelder. Later, when Mann organized a September 6 "weekly redistricting meeting" with an invitation list that was a who's who of Ohio's legislative and executive branch—some, such as Troy Judy, with their personal emails and not their official state addresses—she stated the location simply as "offsite."

In addition to the private meetings, secret locations and personal email use for state business, the plan was to keep maps private for as long as possible. A timeline suggested having draft congressional maps completed by August 19, 2011, but keeping them "in the can" until the legislature returned four weeks later. Asked what was meant by "in the can," a state GOP spokesman claimed ignorance of the phrase's definition.

Behind closed doors at the Bunker, sophisticated maps were being drawn. Ohio Republicans thought they'd done a good job with the lines during the 2000 process, but Democrats did manage to win back the state House during the 2008 Democratic wave. Mapmakers did not want a dummymander to happen again. They created a savvy way to evaluate districts on a precinct-by-precinct level so that they would have a good sense of how the new district would perform even if Democrats had another strong year.

First, they used the percentage of vote received by John McCain in 2008. McCain ran at just under 47 percent, about 5 percent below the average for a statewide Republican candidate, so if you could create a district where McCain would have defeated Obama, you'd know that this would be a solid Republican seat even in an off year for the GOP.

Then they expanded that into something called the "unified index," which tallied the GOP vote percentage in the 2004 presidential race, the 2006 attorney general and auditor races, McCain's 2008 numbers and the 2010 governor's race which was won by the Republican John Kasich. Democrats won two of these races by around 5 percent; Republicans won three squeakers. This index presented an even clearer image of how the district would lean during competitive years. The goal was to create as many districts as possible where the index exceeded 50 percent Republican—again, providing extra insulation even during a Democratic wave.

Emails show that the mapmakers considered trying to draw a 13–3 Republican delegation. That would mean settling for four districts where McCain had polled under 50 percent—Republican-leaning, but potentially competitive if Democrats won big in a presidential year. Even so, the Republicans knew this might be overreaching, and smartly decided not take the risk. Instead, they settled for a solid and nearly unbreakable 12–4 majority, with 11 of the 12 districts safely Republican and only one of them, the 14th, a possible swing district under any circumstances.

Internal documents show that the GOP created a partisan voting index for each of the districts to go along with the unified index; any district R+5 or better was likely majority Republican by that many points. Eleven of the 12 fell between +5 and +11. That meant the district was safely Republican, but not so safe as to waste votes which might help elect Republicans elsewhere. The one swing district, the 14th, was R+3. Democrats, meanwhile, were packed into so few districts that their indexes measured between +12 and +29.

The U.S. House gerrymander was secured by working those same indexes on the local level. The mapmakers did such a good job that it's hard to find anyone in Ohio politics who thinks it can be reversed for perhaps two decades to come.

"We are now have [sic] a majority of seats that lean Republican (50% or better) on 2008 Presidential numbers," wrote Heather Mann that September 2011 in an email that went to Troy Judy, Ray DiRossi, House GOP communications director Mike Dittoe, Ohio House Republican Organizational Campaign Committee executive director Ben Yoho and Chad Hawley, the policy director for House Republicans. The email, also discovered by the Ohio Campaign for Accountable Redistricting, was sent to everyone's Gmail address, and not from a state account.

The next statistic from Mann shows how effective and enduring the Republicans believed the new lines would be. "Previously, to retain a 50+seat majority under 2008 Presidential year conditions, we had to win all seats above a 49.14%; now we only have to hold 50 or more seats that are 50.94 or better." Break down the jargon and strip away the stats: what Mann is saying here is that they drew such an effective firewall that a vast majority of seats are safely in Republican hands even during the most Democratic year these consultants could possibly imagine. The map was rigged so carefully as to make elections unnecessary at best for the remainder of the decade. Democrats could try and undo this, sure, if they could manage to win on these maps in 2020, and take over the apportionment board offices as well. That's a rainbow unicorn picking up the 7–10 split at the bowling alley.

When the cartographers congratulated themselves over email once most of the work was done, it's clear that they were thinking like Chris Jankowski. By spending the money in 2010 and redrawing the lines the next year, Republicans knew they could eliminate expensive swing seats and minimize the number of races they actually had to bother contesting. "We have made significant improvements to many [House districts] on this list. Hopefully saving millions over the coming years," DiRossi wrote to Judy and Mann around midnight on a Friday that September.

"It's 1 AM," Mann replied to them both almost an hour later. "Go to bed you political junkies."

Sometimes it takes a geography genius to decode what a wizard map-maker has done. The best in all of Ohio is Mark Salling, a research fellow at Cleveland State University's Levin College of Urban Affairs, the director of the college's Northern Ohio Data and Infor-mation Service, and a scholar with the university's Center for Elec-tion Integrity.

Gray-bearded, tweedy and affable—the very definition of professorial—Salling works from a basement suite just off Euclid Avenue covered with various maps of Ohio: population density, housing types, highway visualizations. "This is my therapy," he says. "When I have something I don't want to do and I'm trying to procrastinate, I make a map."

If Big Data is the buzzword connected to stats gurus like Nate Sil-ver, Salling is a Small Data guy. Geographic information systems are his thing, the nooks and crannies deep inside the numbers. Salling's office provides the state with the raw data needed for redistricting—which might be why the end results so offended his professional sensibility.

In 2009, when a Democrat, Jennifer Brunner, was secretary of state, her office and Salling's program cosponsored a statewide contest that gave citizens GIS mapping tools and urged them to draw lines based on the legal standards of compactness and contiguity, while keeping counties and communities of interest together. This was not a popular video game. There were only a couple of dozen entries. But every one of them, Salling says, scored higher on those objective metrics than the maps the Republicans produced in 2011.

"I'm not looking at this as a partisan," Salling says. "People on the right complain about big government taking away our rights. Yet the most fundamental right of a democracy, the right to have your vote count, those same people don't seem to be worried about it. It strikes me as insane."

Salling likes to make charts as much as he does maps, and he showed me several, first from the 2001 redistricting, when Republicans managed to draw lines that gave them a higher percentage of congressional seats than the percentage of votes the party earned statewide in every election that decade. Perhaps the most historically significant year was 2006, when Republicans took 61 percent of the seats with just 47 percent of the vote. Then there's a bar graph that shows the percentage of Democratic votes by district. The Democratic districts are skyscrapers; they carry their seats with approximately 70 percent of the vote. The Republican districts are a solid Midwestern mixed-use skyline; they win more, but with vote totals in the high 50s.

Salling argues for a system based on representational fairness, in which there's less of a discrepancy between seats won and percentage of the total vote. "The discrepancy is the result of partisan control of redistricting" he says. "The process of redistricting is critical to partisan political control, and partisan political control is critical to redistricting."

Salling shuffles through another set of graphs, searching for one he has constructed which clearly illustrates how one-party domination of redistricting leads to that party's domination of the state's congressional delegation. In the 1980s, when the Democrats and Republicans had to work out lines together, the state sent a fairly even number of Democrats and Republicans to Washington. After Republicans took complete control of the process in 1991, each successive census gave the state's delegation a stronger GOP majority.

"Democrats just weren't that cutthroat, or haven't developed the approach Republicans have successfully implemented in 2000 and 2010," he says. "If the Democrats were in the same position of power, maybe they would have done the same thing.

"I'm a technician mostly, right? So my big hope is GIS." But will technology, which makes it easier to draw even more detailed lines with each passing decade, make things better or worse? "I think it should help. The more tools that are out there for everybody to use, the better. Hopefully not just one side will use them. I'm not being partisan here.

I'm just making an observation that the Democrats have been dumb about all this for a long time."

If Ohio Democrats have been slow on redistricting, it's not for lack of effort by Kathleen Clyde. Clyde is a third-term state representative from Kent, the largest city in northeastern Portage County, not far from Cleveland and best known as the home of Kent State. She graduated first in her high school class in nearby Garrettsville, and after college returned home to work with a nonprofit trying to develop affordable housing for the homeless. When she couldn't generate interest in poverty issues from her local lawmakers, Clyde got involved on the electoral side and jumped into the 2004 John Kerry campaign, the race so close that Ohio decided it for George W. Bush late on election night. The shenanigans she saw at the polls—long lines in urban precincts, broken or inadequate machines—infuriated her and made her more convinced that the system was broken. After a month to recover from the campaign heartbreak, she applied to law school at Ohio State, determined to work on electoral reform.

Clyde was still fresh-faced and naive enough in her first term to want to be involved in the 2011 redistricting, even though the Democrats had no control on the board. Her minority leader, a veteran lawmaker named Armond Budish, was among the few Democratic voices there, and he likely didn't want to waste his time in public hearings all summer long, knowing that his voice would barely be heard above a whisper. So when Clyde expressed interest, you can almost imagine how he leapt to allow her to sit in for him.

Clyde is poised and politic, careful and clearly ambitious, but over lunch close to the Cleveland airport, she gets outraged all over again. "It was a sham process," she says. "I sat in on this traveling summer committee where they took the apportionment board on the road so we could show the maps to the people. But we didn't have the maps! We went on the road and we didn't have anything to show. So we didn't get very good attendance, and they use that as proof that people don't care. Of course, they're during the day, they're not well publicized—and we don't have any maps. I traveled around the state and saw nothing, just frustration and discouragement from the people who had the where-withal to find out about it and come. They do that on purpose, too. Chaos, confusion, trying to make government look incompetent. It's a very cynical approach designed to keep people from having faith in their government and wanting to participate in the electoral process. When less people turn out, Republicans do better. Especially in Ohio."

Clyde's status as the Democratic apportionment board stand-in did not get her into the Bunker at the Doubletree where the real work was done. "No," she says drily. "No access to the Bunker granted. We got access to things so last-minute that it was almost absurd. I believe we had the first *legislative committee* hearing on the map without actually having maps. Of course, *they* had the maps, but they weren't making them public."

Clyde rattles off the stats: the iron supermajority Republicans hold with 60 seats despite being outvoted statewide. The way the Republicans will use state funds to pay for any court challenges to their maps, while making Democrats scramble to find money to contest them on behalf of what's often a majority of voters. How hard it is to recruit candidates and raise money for a party with no power to make laws.

"I would say that people's votes are not important in many of these districts because of how one-sided they are. I think that our overall representation does not match Ohio. We've seen egregious attacks on voting rights and on women. Ohioans support the right to an abortion, yet we've seen some of the most restrictive actions. We have a number of ultraconservative members of Congress that face primary challenges, and it pushes them so the most extreme candidates win. This isn't the state we are. So Ohioans just shake their heads at, 'Who are these people in Congress?'"

John Boehner is no longer one of those Ohioans in Congress. The House Speaker, whose political team helped wield the pen that delivered the so-far unbreakable Republican advantage, found himself struggling to control a caucus with so many conservatives who saw little need, and even less purpose, in compromise. His job was made impossible by a new breed of post-2010 Congressional Republicans: pure in their conservatism, united in their distaste of dealmaking with Democrats and President Obama, and certain that they represented districts where their only electoral challenge was by someone even further to the right. Boehner's top deputy, Eric Cantor, once a conservative young Turk himself, was first to go, losing a summer 2014 primary challenge to an even more hardline Republican backed by talk-radio power Laura Ingraham. In September 2015, Boehner announced his resignation, yielding in the face of pressure from the House Freedom Caucus. That group contained approximately 35 GOP members, about half of them from the South, from districts so Republican that members felt no need to moderate their views. Indeed, moderating their views was the only thing that could push them out of office.

"The problem is, there are 30 to 40 members that have now decided they can block a Speaker from being elected on the floor of the House—'cause you got to get 218 and Republicans margin is only 27 or 28," Cantor told an interviewer in the fall of 2015, decrying the "vocal minority" who made Republicans look dysfunctional. Redistricting had made the Republican Party too conservative even for what had been the most conservative, revolutionary edge. Meanwhile, Donald Trump, Ted Cruz and Ben Carson all showed, at one point, great popularity or even dominance in the party's race for the White House, while establishment candidates including Jeb Bush, Chris Christie and Ohio governor John Kasich spent 2015 failing to gain traction amongst a GOP base that had moved further to their right.

The Republican Frankenstein—created in part by safer and safer seats, held by more and more conservative members, which in turn generated deeper and deeper frustration among the conservative base when congressional majorities did not lead to exactly the policies they hoped to see—had become uncontrollable. Boehner would once have been able to count on a Washington, DC, office for five years after leaving the speakership. Freedom Caucus hardliners sought to eliminate even those funds and to put the money toward deficit relief.

Tom Whatman, meanwhile, once Boehner's top political aide, found himself in the fall of 2015 working on behalf of Ohio Senator Rob Portman's reelection campaign, who was eager to build connections to Democrats who might cross party lines to support the veteran incumbent. Portman, a Republican, feared that a 50–50 Midwestern bellwether like Ohio would reject a candidate like Cruz or Trump, jeopardizing his own reelection. Those lopsided congressional lines would not protect him in a statewide race.

By 2015, Republicans found themselves willing to support modest redistricting reform. Ohio voters backed, with a majority of over 70 percent, a November 2015 referendum which added two new members to the Apportionment Board which draws the state legislative lines. Under this plan, unless two members of the minority party on the board voted for new maps, the maps would have to be redrawn after four years instead of ten. The board was also instructed to "attempt to draw" a map that does not favor either party, and corresponds to overall voter preferences. Clyde and many reformers saw it as half a loaf, as it only affected state legislative lines and did not do anything to address the state's tilted congressional maps, but it at least showed that there is widespread public support for reform. Nevertheless, it was hard to miss the irony: Ohio's ratfuck was so complete that even its master designers couldn't pull it back or control its extremes.

CHAPTER 7

DEMOCRATS

"They Just Whistled Past the Graveyard"

The Democrats who jubilantly celebrated victory in Grant Park on election night 2008 believed that the evolving face of America would make the party's ascent inevitable. Democrats dreamed that America's changing demographics would lead to another decade of triumphs and a new permanent majority. The actual numbers proved quite different. After the 2014 election, the last of the Barack Obama era, and a Republican wave almost as complete as the GOP's 2010 tour de force, the Democrats were virtually wiped out almost everywhere beyond the White House and the coasts.

By 2014 Republicans controlled 32 of the nation's 50 governorships, a gain of 10 since 2009. Republicans doubled their advantage in state legislatures, holding 33 of 49 state Houses and 35 of 49 state senates. (Nebraska's unicameral legislature is officially nonpartisan.) Democrats held 816 fewer state legislative seats than they had before Obama took office, a number the *New York Times* ranked as among the very worst performances since the 1800s. "These are historic highs," Tim Storey of the National Conference of State Legislatures told me. "It's almost stretched as far as it can possibly go. Republicans control more legislative chambers than ever before—

and almost as many seats nationwide." But perhaps the more ominous number for Democrats is this: only 36.6 percent of registered voters bothered to go to the polls in 2014, the lowest turnout since World War II. There's no demographic advantage big enough to conquer the level of apathy Democratic voters have felt in nonpresidential election years since 2006.

When a party loses this many governorships and state legislative seats, not only do they end up on the wrong side of redistricting, but the bench of future stars for higher office thins as well. That's how you end up with an election like the one in 2016, with a baker's dozen of Republican senators and big-state governors seeking the presidency, while Hillary Clinton runs against a 74-year-old socialist and a former Maryland governor best known for inspiring a character on HBO's *The Wire*.

How could this happen to the Democrats? How could a party with such a genuine demographic edge get out-organized, out-strategized and out-energized in election after election? I went in search of the party's wise men and would-be Paul Reveres, the people who'd warned of the importance of redistricting, but whose shouts vanished into a black hole of complacency, overconfidence and unimaginative thinking.

After the Republican rout of 2010, Steve Israel, a New York congressman then in his sixth term representing suburban Long Island, took over as chairman of the Democratic Campaign Congressional Committee. If Washington is a city filled with unpleasant jobs, Israel stepped into one of the most hopeless. The DCCC chair serves a two-year sentence as a party road warrior, raising money, barnstorming chicken dinners and county barbecues and, most importantly, trying to recruit congressional candidates who might actually be able to flip a district. A successful term pole-vaults a politician into leadership, maybe even majority leader someday. On the other hand, no ambitious mayor or state senator wants to sacrifice a career—let alone endure those barbecues every weekend all summer and fall—only to lose 58–42 in an unwinnable district. So the chairman bounces from one

Hampton Inn to the next, Milwaukee to Dayton then Dubuque, mar-
shaling every drop of persuasion and a dash of Washington glam-
our to arm-twist the hopeful and the recalcitrant into campaigns
all their own, while strong-arming less promising candidates to the
sidelines.

Steve Israel spent four years doing this. Two congressional terms.
That's 208 weeks of Friday cab rides to Reagan National or LaGuar-
dia airport. His second marriage collapsed. The late nights, the
loneliness, the long hours and flight delays home from Tucson, or
wherever the hell he was on Sunday evening—it all proved so inter-
minable that the only way Israel could deal with it was by writing a
novel on his iPhone that was a vicious satire of Washington ridiculousness.

You can see why all the travel and all the time must have seemed
worth it. The 2010 spanking meant that almost any competent job
would look good by comparison. Also, 2012 brought a presidential
cycle. Democrats actually turn out to vote in presidential years, after
all, and that enthusiasm trickles down the ballot and helps elect senators and congressmen. Barack Obama's reelection was never seriously
in doubt once the GOP field narrowed to Mitt Romney, Rick Santorum
and Newt Gingrich—respectively, the former governor whose health-
care plan was the model for Obamacare, a senator who lost his reelection bid by 20 points, and a House Speaker who resigned under an
ethics cloud and rumors of infidelity.

That, of course, was before it became clear how the Republicans
planned to push their 2010 advantage into a durable and lasting majority. As he studied the new districts and crisscrossed the country scar-
ing up ambitious legislators to run in them, Steve Israel may have been
the first national Democrat to realize how ratfucked his party was—
and how long it would last.

"What shocked me when I first came into the DCCC was when I
learned that the expansive battlefield that I thought I would have at my
discretion was actually a pretty small map," Israel says. We're in his
congressional office and there's a buzz because the president has just

been by on an unsuccessful arm-twisting mission of his own, collecting liberal votes for the Trans-Pacific Partnership trade agreement.

"We're all out there talking about 75 to 100 competitive districts nationwide—the politicians, the pundits, the news media. That's the big lie," he says. "After you actually look at redistricting, in the 2012 cycle, it was about 35 to 50. And then in the 2014 cycle, when I did it again, the map had shrunk even more. There are a couple dozen competitive districts. Maybe. Truly competitive districts: 20 to 30, at most. And when you need 32 seats to take the majority back? It becomes a bank shot."

Israel laughs a little ruefully at this. He likes the billiards metaphor but he dreamed of rising in the leadership, and this wound remains raw. He's charismatic, disarmingly direct, a salesman so likable he could probably sell Twitter followers to Beyonce. But he couldn't come close to taking back the House in a year when Barack Obama won 332 electoral votes and carried the national popular vote by 5 million. Republicans were defending 242 seats after their 2010 sweep; you'd have to go back to Harry Truman's presidency for a more target-rich environment and a year when the GOP was defending more potentially vulnerable seats. Israel managed to take back 8 of them.

"You can have the best recruit, the best candidate, the best fundraising. But if you have an uncompetitive district, there's no path," he says. "The one thing we could do to reverse the polarization here and find compromise is nonpartisan redistricting. It just levels the playing field. Our debate right now—the Republican majority, the sequester, the shutdowns, the loss of faith that the American people have in our government—are all rooted in one thing: we have too many far-right and far-left districts in the Congress."

The far-left districts creatively cram Democratic-inclined voters into a small number of districts. The incumbent wins that with 70 percent of the vote and never faces a real challenge. The Democrat elected feels little pressure back home to work with anyone outside his or her caucus. Meanwhile, the rest of the state is left for Republicans to creatively carve districts they carry with 60 percent majorities. Not as safe, but just as unbeatable—and there's many more of them. They also feel no need to take into mind perspectives beyond their own.

"I mean, the math proves it," Israel says, and you hear the anguish of every night at the Doubletree bar with a burger and a bad Syrah, as he tapped another grouchily satirical line of his novel into his smartphone. "Look, we won 1.5 million more votes than they did in 2012 and we only picked up eight seats. Now that tells you that this whole thing was jury-rigged in order to stop Democrats from playing in competitive districts. And it worked brilliant for them. I'm just sorry we didn't figure that out in 2008."

As Israel sees it, that's the year when Democrats really screwed up. He thinks the party should have been thinking ahead *then* to redistricting and down-ballot races. Instead, they used Obama's landslide and big wins fueled by Iraq–Afghanistan war exhaustion and Great Recession anguish to run up a huge majority in Congress. Democrats neglected the states. The party planned for nothing. Redistricting, he said, never seemed to cross the mind of the Democratic leadership or strategists. It was, he says now, "a catastrophic strategic mistake." In 2006 and 2008, Democrats "won districts that we had no business winning. But we started losing state legislatures and governors across America—and that's what destroyed us in 2010 and 2012. Had we devoted resources to protecting Democrats in state Houses across America, the Republicans still would have won the majority in 2010. But we would have had a seat at the table in redistricting and we might have been able to take it away from them in 2012.

"The DNC," he says, shaking his head, "they just whistled past the graveyard. I don't understand why." Sure, that dropkicks the blame to a different committee *and* the election cycle before Israel got involved. Told you he was a smooth salesman. But Israel is frank, and depressingly so, when asked when Democrats might stand a chance of competing again for control of Congress.

"We're not going to win anything in 2016. It ain't gonna happen," he says. "We have to put shovels in the ground now and start building a foundation upon which we can build an infrastructure that will get us playing in states in 2018, winning in 2020 and taking back the majority in 2022. That's the strategy we've got to embark on if we want any hope. It's a six-year rebuilding plan that embraces state elections, the judiciary and Super PACs."

Shovels for a foundation for a six-year rebuilding of an infrastructure just to be competitive not this next time but the time after, for a shot at winning the time after the time after that. That seems like the kind of long-term strategy someone ought to embark on now. It sounds like a bank shot.

"The Republicans have always been better than Democrats at playing the long game. And they played the long game in two fundamental ways. Number one, on the judicial side. They realized they had to stock courts across the country with partisan Republican judges and they did it," he says. "The second long game was on redistricting. The center of gravity wasn't an immediate majority in the House. It was rebuilding the infrastructure in courts and state Houses across the country so when they got the majority back they could stay in it for a long, long time."

What Israel is praising sounds massive and insurmountable, but really it's the work of Chris Jankowski, the RSLC and a small group of really smart strategists with a brilliant plan. I suggest that what the Democrats somehow need to unravel is a triple gerrymander—courts, state Houses, congressional lines—and that the true genius of the GOP plan is that it's not exactly easy to do on their new maps.

"No, I say it's a quadruple gerrymander," Israel says, one-upping me, "because by gerrymandering the courts they got the *Citizens United* decision."

Dark money likes Democrats okay, but the corporations and billionaires who spend it really love Republicans. So I suggest that considering the electoral and fundraising challenges—and the Democrats' strategic ineptitude—one plan might be to make the case directly to voters. Argue that redistricting matters. Appeal to fairness, to the idea that elections only matter when the side with the most votes wins.

Connect the dots, and show that people won't get the policy actions
they want until the process is fixed. In Pennsylvania, I saw candidates
and voters fired up about gerrymandering and well aware of the problems it caused. But Israel brushes this idea aside like I am some googly-
eyed idealist.

"I've sat in on countless meetings with the campaign reform folks
and the redistricting folks," he sighs, "and this argument that you can
take this to the public isn't going to work. We're in an economy right
now where people are trying to figure out if their paychecks are going
to stretch to the end of the month. You want me to talk about redistricting? Their response is, 'What else is new? Stop telling me the
deck is stacked against me. I know it is. Tell me what your economic
solutions are for that.'"

But if the two are connected, I suggest—playing GOP mastermind
wordsmith Frank Luntz for a moment, the man who turned the estate
tax into the death tax and can discover the right language to sell any
policy—they've stolen the people's House . . .

"Never gonna happen," he interrupts. "It's a dramatic argument,
but if you were to poll it, it doesn't move voters. There's only one way
this is going to work, and that is for Democrats to do what Republicans
did. Figure out how to win state Houses, lay out the infrastructure. We
know what works because the Republicans made it work. We use their
tactics: go in and beat Republicans in state Houses and state capitals—
and then engage in fair redistricting. The only way to do that is to play
by their rules so you can change the rules."

There's something profoundly frustrating about this: the Democratic congressman who had the closest look at the Republican strategy sees no way to countervail it other than by replicating it. That
sounds like a recipe for exactly the arms race Jankowski mentioned.
Democrats don't win those. Republicans will be ready for them on
favorable maps. One need not be a googly-eyed idealist to be skeptical
of the idea that Democrats will raise all this money and then change
the redistricting rules they've had every opportunity to address before
but never have.

"I'll tell you one thing," Israel says as he walks me to the door. "This wouldn't have happened if Martin Frost was still here."

Martin Frost is a Texas Democrat who served from 1979 until 2005. He and John Tanner, a Tennessee congressman who held office from 1989 through 2011, were the two Democrats in previous Congresses who really understood the long-term ramifications of redistricting and agitated, usually alone, for action. Both are long gone from the Hill, but I find them where I half expect to: steps from K Street, along the DC legal and lobbying corridor where former pols put their years of experience to work for big business.

Frost's official bio at the law firm Polsinelli actually boasts that "he knows personally virtually every member of the current Democratic Leadership and most of the ranking Democrats on key House Committees." Neither Frost nor Tanner was so busy that they didn't email me back within minutes to confirm an appointment. Taken together, their stories explain why the Democrats lacked a redistricting strategy and why they risk being a permanent minority in the House.

Powerful Washington offices don't look that way from the outside; influence hides inside nondescript buildings. Washington banned skyscrapers in 1899 by limiting new buildings to a height of 110 feet; minor modifications over the years have essentially capped towers at ten or twelve floors. That has preserved the impressive Capitol and Washington Monument views from most of downtown, and with it the myth that power resides in dominating structures and not these drab towers.

That changes with your first glimpse behind closed doors. The staff lists may read like a list of *Crossfire* guests from a previous decade, but the message is clear: this is where the real work gets done. Step off the elevator and it's another world: vaulted ceilings, spiral staircases between floors. You check in with one receptionist, get led to a second bank of elevators, and another assistant arrives to escort you down the private staircase. I feel like superspy Claire Danes of *Homeland* being led to a clandestine meeting with a terror leader, and half expect to be offered a blindfold. Instead, I get a cappuccino and a welcome from

John Tanner, who has a corner office at Prime Policy Group, complete with putting green.

It's a cushy, conventional landing for an eleven-term congressman from Tennessee, especially one comfortable straddling both sides of Washington's partisan divide. In 1995, Tanner cofounded the Congressional Blue Dog caucus, a coalition of largely white Democrats from rural and Southern districts who tilted right on guns and God, social issues and spending. They were centrists who sought compromise, and even though the result was usually to move Democrats subtly right, their ranks were, ironically, decimated by GOP redistricting policies that made it nearly impossible for Southern Democrats to be elected outside of majority-minority seats.

Exhausted by the partisanship and well aware that his reputation for reaching across the aisle would not earn him any sympathy when Tennessee Republicans redrew congressional lines after the 2010 census, Tanner chose not to seek reelection. He landed at Prime Policy, as lobbying and government relations may be the last place in Washington where bipartisanship still pays—and pays well. The firm's clients include AT&T, Chevron, Google and the National Rifle Association, along with big pharmaceutical and energy companies. Their website boasts that 54 members of the House and Senate have staff alumni at the firm.

Before he joined the Gucci Gulch backslapper brigade, Tanner repeatedly tilted at Washington's loneliest windmill: redistricting reform. As his fellow Blue Dogs disappeared, the white Southern Democrat went extinct and congressional partisanship hardened, Tanner was moved to take action. In three successive Congresses, under both Republican and Democratic control, he tried to put a stop to partisan gerrymandering. He proposed national standards that removed the power to draw lines from state legislatures and handed it to bipartisan commissions. His plan also prohibited redrawing lines more than once in a decade, putting an end to Texas-style chicanery which allowed Tom DeLay to remap congressional districts after Republicans took over the state legislature in the mid-2000s.

Understandably, this was not an issue that made Tanner a lot of friends.

"Here?" Tanner snorts. He pushes at a cup of coffee. "Ha! They're drawing their own districts. I had many members come up to me and say, 'What are you doing?' They have deals. 'Don't come around here fucking with the maps. I won't fool with your map if you don't fool with mine.'"

Tanner first introduced his plan in 2005, when Republicans ran the House. George W. Bush cut taxes and put the Iraq and Afghanistan wars on a credit card, and the Republicans in charge provided the blank check, he said, rather than insisting on proper congressional checks and balances. Republicans didn't want to do anything that might cast the party in a bad light. "Hell yes, that's because of redistricting!" he says, still grumpy about the lack of oversight. Tanner knew it would be an uphill battle then and, indeed, it never earned as much as a committee hearing. When Democrats took back the chamber after the 2006 election, he thought he might convince his leadership to listen. He buttonholed Speaker Nancy Pelosi and Majority Leader Steny Hoyer until they wriggled free.

"I told them, if you don't do this, all the population growth is under Republican control. The only stronghold left for Democrats is inner cities," Tanner says. "Barack Obama only carried like 600-something counties out of 3,000 nationwide—but he won the election! They didn't want anything to do with it."

Tanner remembers Pelosi saying, 'That's a good idea. We'll take a look at it." But he couldn't get a hearing on the bill in either 2007 or 2009, the last years of Democratic control. The hardline partisan warriors, he suggested, never really want to reform the process. They might fight to take away the other side's advantage, but never, ever, do they want to risk their own. Their donors don't contribute to help reform the system or build toward disarmament.

Pelosi and Hoyer must regret that decision now, I suggest, in their new role as permanent leaders of a minority. Tanner snorts again. "The hard left, the hard right, they're drawing their own districts, basically," he says dismissively. "In theory, you are perfectly correct. In practice, it's just not something anyone wants to take up. The majority of the delegation draws the damn lines. That's what happens, practically speaking. I went through it three times. There's a lot of power connected to that system."

The result, he says, is that the middle collapsed. Congress divided and members went to their separate corners. There's an old joke in Oklahoma that the only thing in the middle of the road has probably been run over. However, even in a time of increasing ideological polarity, a 2014 Pew Center poll on partisanship still found that a majority of Americans wanted the two parties to work together and find common ground.

The study, one of the largest and most exhaustive on political polarization, found hardened partisanship among the bases of both parties, and a growing sense that the opposing party's views were a threat to the country. But, the study's authors concluded:

> These sentiments are not shared by all—or even most—Americans. The majority do not have uniformly conservative or liberal views. Most do not see either party as a threat to the nation. And more believe their representatives in government should meet halfway to resolve contentious disputes rather than hold out for more of what they want. Yet many of those in the center remain on the edges of the political playing field, relatively distant and disengaged, while the most ideologically oriented and politically rancorous Americans make their voices heard through greater participation in every stage of the political process.

The problem with our politics is not that all of us are more partisan, or the Big Sort. It's that we have been sorted—ratfucked—into districts where the middle does not matter, where the contest only comes down to the most ideological and rancorous on either side. Because the Republicans drew the majority of these lines, there are more rancorous Republicans than Democrats. And because Republicans such as Virginia congressman Eric Cantor and Utah senator Bob Bennett, and not Democrats, have been pushed from office from an ideologically motivated activist wing, it's Republicans who have become more rigid and less willing to search for common ground. Tanner says that the "mind made up" caucus is the vast majority of Congress, and it has ground everything to a halt. Add in a willingness to obstruct and the fact, confirmed by the Pew poll, that partisans define compromise as a deal in which their side gets more of what they want, and you begin to see why gridlock abounds. The House is polarized, it's ossified, and responsive only to its extremes. Primary voters, the most partisan and polarized, matter most, their passions inflamed by talk radio and media echo chambers.

"I'd say 300-plus seats are responsive to the most partisan elements of our society," says Tanner. "The middle? Where most of the people are? There is no middle here. And when you lose the middle, you lose the ability to govern a diverse society like the United States of America. We can't even do the small problems now, much less the big ones.

"I saw the gridlock," he continues. "These guys are trapped in this system wherein the only threat is from their base in a primary. I was talking to a member from New York yesterday, a friend of mine, and he said, 'My only threat is from the far left in a primary.' A Republican, if they stray from the rigid ideology of the far right? Shit. They put themselves in political peril. They know better—some of them—but it's not worth the political fallout to wander into the sensible center and try to sit down and work something out. No one will do what they all know has to be done to keep the country from going adrift. Is that because of redistricting? Hell, yes."

Tanner, who is seventy-one, speaks with appealingly frank disgust for a man who now makes his living based on his relationships with these politicians. Disappointment and weariness seem set in his face and behind his eyes. "Me? I'm a fossil." The Democrats, he says, "have always been, in my view, a little Pollyanna-ish about things and don't want to play much hardball, or whatever the hell you want to call it." As for the Republicans: "It is just a raping of the legislative process.

They don't have any kind of respect. Not even for the institution. This country started the day they got here.

"Democracy? The people's will? It doesn't matter. Seventy percent of the people like Obamacare, the polls say. It doesn't matter. We get 50 votes to repeal it. That's redistricting, too. The average citizen is a pawn. Without the protection of a fairly drawn district, the citizen is a pawn of billionaires who use the map of the country as a checkerboard to play politics on.

"Another corrosive effect? If you asked me the difference between when I came in 1989 and when I left in 2011, I would say it's the attitude of incoming members. Back in '89, when you got elected, you actually wanted to come here and make things better. Fix problems. Democrat or Republican, it didn't matter. We went to the Kennedy School at Harvard for our orientation all together."

In Tanner's mind, this changed in 1994 when Newt Gingrich engineered the Republican takeover of Congress and claimed a mandate for a conservative "Contract with America" after a midterm election with 38.8 percent voter turnout. That helped lead to the 1995 government shutdown and the impeachment battle in Bill Clinton's second term, which only further polarized the nation.

"When Gingrich and his band of thieves came in '94, he banned the Republicans from going to Harvard. Now these guys come here to press an ideological position and the end justifies the means. That's why the whole thing has broken down. And that's redistricting, too."

A few minutes later and a few blocks away, on I Street, Martin Frost greets me at Polsinelli. If Prime Policy has the feel of a secret clubhouse—call it Willy Wonk and the Lobby Factory—Polsinelli is all sleek, white, modern, glass. It's hard to believe the man before me is the last hardened Democratic street fighter to have served in the House, the man who singlehandedly gave the entire Texas Republican party fits for a decade and a half. Frost doesn't look the part of an aggressive warrior. He's a little hunched, hidden behind owlish glasses that recall the Reagan era. He escorts me into a conference room with a well-appointed cookie tray. He speaks with the surety of someone who has always been the smartest person in the room.

The importance of redistricting hit home for him after the 1990 census, when Texas gained three congressional seats under reapportionment. Frost represented the Dallas–Fort Worth area, and it became clear that one of the new seats would be a majority African American seat there—which had the potential to cut into his base. Frost wanted to stay in Congress and understood well that a new majority-minority seat could pack Democratic votes he needed into a single separate district. He wanted a plan that would create new districts for minorities in Texas while not harming the Democrats who held neighboring seats, including himself. And he knew that Republicans would do their best to "bleach" those surrounding seats. "The survival of white Southern Democrats would be determined by how many black voters were left over for their districts after the new majority black seats were created," he wrote in his book *The Partisan Divide*. So Frost "started asking the question, 'Who is doing redistricting for the Democratic Party?' I wanted to talk to that person. I was stunned by the answer: 'No one.'"

Texas in the 1980s was trending bright red, but Democrats still controlled the legislature and the governor's office, and therefore congressional redistricting. They came up with a plan that added three new minority districts without dismantling the bases of the incumbent white Democrats, which Frost calls "a classic example of what could be done when all members of a state Democratic delegation worked together for the common good." Texas Democrats extended their advantage in the U.S. House from 19–8 to 21–9. The Democrats' gerrymander held until Republicans finally took the state house in 2002, and House Majority Leader Tom DeLay pushed the legislature into a mid-decade redistricting plan. The spectacle included Democratic House members fleeing the state for Oklahoma during summer 2003 in an attempt to deny a quorum. Democratic senators bolted for New Mexico. All that merely delayed reality. Legislators could camp out away from their families and jobs for only so long. Time was on the

Republicans' side, and in early fall they were able to pass their plan. It redrew the lines of the most powerful Texas Democrats in the U.S. House, and in 2004, Republicans knocked off Charlie Stenholm, Nick Lampson and Frost himself. One Democrat switched parties, another retired, and by mid-decade Republicans had grabbed a 19–13 advantage. Frost returned to the law and DeLay was nabbed by the law: he was convicted on charges related to the corporate campaign contributions which aided state Republicans in taking back the House. (An appeals court later tossed out the verdict.)

Texas is a classic example of exactly how important it is to control

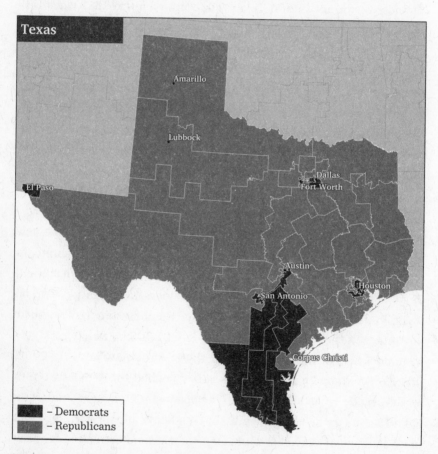

"We just got overcome on the political side," says Martin Frost of Texas's red congressional map.

the lines. Under the Frost gerrymander, Democrats were able to control the congressional delegation despite the state's conservative bent. By the time Republicans could right the lines, the state's growing Hispanic numbers had some analysts predicting that Texas could turn blue by 2020 or 2024. After the 2010 census, the state gained new seats in Congress due largely to Hispanic population growth, but Republicans were able to craft the new seats in the conservative Dallas suburbs, and the GOP retained the advantage. Lawsuits filed by Hispanic voting rights groups helped make public the Republican strategy, which was based on a careful study of Hispanic voter turnout statistics. Through Maptitude and other analyses, line-drawers were able to zero in on specific Latino voters and neighborhoods which were more likely to come out to the polls than others. The switches looked neutral under the Voting Rights Act, and even made some districts appear more competitive. In fact, sophisticated voter analysis made it possible for Latinos and Hispanics to look more powerful in the district than they actually were. This tactic would also be utilized by mapmakers in Wisconsin, who wanted to create Milwaukee-area districts that looked Hispanic but voted Republican.

The problem for the Democrats is that despite these repeated, naked lessons in the importance of line-drawing, no one continued Frost's work after he left the House. "For a while we fought them to a standstill, because we had good legal talent and technical help on line-drawing and strategy. Then we just got overcome on the political side," Frost says.

How is that possible, I ask, and Frost at first demurs. "I'm not the right one to ask that question to," he says, but then admits that he thinks about it all the time. He has concluded that race matters, and that the party's largely coastal and white leadership simply doesn't understand what it is like to run for office as a Democrat outside of, say, Pelosi's San Francisco or Hoyer's district of liberal, wealthy federal government employees in the Maryland suburbs of Washington, DC.

"Often, leaders in the Democratic Party come from safe, white districts. So they don't worry about these kinds of things, because nothing can be done to them. You can't do anything to Nancy Pelosi's district.

George W. Bush got 15 percent of the vote in her district. So, white Northern leaders don't think of this the same way that white Southern politicians think about it. We instinctively understand the problem, but white liberals—particularly from the north—didn't really focus on this very much. They said, 'Well, everything's fine. We'll just continue what we're doing,' and didn't make this a priority.

"I argued for twenty or thirty years about the importance of paying attention to state legislatures, but I couldn't get enough people in the party to really embrace that. The Republicans understood this and had a strategy. We didn't. Let me tell you a story. I don't think I've talked about this."

Martin Frost's story starts in June 1964, when he arrived at the *Wilmington News-Journal* in Delaware, a cub reporter straight out of journalism school. On his first day, the Supreme Court decided *Reynolds v. Sims*, one of the key redistricting cases of the 1960s, which ruled that state legislative districts needed to be as equal in population as possible. Before that decision, many states had not redrawn their lines in decades, diluting the votes of urban residents and minorities as city populations exploded. Chief Justice Earl Warren authored the landmark opinion that this violated the Constitution's equal protection clause, triggering legislators nationwide to break out maps, pens and something new: computers.

"There was a guy in Wilmington, Delaware, his name was Sid Hess, who worked for one of the chemical companies," says Frost. "For some reason, he had gotten involved in the computer applications of redistricting. This was in 1964! So I did a story about this, and I didn't do a very good job, and Sid and the other guy he worked with came in and rather than balling me out, said, 'We'd like to spend a little time with you and educate you on what we're trying to do and how this works.'" By happenstance and coincidence, Frost got fascinated by the political, legal and technological implications of redistricting at exactly the right time. This would serve him well twenty-five years later, as a congressman from a Texas district certain to be redrawn after the

1990 census. Frost knew the Voting Rights Act and saw the writing on the wall.

"It was obvious to me that because of the Voting Rights Act, there were going to be a number of African American districts created in the South in 1991 and 1992, as there should have been. There were a number of states that still had no black congressmen. That's when I got motivated. I said, 'Look! I'm about to be the target of this. I'd like to survive.' And that's when I went and said, 'Who's in charge of redistricting for the Democratic Party?' And the answer was no one. I would say, 'Oh, come on—you must be kidding!' No, no. No one's in charge.

"The reason that I was so concerned about this was I came from a Southern state, and I understood how tough this was, and that you had to fight these guys. This was hand-to-hand combat if you were to survive in the South, and you had to make this an absolute priority in terms of devoting the financial resources—the technical help and the legal help—to try to elect people to the legislature. People from other parts of the country didn't fully appreciate how tough this was. And it's not because I'm any smarter than anybody else. I came from the South, where this was really tough."

For years, Frost explains, senior Democrats acted like they knew all the people in their state capital and could just contribute lavishly to the campaigns of state representatives back home, then go cut a deal for themselves when redistricting came along. When Democrats controlled the House for the four decades before the 1994 Gingrich revolution, redistricting worked with a wink, he said; it was an incumbent protection racket on both sides. "Even if the Republicans were in control, they thought they could make their own deals. It turned out, they couldn't," he says. "That's why prior to the referendum in California—prior to the commission—everyone got reelected." The numbers back that up. In 2000, the last redistricting in California controlled by politicians before voters, in a referendum, gave the responsibility to an independent commission, Democrats owned the entire process, but used their advantage to ensure reelection for everyone, Democrat and Republican. California had 50 districts in

2002, and as the *New Yorker*'s Jeffrey Toobin noted, not one challenger cracked 40 percent of the vote.

"That was not a strategy that was going to work long-term," Frost says. "Once the Republicans had the numbers, then it was to hell with all you people. I'm not making any deals with you folks!"

That one-two punch, he explains—the Lee Atwater–Ben Ginsberg strategy to pack Southern Democrats into majority-minority districts, combined with the national GOP's attention to controlling state legislatures in order to own redistricting—decimated the Democrats in the House.

"The only way we could have prevailed in the South, ultimately, would have been if we had had enough money to really do a good job on the legal side, and if we had somehow been able to at least keep some more Democrats in legislatures," Frost says. "We might have lost some control of these Southern legislatures anyway, but we needed to keep as large a critical mass as possible. We weren't going to be able to control Southern legislatures indefinitely." The demographics and the politics had shifted too rapidly. "You could in the North, if we played the game correctly. We didn't do that. 1994 should have been the ultimate wake-up call. But what was going on in the House was not a priority for the DNC. The DNC was a presidential committee. The Republican National Committee saw things differently. They financed what Ginsberg did. Democrats never really understood this."

Frost became chairman of the Democratic Congressional Campaign Committee after the 1994 rout, but he could never convince anyone else in power to take redistricting seriously. I tell him what Israel told me: this wouldn't have happened if Martin Frost had still been around. Frost gives a quick nod and you can tell he agrees.

"No one else in the party cared about this or understood how important it was, for whatever reason," he says. The Republicans not only got it, but they knocked out the one Democrat who did. "Maybe I wouldn't have been able to change history, but we sure as hell would have gone down fighting." There's no point in fighting now, he said. The 2010s are lost for his party, no matter what. "This decade?" He waves his hand dismissively, as if the idea itself is ridiculous. "This decade is gone. It didn't have to be. If the Democrats had put the same type of emphasis on redistricting that the Republicans did, there might have been a different outcome. Could have been, could have been. We'll never know."

Now, he says, the only thing that matters is what happens in 2020. "If external events cause a massive Democratic landslide in a presidential year, then we have to get back into the legislatures and take no prisoners. But that takes a lot of money and a lot of time and a lot of dedication." His voice trails off and an assistant interrupts. There is a lunch to attend and a car is downstairs. I don't get to ask my last question about whether he has any confidence that the Democrats will mount that concerted strategy. I have a feeling I know the answer anyway.

It's not that the Democrats aren't trying. In August 2014, the Democratic Legislative Campaign Committee announced the formation of Advantage 2020, a Super PAC hoping to raise $70 million to spread across the 2016, 2018 and 2020 cycles to help Democrats become more competitive in state legislature and other down-ballot races. Its director, Mark Schauer, understands the crushing 2010 GOP wave as intimately as anyone. "I lived it," Schauer tells me, calling from Washington, DC, the afternoon after Advantage 2020's first redistricting summit in December 2015. "It was a wipeout." That year, Schauer lost his seat in Congress to Republican challenger Tim Walberg by 11,000 votes—50.2 percent to 45.4 percent—despite Bill Clinton headlining a pre-election day rally in Schauer's hometown of Howell, Michigan. Polls in the days just before the election showed the race a dead heat; every undecided voter must have gone with the Republican challenger. Schauer lost again in 2014, this time as the Democratic candidate for governor; he was bested by incumbent Republican Rick Snyder by some 128,000 votes statewide, or 50.9 percent to 46.9. Both 2010 and 2014 were midterm election years, and from his defeats Schauer took the lesson that Democrats need to get better at turning out voters in non-presidential years. He might be leading the Democrats' 2020 version of

REDMAP, but he doesn't sound particularly impressed by the GOP's 2010 strategy.

"Don't give them too much credit," he says dismissively, to open our conversation. "I mean, they certainly deserve credit for having a plan, and understanding the importance of redistricting in 2010, and putting resources behind it, and putting money into state legislature races. But they got lucky with a tidal wave election in 2010."

Schauer is remarkably upbeat and on-message for a man with such an unenviable task. Perhaps that's because he's the one not giving the GOP enough credit. He says the Democrats have three election cycles to turn things around, and since two of the three are presidential years, he's hopeful that turnout will be in his favor. He's also counting on legislative term limits in Michigan, Ohio and Florida to lessen the power of incumbency and give Democrats a shot to flip districts, and even chambers. When I suggest that he still needs to win in districts drawn with powerful mapping technology to favor the Republicans, his shrug is clear through the phone. "Yeah, the maps are a given," he says. "We are developing state and chamber-specific multicycle campaign plans, taking advantage of the fact that we've got three cycles to do this." Everything need not be done at once, he suggests. Democrats simply need to strategize how to get a seat at the table in states like Michigan, Ohio, Pennsylvania and Wisconsin. That means flipping one chamber or winning a governorship. A voice in the process would lead to less tilted maps, he says.

Democrats only raised $10 million for these efforts in 2010, compared to the $30 million REDMAP plan. Their budget of $70 million for the next three cycles is a sign of seriousness. However, that number is a goal. The more Schauer talks, the clearer it becomes that even he doesn't believe he'll have anywhere near that much money to spend. "Look," he says, "there's a long way to go and, yes, a lot of questions about whether the commitment is there overall, including from funders." In 2010, he tells me, Democrats were unprepared for the REDMAP paradigm shift. They were planning for map-drawing and legal challenges, for the fights of the 1990s and 2000s. "There wasn't, from my vantage point, a proactive strategy about going to the source of how you impact a redistricting process," he says. "I think this looks much different than how things looked a decade ago at this time."

He's right about that: 2020 does look different, in that this time both parties have started thinking about redistricting six years before the census. The challenge he faces, however, is that the Republicans are waiting for him. Unlike REDMAP, which caught Democrats by surprise no matter how much the Republicans declared their intentions, the GOP fully expects the Democrats to try to run the same play. And so in the summer of 2015, the Republican State Leadership Committee announced that it would commit $125 million—almost twice what the Democrats were merely hoping to raise—to a three-cycle REDMAP 2020 plan designed to defend GOP chambers and expand deeper into the states they missed in 2010. "This isn't a triple bank shot," insists Schauer bravely, even though his opponents are likely to battle with, at a minimum, triple in the bank.

CHAPTER 8

FLORIDA

"Tampa Is Far from Perfect"

F lorida is a unique slice of Americana that seems equally strange in the crime noirs of Carl Hiaasen, the comedies of Dave Barry or the literary fantasies of Karen Russell. It is the land of hanging chads and Elian Gonzalez and George Zimmerman and Terri Schiavo, the place where pastors burn the Koran or eat cockroaches to get attention, the state where tabloid headlines such as "Florida man beats up pizza delivery boy who forgot garlic knots" seem to regularly go viral. It has a Tea Party governor who accidentally distributes a phone sex number during a press conference. It has the most bugs and in some surveys the most snakes—and that's not counting the political operatives.

In November 2010, however, Florida voters did something smart, revolutionary and unlike almost any other state: they took control of redistricting. Voters approved a set of two constitutional amendments, known as Fair Districts. One governed state legislative districts, the other congressional districts. It passed with 63 percent of the vote and significant bipartisan support during a year that was otherwise a Republican wave. The text was unambiguous and sent a clear message to state legislators: you might have the responsibility for drawing the lines, but you'll color within specific new boundaries and with a spirit of fair play.

"Legislative districts or districting plans may not be drawn to favor or disfavor an incumbent or political party," the amendment read. "Districts shall not be drawn to deny racial or language minorities the equal opportunity to participate in the political process and elect representatives of their choice. Districts must be contiguous. Unless otherwise required, districts must be compact, as equal in population as feasible, and where feasible must make use of existing city, county and geographical boundaries."

The Republicans who governed Florida's political establishment were not willing to let go easily. They'd worked too hard to gain this advantage. When Jeb Bush was elected governor in 1998, Republicans held the governor's office and both houses of the state legislature for the first time since Reconstruction. They wasted no time in drawing a solid and enduring gerrymander that retained GOP control of the state legislature and congressional delegation for the next decade, despite the advantage Democrats held statewide in voter registration.

After the 2000 census, Florida's booming population brought two new Republican congressional seats. GOP redistricters wielded a sharp pen and brilliantly designed the two new districts. As University of Central Florida political science professor Aubrey Jewett described, Republicans carved a new GOP-leaning seat in the east-central part of the state for then House Speaker Tom Feeney. They also sketched a Republican Cuban seat in the Miami area for Mario Diaz-Balart, then the state senator who chaired the committee overseeing congressional redistricting.

By 2002, they'd built themselves an 18–7 advantage, which meant they held 72 percent of the congressional seats—double the percentage of registered Republicans in the state. By 2008, the Democrats' deficit was merely 15–10. To understand how the effectively the lines were drawn, consider this: Florida voters handed the state's 27 Electoral College votes to Barack Obama that year. Obama outpolled

John McCain by 50.9 to 48.1 percent, besting the Arizona senator by 240,000 votes. But because of Florida's funky district lines, Obama carried only 10 of Florida's congressional districts, while McCain won 15. The indexes used by mapmakers in 2001 were strong enough that the GOP delegation could endure a Democratic win.

In 2010, Republicans captured supermajorities in both the state House (81–39) and senate (28–12), even while Democrats maintained a 41 to 36 percent edge in voter registration. Once again, Florida's population growth brought the state two additional congressional seats. Once again, Republicans controlled every aspect of redistricting, but this time, the GOP would have to grapple with the new Fair Districts amendment.

Locking in those two new seats would require a secret strategy, not just creative line-drawing; the Republicans would have to be more Mata Hari than Picasso. The party's brilliant and competitive strategists were more than up to the challenge. It would take more than four years and several court challenges before the state Supreme Court ruled the plan unconstitutional, forced lines to be redrawn, and revealed the lengths to which Republican consultants would go to in order to rewire legislative and congressional districts in their favor.

The Republican Party of Florida is located on E. Jefferson Street in Tallahassee, across the street from the John Gilmore Riley House, a national historic monument honoring a man born into slavery four years before the Civil War who died a millionaire and an honored, trailblazing educator. It's the kind of story of uplift and liberty that both parties like to claim as their own in speeches and thirty-second advertisements, as flags unfurl and an obligatory Bruce Springsteen anthem plays. And then they retreat behind closed doors and return to job one: maintaining power.

Years later, the story would emerge in depositions and cross-examination. As it turned out, just weeks after the Fair District amendments passed, the smartest Republican strategists gathered at party headquarters to plot their next steps. If redistricting was

Florida's second favorite sport after college football, this was a room filled with the Steve Spurriers and Bobby Bowdens of the political swamplands. Dean Cannon, then Florida's House Speaker, sanctioned the meeting. In attendance were Cannon's redistricting adviser Alex Kelly, Chris Clark, the top legislative aide to state senate president Don Gaetz, and some of the GOP's mastermind consultants.

There was Frank Terraferma, the Director of House Campaigns for the state party, dubbed the "genius mapmaker" by a Republican National Committee emailer. "Does he age? Does he ever get tired? Is his brain part computer?" asked a state politics blog, counting down Florida's brightest political minds. There was Rich Heffley, a long-time friend of Gaetz, who would serve as a $10,000-plus-a-month "redistricting consultant" to the state GOP, according to later court testimony—and whose firm, Strategic Direction, had invoiced some $6.4 million to the Florida Republicans since 2000. "If you're picking sides in a political dodgeball match," praised a fellow consultant, "pick Rich first."

There was Marc Reichelderfer, a veteran whose Twitter photo portrays him all laidback and hipster glasses at the Republican convention, who built longstanding relationships in an unconventional way—with kindness, friendship, and deep relationships. And finally, Pat Bainter of the consulting firm Data Targeting, the kind of guy who gets called in headlines "the most influential man in Florida GOP politics you don't know." That story described Bainter as a "Wizard of Oz in state politics. His firm's presence can be felt nearly everywhere, but little is known about the man pulling the levers." That's not an accident, as a *Naples Daily News* story noted; his company has no sign and lists a different address online, while Bainter had done only one media interview in the previous three decades.

Another participant, according to testimony, was Ben Ginsberg—yes, the same Ben Ginsberg—serving as personal counsel to Heffley, Reichelderfer and Terraferma. Much of that group would reassemble in January, including Gaetz himself.

It would later be suggested that the only purpose of these meetings was to tell the consultants that the new Fair Districts amendment meant they could not have a seat at the table during this redistricting cycle. And if it seems strange that two secret meetings would be required to tell operatives and partisans that they couldn't be involved, well, it would seem that way to a furious trial judge who would suggest that these initial meetings were really about finding a way around the new amendment—that the legislative leaders, their aides and the consultants had engaged in a complicated and highly concealed scheme to run two redistricting processes, one public, and one very private.

The agenda might have remained clandestine if Reichelderfer hadn't distributed a memo with questions like this: "Communication with outside non-lawyers—how can we make that work?" and "Evolution of maps—Should they start less compliant and evolve through the process—or—should the first map be as compliant as possible and change very little?" Partisan intent infected the process from the very beginning. It was part fox guarding the henhouse, part victorious electoral conquerors determined to lay claim to their spoils.

"This group of Republican consultants or operatives did in fact conspire to manipulate and influence the redistricting process," wrote Judge Terry Lewis in the summer of 2014, in a scathing ruling which declared at least two districts unconstitutional and sent the maps back to be redrawn. "They made a mockery of the legislature's proclaimed transparent and open process of redistricting by doing all of this in the shadow of that process. . . . They were successful in their efforts to influence the redistricting process and the congressional plan under review here. . . . They managed to taint the redistricting process and the resulting map with improper partisan intent. There is just too much circumstantial evidence of it, too many coincidences, for me to conclude otherwise."

Rich Heffley disagreed strongly in an interview with me, picking up on the word circumstantial. "The ruling was a textbook case of judicial overreach," he said. "Lewis even admits on page 22 of his opinion his entire case is circumstantial. In his fanciful writing he muses as evidence meetings that happened before there was even census data or a redistricting mapping program. What impact could those have had?"

Other than leaving a trail of emails and those coincidences and circumstantial evidence, the Republicans did a brilliant job, both with their behind-closed-doors plan and with the gerrymander itself. Two expert redistricting scholars, Jowei Chen of the University of Michigan and Stanford's Jonathan Rodden, built a simulation model to predict whether it was possible that these maps could have produced such a partisan outcome without being built with partisan intent.

Their conclusion, as filed with the court: "An extreme statistical outlier . . . falls outside the range of partisan bias that could be expected from the non-partisan districting process. . . . [it's] virtually impossible for a nonpartisan districting procedure to produce a congressional plan as extreme as the Florida Legislature's enacted plan."

These GOP operatives and consultants covered so many tracks that they would only be undone by equally determined lawyers representing the Fair District coalition and the League of Women Voters. There are thousands of pages of exhibits, depositions, testimony and private emails in the trial record, and when you read them, the entire picture of this audacious power grab comes to view.

Consider the very strange case of Alejandro E. Posada, a twenty-one-year-old junior studying economics at Florida State University in the spring of 2011. He was a member of the College Republicans. He was thinking about his senior year, about an upcoming internship with the state Republican Party, about finding a job after graduation.

That Monday, June 20, Posada testified at one of the public redistricting hearings in Tallahassee. Watch the video recording of his sixty seconds at the podium and you will experience his high anxiety. He wore a new suit with a pink tie. He carefully parted his hair. He signed in as a possible speaker by providing his name, address and telephone number. When given an opportunity to address the panel, which included Gaetz and then House Speaker Will Weatherford, he praised the politicians.

"I think one of the primary goals of this process has to be transparency and I think y'all have done a great job here today," Posada said. "I think something that needs to be of primary concern is that we don't rush anything here because I know there's been a few people that have come up and said we need to get this taken care of now, immediately, we need maps now, what-have-you. But I think it's important that in the interest of transparency that everyone's views be allowed to be heard."

So perhaps it wasn't completely coincidental when an Alex Posada, using the Gmail address alexposada22, submitted a set of congressional maps to legislators on Halloween afternoon 2011, through a portal on the committee's website which allowed public submissions in the name of, yes, transparency. After all, Posada had a proven interest in redistricting. He'd spent that Monday afternoon at the Knott Building sweating through a suit and talking ever so earnestly about transparency and listening to the people, about not hurrying these maps and carefully considering all the possibilities. Maybe he really did go home, download the district-drawing software, and get to work crafting the exact lines that the committee would ultimately sign into law.

Because some of that actually happened. A little after 3:30 on October 31, just ahead of the deadline, an email arrived from alexposada22@gmail.com with a set of Florida congressional maps attached. This Alex Posada lived in Tallahassee, just like the Alex Posada who gave that nervous testimony. They shared the same street address and telephone number.

The maps were received by Alex Kelly, the House Redistricting Committee's staff director, who replied almost immediately: "Got it—we'll let you know if we have any questions." But while there's no paper trail of anyone from the legislature asking Posada any follow-up questions, six of his districts, precisely as they were submitted to the committee that Halloween, did make the final map. It was a win for democracy and transparency.

Maybe it was just a win for what-have-you. Alex Posada finished his internship with the state Republican Party, graduated from Florida

State, spent a few months as an executive assistant at a consulting firm run by Speaker Weatherford's brother, then pretty much gave up on politics. He certainly never gave redistricting another thought. He moved to Orlando and started working construction.

And the maps? They formed the boundaries of 25 percent of Florida's new congressional districts. As lawyers for the League of Women Voters and other groups combed through hundreds of maps and reams of data produced by GOP consultants, uncovered through the discovery process, they noticed something very odd. Those seven districts supposedly drawn by Alex Posada perfectly matched the seven districts drawn by "genius mapmaker" Frank Terraferma.

When he testified in Judge Terry Lewis's courtroom, Terraferma readily conceded that the maps were his. "I agree without any doubt that I drew those maps," he said. He expressed astonishment at how Alex Posada could have obtained them, and who might have sent them to his colleague Alex Kelly at the redistricting committee. Terraferma would admit that he did sometimes bounce maps back and forth with Rich Heffley; however, he denied coordinating with him. These were maps that the two had started sharing as early as July 2011. And yes, he used the fancy Maptitude software purchased by the state Republican Party. But that wasn't for any real purpose, he said. It was an exercise. He drew the maps "for a variety of reasons," mostly just because "it's fun."

"It's apparently a fact that some people admitted these maps," he said. "I wasn't aware. . . . I don't know what other people did with stuff that I may have drawn."

Vince Falcone of the law firm King, Blackwell, Zehnder and Wermuth phoned Alex Posada to ask whether he had submitted any maps. Yes, Posada said, he had, then hurriedly hung up. Posada's hesitancy and rush earned him a subpoena.

Posada began his deposition, delivered under oath, by apologizing for his initial lie. He testified that he had panicked when the call came—not because he was trying to protect anyone, but because he had no idea what to say. He had not submitted any maps. The address and phone number given in the email were his, but he'd never had that email address. He'd never allowed anyone to submit maps under his name. And an email that the committee had received from his Florida State email account—a real one—did not come from him. "I have no recollection of sending any email of that kind ever," he said. "I don't have any recollection of ever giving anyone access to my email or redistricting or anything of that nature.... I have zero, zero knowledge of that email or how it was sent or why or any of this."

He did recall someone asking him to attend a public committee hearing, but could not remember who that might have been. "I guess I made a statement or something at that meeting, but I don't really remember what it was. . . . I mean, this happened when I was in college." He had no real interest in redistricting at all. "Not that I can think of. I mean, it's been what, three years now. I mean, I'm sure it sounded interesting at the time. I really don't remember. That was a long, long time ago. . . . I don't remember specifically all the things that I, you know, had an interest in three years ago." No one, Posada said, gave him a script to read. He never talked about it—or heard anyone talk about it—during his internship. He never talked about it—or heard anyone talk about it—as an assistant at Strategos, the consulting firm where the House Speaker's brother was a partner. He didn't know anything about this at all. That much, at least, really was transparent.

When Rich Heffley took the stand—in testimony that was largely heard in a closed courtroom and kept almost entirely under seal until very recently—he didn't have much light to shed either.

"I won't say what my mom taught me about assuming things, but I will tell you that I don't know Mr. Posada. I didn't have anything to do with submitting maps, and I don't know how they got in the public domain," he said. Heffley testified that he never submitted maps, never submitted maps under anyone else's name, and never told colleagues how to utilize maps. Pat Bainter—in an even more tightly closed courtroom than Heffley—said the same thing.

The massive paper trail and Judge Lewis's ruling tell a different story. They lay out a meticulous plan to undercut the public process while maintaining some vague deniability for a careful communicator. The surreptitious plot seems fairly clear: The consultants perfected maps. Other consultants helped recruit private citizens as go-betweens to submit them as seemingly uninterested parties and even more to speak in favor of their adoption. Terraferma, Heffley and Data Targeting's Pat Bainter would all say that their efforts were just for fun, but they were also very highly paid, very active, very obsessed, and very secretive.

Heffley, in his interview with me, however, insisted that "nowhere in the Florida constitution does it mention public citizens or their intent. It is the legislature who must comply with the amendments. There is no real evidence that we had any impact on intent. In fact, I didn't draw one single line, district, or map.

"More directly, if we were going to try to influence the process, wouldn't we have drawn maps that would have gained seats for the Republicans? Maps at all levels cost the GOP seats in Congress, and the Florida Senate and House. Would we really have run an elaborate shadow process to lose political strength?"

And while all of the GOP operatives can deny knowing Alex Posada, or how his map was submitted, buried in more than 500 pages of Bainter's emails is a five-page list of names sent between Robert Krames of Bainter's firm and Andrew Wiggins at the state Republican Party. Individuals the firm believes would somewhat unwittingly work on their behalf. Twelve from the bottom of the last page? The name Alex Posada.

Bainter fought the release of his emails almost all the way to the Supreme Court (Clarence Thomas declined to hear the case), and did manage to keep them under seal for many months. When he testified, behind closed doors, he acted nonchalant about redistricting. This is an actual exchange he had with Fair Districts attorney Michael DeSanctis:

"Why were you drawing maps?" DeSanctis asked.

"Intrigue," replied Bainter.

"Intrigue about what?"

"What do you mean by 'what'?"

"What do you mean, 'intrigue'?"

"It was a pretty intriguing process."

"What? Well, one might be intrigued by the redistricting process and still not take it upon himself or herself to actually draw maps. So I'm wondering . . . what was going through your mind?"

"It was a very fascinating item. And I found it very interesting. I never actually completed a map. I found it way too tedious."

In fact, no detail was too tedious, as revealed by the emails Bainter fought so furiously to keep private.

"We will NOT exactly copy this map, but it does give you something to go on. In particular take note of the new Hispanic Central Florida District," Bainter emailed his staff in October 2011, attaching a map drawn by Terraferma.

Emails from July 2011 show him pushing a novel legal theory that he "spoke to the attorneys [about] several times today." Bainter wanted a way to pack more Democratic voters into solidly Democratic districts, so that Republicans could spread their voters around more strategically. They gave him a novel idea: districts could vary in population by up to 5 percent as long as they claimed that the goal was preventing retrogression—a term meaning the lessening of minority voter strength. "So, in affect [sic], we are green lighted to, for example, make some of the panhandle districts light, but as much as minus 5% in order to be able to bring more population to some of the minority districts," Bainter wrote.

Anthony Pedicini of Strategic Image Management, a Florida-based political consulting firm, needed only seven minutes to send back a one-word response, the email equivalent of a high five: "Yeah!"

In late October—right after the consultants traveled to Washington to meet with Ben Ginsberg and stay overnight at his home—Terraferma emailed the state senate plans to him and other consultants. Bainter had but one comment: "Just need to overlay the home addresses on this to make sure. . . ." What he meant is that they would need to double-check the home addresses of the incumbent senators to ensure they hadn't accidentally excluded someone from their district. Now recall that the Fair Districts amendment made clear that maps were not to be drawn with partisan intent or to protect incumbents.

Another email chain, this one involving Bainter, Heffley and Terraferma, which started on October 26 and continued on November 1—the deadline for maps to be submitted by the public—had the subject line: "Here is a completed congressional plan though Tampa is far from perfect." It attached a set of maps called "Congress Complete," which were a modified version of Terraferma's July maps, and bounced between Terraferma and someone named Jim Rimes, with Heffley cc'd, before Terraferma forwarded it to Bainter. Bainter responded, "You want this submitted?" The response came not from Terraferma but from Heffley: "He wants more time to revise. What do you think the deadline is for us to get something to you?" "I would say 3 if it has to be in by 4," "Has to be in by 5," Bainter replied. "Has to be in by 5," Heffley answered.

A little after 3:30 P.M. on October 31, alexposada22@gmail.com submitted his map. As well as containing six districts identical to Terraferma's July map, it contained eleven identical to Congress Complete. But, since Tampa was far from perfect, Terraferma subsequently redivided his 11th district across Pinellas County, creating two Republican-leaning districts where there had been only one.

In an email dated November 22, 2011, with the subject line "Map Overview," Bainter laid out a district-by-district analysis of the state senate maps, which he calls "our final version of this thing." He got deep into the nitty-gritty; his sample comments included "much more compact than it has ever been," "this configuration increases AA [African American] representation from about 33 percent to about 41 percent," "purposefully remains west of the highly populated coastal areas." The consultants seemed pleased with the maps. "I count 28 R seats, 29 if you were able to pick up the new Hispanic seat in Orlando," Bainter wrote.

The key question was, "You want this submitted?" While the Republican consultants bounced draft maps back and forth, Bainter's staff was briefing lawmakers, designing scripts, coaching citizens on what to say, lining up names under which to submit maps.

In his testimony, Bainter tried hard to paint his activities in a civic light. He said he was interested in getting people involved in the democratic process. On October 10, Bainter emailed two staffers, Matt Mitchell and Michael Sheehan. "Please get with me first thing this morning re maps," he wrote. "We've got a job to do." Together, they ensured that the voting-age population stats were on the maps. Sheehan told his boss that the maps were ready for submission. The exact maps they exchanged that day ended up being submitted under the names Micah Ketchel and Andrew Ladd.

The next day, Bainter emailed Sheehan and Mitchell again. "Stafford is getting me 10 more people at least. We could start by submitting the map [Reichelderfer] sent us." Stafford was Stafford Jones, a Republican county chairman. Sheehan replied with a state senate map; later, that map was found to have been submitted under the name of Christine Jones, Stafford Jones's wife.

Later in October, Bainter sent Heffley an email with a state senate map and accompanying political-performance history. Bainter passed it along to a state Republican Party official. That map was submitted under the name Delena May.

It worked. In public statements, the legislature said that it had used not only the Posada maps, but also state senate maps submitted by Alex Patton, Christine Jones, Remzey Samarrai, Delena May, Andrew Ladd, Micah Ketchel [some of whom submitted maps for multiple districts]. All of these maps were actually submitted by GOP operatives.

Bainter, in his combative testimony, presented a very simple face on these actions. "Well, we certainly had, again, a number of citizens out there that—that wanted to be involved," Bainter said. "And, yeah, so we absolutely would—would give them the opportunity, if we had maps sitting around that—that could be submitted, it seemed like a good idea to do that."

Asked whether Reichelderfer, Heffley and Terraferma knew that these maps would be submitted in this way, he said: "Again, I—the mischaracterization needs to be cleared up. I think they certainly knew that—that we had a broad network of grassroots folks that wanted to participate in the process, and, you know, to that end seemed like, again, a really good idea to be able to allow those citizens the opportunity to participate." While one might applaud these consultants for stirring up grass roots support, one can also see how they used friends, family, and fellow partisans to avoid the intent of the Fair Districts amendment.

Bainter argued with the plaintiffs' attorneys when they described him as an "operative," a term he considered insulting, and eagerly defended his right to participate in a democratic process like redistricting. Nevertheless, the emails show how hard the consultants worked to create the appearance that they were not involved. Just before the deadline for submitting maps to the committee, Bainter emailed Sheehan and Mitchell wondering, "Do we need to be a bit more 'creative' about how we are naming these [maps]? Seems like there is some coordination here." Sheehan responded that he had submitted the file with "a different name." Bainter replied, "Lets [sic] be extremely careful."

"Want to echo Pat's reminder about being incredibly careful and deliberative here, especially when working with people who are organizing other folks," wrote Mitchell on November 29, just before legislative meetings were held on the maps.

"Must be very smart in how we prep every single person we talk to about all of these. If you can think of a more secure and failsafe way to engage our people, please do it. Cannot be too redundant on that front. Pat and I will probably sound almost paranoid on this over the next week, but it will be so much more worthwhile to be cautious."

And then there were the scripts, also discovered in the sealed emails. There was advice for citizens, sent from Terraferma to Bainter:

- DO Identify oneself as an individual, city of residence and state years of residency in area.
- Do NOT identify oneself orally or in writing (on speaker card) as a part of the Republican Party. It is more than OK to represent oneself as just a citizen.
- DO identify like communities of interest/geographic areas that could form the basis of a district.
- DO NOT reference partisanship in any way, Dems, Repubs etc or mention names of incumbents.

- DO NOT be concerned if your testimony has been stated by previous speakers or is in contrast to the majority of preceding speakers.
- Please DO THANK the Legislature for listening to citizens first BEFORE producing maps.
- Citizens speaking will NOT be questioned by anyone. Speakers say what they want and depart.

They could say what they wanted, of course, but they could also get specific advice on what to say from Data Targeting. "As requested, talking points for folks in Lake + Volusia area," wrote Data Targeting's Mitchell in a note to a colleague at a firm called Electioneering Consulting, cc'ing Bainter and Krames in his office as well as Wiggins, at the state GOP.

The scripts and proposed emails included such lines as:

"Senate District 20 is an excellently drawn state senate district. My home area of Lake County is smartly divided on a north-south plane, rather than just tossed into a bunch of different districts with no regard for Lake's unique differences. As Amendment 6 demands, the district also follows county, city and highway lines very well throughout, including keeping The Villages and Ocala in one piece. Very smart work from the committee on this district. I approve!"

"It's not the prettiest district, especially where it slides into Orlando. But south Lake County residents like me would be well-represented under this map, and obviously I'll say that's a good thing."

"District 8, where I live, still looks a little strange to me. I guess it's because we had to draw a minority access district in Jacksonville, which for some reason swoops into Volusia County and even Daytona Beach, which seems ridiculous to me. But it is a little bit better than how it's drawn now. It's more compact, and there's less of Jacksonville in it, so it's a more unique

First Coast district rather than just another Jacksonville seat. As a Volusia resident, that's something I'm glad to see. Thanks again for your hard work in putting this together."

"We are political junkies," the lobbyist and GOP adviser Marc Reichelderfer testified during the first trial. "Drawing maps is kind of like doing a Rubik's Cube." He drew maps "for a variety of reasons," he said, mostly just because "it's fun."

He dismissed the importance of the fact that he had received maps before they became public, given to him on a flash drive from friends working on the House committee, maintaining that he was interested merely out of personal and professional curiosity. "The fact that they're on my computer," he suggested at the trial, "doesn't tell me how they got there." Judge Lewis did not buy that coincidence.

Heffley sees it differently—indeed, he suggests that it's the liberals who have done the ratfucking. "The ultimate irony," he told me, is that "the liberal group who formed, funded, and passed the 'Fair District' Amendment became the plaintiffs who challenged the maps drawn by the legislature. In the course of the trial, the same group of Democrat partisans then drew and submitted their own maps to the courts. The courts then selected their maps with none of the scrutiny or requirements those very same people professed were necessary to ensure 'Fair Districts.'"

Add all of it up—the brainpower, the secrecy, the scripts—and you have what may have been the most determined ratfucking efforts anywhere during the 2010 cycle. If we were truly Big Sorting ourselves into homogenous and like-minded districts, if the boundaries truly didn't matter, our highest-paid political minds wouldn't have been working around the clock, risking their careers and reputations, to tweak the maps to give exactly the result they wanted. Politicians who believe their ideas will win in a fair fight don't resort to this kind of chicanery. Indeed, not all of them do. Redistricting does not have to work this way. But in 2011, Florida was hardly the only state where extreme secrecy ruled.

CHAPTER 9

WISCONSIN

"They Put My District in a Woodchipper"

Andy Jorgensen still remembers the smirks on the faces of his Republican colleagues. The former General Motors assembly line worker had been elected to the state assembly in 2006 to represent the 37th district, largely blue-collar towns in the southern part of the state, not far from Illinois, and, as a three-term Wisconsin state representative, was seen as a rising star in Democratic politics. But redistricting after 2010 fractured his Democratic-leaning district, scattering his votes among four newly designed Republican-leaning districts. "They put my district in a woodchipper," Jorgensen tells me.

Jorgensen lived in Fort Atkinson, about three blocks from the new 43rd assembly district, which looked like the seat he'd have the best chance of winning. So he put his house up for sale and moved into a two-bedroom apartment inside the 43rd with his wife and three kids. "It became a mission of mine to fight the gerrymander," he says. When he managed to doorknock his way to victory over GOP lawmaker Evan Wynn, Republican colleagues in the house knew exactly what he had had to overcome to return to the chamber.

It's usually a solemn but joyful occasion when new legislators take their oaths of office, but when Republicans saw that Jorgensen was back among them after the 2012 election, they laughed at the political hazing they had put him through. He recalls feeling like he was back in junior high. The cool kids had tried their best to get rid of him. It didn't work. But the following terms would not be an enjoyable time to be a Democrat in the minority in Wisconsin.

The story begins almost two years earlier, as one of the worst blizzards in 130 years pummeled Madison, Wisconsin. Governor Scott Walker, a conservative Republican newly elected on a promise to cut taxes and spending, declared the first days of February 2011 a state of emergency and did what he'd always dreamed of doing: he shut down the government.

Classes were cancelled at the University of Wisconsin–Madison, so more than 1,000 students took to Bascom Hill for a massive snowball fight, firing snowball slingshots and blaring vuvuzelas as they marched into battle against competing dorms. Nineteen inches of snow made getting around impossible in the capital city and stranded Green Bay Packers fans desperate to fly to Dallas for that weekend's Super Bowl. Wind-chill factors nearing 30 below didn't help; neither did snowdrifts created by 60 mph wind gusts. "It created drifts the size I haven't seen in 34 years here," the weary Madison streets superintendent told a reporter. Groundhog Day festivities were canceled, because, really, what was the point?

Yet the headline trumpeted in the *Milwaukee Journal-Sentinel*— "Wisconsin is closed for business"—wasn't entirely true. The lawyers and political operatives planning the state's redistricting powered through the storm. "I will likely make it in later this morning," wrote powerful Madison litigation attorney Eric McLeod, a partner at the firm of Michael Best & Friedrich, to Adam Foltz, the key redistricting aide to Assembly Speaker Jeff Fitzgerald, that Wednesday morning. "My house was literally drifted in, couldn't open doors. It's like that all over obviously. Just finished shoveling and plowing."

McLeod wanted to keep Foltz on task. His powerhouse firm was seen by many in Madison as essentially in-house counsel for Walker and the state GOP; the Milwaukee newspaper reported that McLeod

was among three Michael Best attorneys who provided a conservative state Supreme Court judge, Michael Gableman, with thousands
of dollars of free legal counsel when he faced an ethics charge. (Best
clients seemed to enjoy such an advantage at the Supreme Court that
when they lost a case more than a year later, the *Journal-Sentinel* was
so shocked that its headline read "Justice Gableman Rules Against
Michael Best.") The Best firm said it "was confident the arrangement
comported with state ethics laws."

Redistricting headquarters was a conference room in Michael Best's
modern glass building, a quick walk across South Pinckney Street from
the state capitol, but a world away in privacy. McLeod, the very image
of a young Republican lawyer, his reddish-brown hair squarely parted
on the left, helped coordinate a highly connected team. The brain trust
centered around Foltz, a young Paul Ryan lookalike, and Tad Ottman,
a science fiction enthusiast and savvy young Republican mastermind
from senate president Scott Fitzgerald's office. The legislature also
hired Joe Handrick, a former state representative turned lobbyist and
one of the state's true redistricting experts. The federal lines were in the
hands of Andrew Speth, a trusted Paul Ryan aide and a longtime friend
of Republican National Committee chairman Reince Preibus.

Republicans had swept control of state government in 2010, just in
time for redistricting. Walker succeeded a Democratic governor who
chose not seek another term. Thanks to REDMAP's help and the anti-
Obama wave, Republicans turned a 50–45 deficit in the state assembly into a 60–38 advantage. They also flipped the state senate, from
an 18–15 Democratic edge to 19–14 Republican. Chris Jankowski and
the RSLC spent $1.1 million on Wisconsin races alone, largely on TV
ads. "We'll be providing air cover," he told the *Wall Street Journal* at
the time. GOP-aligned organizations came flooding in with thousands
of dollars in ads, and polls trying to identify issues that might bring
Republicans out on election day.

When Republicans won, the party wasted no time in pushing a bold
Wisconsin Badger-red agenda on this solidly purple state, one with
a history of electing both progressive heroes such as Senator Robert

La Follette and populist embarrassments such as Senator Joseph McCarthy. They proposed a budget which slashed state spending and took aim at the collective bargaining rights of public employee unions, both priorities of the big-money funders who had helped the GOP capture the governor's office and the legislature. Democrats pushed back with an aggressive recall campaign targeting GOP state senators.

Time was tight. Republicans knew they had to push ahead quickly with redistricting in case Democrats recaptured the senate in the unpredictable summer recall elections.

What Tom Hofeller's maps and GOP consultants came up with was one of the greatest gerrymanders of the year—as secretive as Ohio's private bunkers, as enduring as North Carolina, and as frowned upon in the courts as Florida. In 2012, Wisconsin voters would cast 174,000 more votes for assembly Democrats than assembly Republicans, yet Republicans won 60 percent of the seats. "It's everything antidemocratic and it's everything corrupt," Representative Jorgensen told me. "This is a corrupt way of taking power you didn't win. This is an episode of *The Sopranos*."

It took three lawsuits from citizens and government watchdog groups, thousands of pages of court transcripts and depositions, hundreds of not-carefully-enough-worded emails, several furious decisions from bipartisan panels of judges, two election cycles, and a new political science measurement to uncover the brilliant story behind the 2011 Wisconsin gerrymander.

The new lines were so stout that they delivered impressive majorities for Republicans in both congressional and state legislative races in 2012, even as Democrats won big statewide. President Obama captured 53 percent of the vote and earned the state's 10 electoral votes. Tammy Baldwin was elected to the U.S. Senate with 51.5 percent of the vote. And Republicans managed only 49 percent of the aggregate vote in the eight congressional elections—but won 5 of the 8 seats.

At the state legislative level, Republicans won 56 of 76 contested assembly races—74 percent of the seats—with just 52 percent of the vote.

When you add in the handful of seats Democrats won uncontested—and you should, as Republicans packed so many Democrats into those districts as to make themselves intentionally uncompetitive there—then the Democrats would have won the statewide vote by 200,000. In state senate races, Republicans snagged 6 of 11 contested seats (flipping two Democratic districts in the process), despite Democrats earning 51 percent of the votes.

"There is no question—none—that the recent redistricting effort distorted the vote," University of Wisconsin–Madison political science professor Ken Mayer told the Wisconsin Center for Investigative Journalism. "Nobody takes seriously the notion that the legislative plan for congressional districts wasn't politically motivated."

Mayer is one of the experts working with William Whitford, a former Wisconsin–Madison law professor, and eleven other plaintiffs who filed suit in July 2015 arguing that the partisan gerrymander violated both the First and Fourteenth Amendments of the U.S. Constitution. "We're particularly frustrated because we feel like our votes don't matter," said Whitford at a press conference announcing the action." A regretful former state senator, Dale Schultz—a Republican who voted for the 2011 maps—stood at his side. "I myself am guilty of the very actions I'm joining in trying to stop. As a former senate majority leader I could have—in fact I should have—introduced meaningful legislation which ended partisan redistricting."

Mayer and the plaintiffs base their argument on a new standard called the efficiency gap, developed by University of Chicago law professor Nicholas Stephanopoulos and Eric McGhee, a research fellow at the Public Policy Institute of California. They posit that that between "cracking" and "packing" districts—dividing voters of one party across a number of districts, or cramming them into a small handful—you can measure the number of wasted votes. The efficiency gap is the difference between the parties' wasted votes divided by the total votes cast. Gerrymandering, then, becomes the art of wasting more votes for the other side. This measurement shows what they call the "undeserved" seat share—the proportion of seats that one party would not have received if lines were drawn in such a way that both sides had an equal number of wasted votes.

Stephanopoulos and McGhee found that their metric remained stable between 1972 and 2010, with a median of almost exactly zero. After 2010, the efficiency gap across the country skyrocketed to the highest level in the modern era, and the Wisconsin numbers were some of the most pro-GOP in history. The lines drawn in 2011 produced a 13 percent gap in 2012 and a 10 percent gap in 2014. They call that the twenty-eighth worst efficiency gap in modern American history, out of some 800 that they ranked over the last five decades. Based on this research, "There is close to a zero percent chance that the current plan's efficiency gap will ever favor the Democrats during the remainder of the decade."

So how did Republicans pull this off? Ingeniously, and quietly. The plan was launched the day before the blizzard struck Madison. "Now, off to the races," another attorney, Jim Troupis, emailed McLeod, Ottman and Foltz, summing up a meeting that morning and lining up the checklist for moving forward. Handrick would begin working through map options. A political science professor and conservative redistricting expert in Oklahoma would be retained. Foltz and Ottman would begin meeting with each Republican legislator. Most importantly, billing for the attorneys was resolved—"monthly statement of amount due from the Trust—a one line total. . . . Once initialed MB&F will issue appropriate payments." The "Trust" was vague, the one-line total just as opaque and the appropriate payments vaguer still. However, before this was over, the lawyers alone would clear $400,000, as the *Journal-Sentinel* reported.

The group stayed small and tight. Nothing was to leave the Michael Best war room. Only Republican legislators were briefed on the maps. Before being briefed, they had to sign a confidentiality agreement. Every single one did. "Four decades in office," said senate president Mike Ellis to a reporter, "and I've never been asked anything like it. . . . It was a pain in the you-know-what," he added.

The legislators were not shown much. According to official policy, which emerged through the discovery process, "Legislators will be allowed into the office for the sole purpose of looking at and discussing their district. They are only to be present when an All Access member is present. No statewide or regional printouts will be on display while they are present (with the exception of existing districts)."

The agreement the legislators signed asserted that McLeod had "instructed" Ottman and Foltz to discuss the redistricting process and then claimed an attorney–client privilege for all conversations—one more level of secrecy. In a later lawsuit, a three-judge panel, outraged by the claim of privilege, would describe this as part of a "charade" designed to "cover up a process that should have been public from the outset."

Very little was public, and the emails released by the Wisconsin courts show that even more was scripted. A list of talking points was found on Foltz's computer, counseling Republican lawmakers to play up the importance of minority districts: "Minorities must be given the opportunity to elect the candidate of their own choosing." That this made surrounding districts more conservative was so clear that it did not need to be spoken. Republican lawmakers heading into public hearings were warned not to be confused if party leaders gave lip service to concepts such as democracy; what mattered was what they said behind closed doors to one another, and not to the public in official meetings. "Public comments on this map may be different from what you hear in this room. Ignore the public comments," legislators were instructed.

According to the document's tracked history, it was created by someone with the user name AFOLTZ. When Adam Foltz was asked about this during another kind of official meeting, in a courtroom, he testified that he had *probably* helped write the talking points, but he couldn't entirely remember. Why were they created? Couldn't remember that, either. The advice to ignore what was said in public? "I honestly don't know exactly what it's referring to there," he said. Foltz continued to insist that even though he did look at political criteria, and even though lawyers at Michael Best had told him to share the maps with Mike Wild, a redistricting director of the Republican National Committee, partisan performance had nothing to do with the lines.

The three-judge panel rejected that notion directly. "We find those statements to be almost laughable," they wrote.

Dig deeper into the transcript and you can see why the court reached that conclusion. There are, for example, identical word-for-word declarations by both Ottman and Foltz that neither had any idea why each had an external hard drive fail. "I cannot explain why one external hard drive became corrupted," each man told the court in a separate document. "In any event, I never did anything to destroy or interfere with any hard drives."

Fortunately, a cache of emails largely among McLeod, Ottman and Foltz was preserved—though Foltz and Ottman were both emailed on their personal Gmail accounts. The emails—made public in summer 2012—tell a story that the lawyers, operatives and consultants obfuscated both in courtrooms and in public hearings. Even the eighty-five pages that emerged during discovery—a small percentage of all the communication—make the narrative clear.

Wisconsin Republicans wanted to pack as many Hispanic voters as they could into Milwaukee districts, therefore bleaching surrounding districts whiter and more Republican. They used Maptitude to overlay complex algorithms on a block-by-block basis. How had these blocks voted in each election between 2000 and 2010? What could be predicted about how these districts would perform over the next decade, if consumer spending and income patterns were added to the algorithm?

The emails also included a memo, marked "privileged and confidential," from Troupis to McLeod, Ottman and Foltz, laying out the "areas we will be most interested in as we look at the maps this next week . . . these we can count-on as issues that must be faced from a legal perspective."

Under sections subtitled "African American Concentration" and "Hispanic Concentration," Troupis highlighted the need to plan ahead. One criterion for both: "Change over 10 years in the %population/ %voting age." He wanted to ensure the gerrymander would endure. They needed to think in advance about how to sell the lines: "Expected arguments for and against the proposed district" made the list, and in a subsection marked "Political Change," so did spin. They were tasked with determining "Defense showing that the D's can still win a majority—i.e. sufficient districts in the winnable category."

On Wednesday, July 13, 2011, Ottman emailed Foltz and the Michael Best attorneys to say the best he could do was pack the Milwaukee state senate district so that the Hispanic voting age population was 40.8 percent. "There was no configuration that we could come up with that raised that by more than about 1 percent," he wrote. But just seventy minutes later, he hit upon a favorable formula that he'd previously thought impossible. "By wildly gerrymandering the 7th Assembly District, I can move the HVAP in the Senate seat from 40.8 to about 42.6."

But while Ottman manipulated the lines to pack the Hispanic populations in, the Republicans hired Professor Keith Gaddie to do something even shrewder. Gaddie provided complex algorithms of his own, also with the effect of optimizing the Hispanic percentages. He estimated both low Hispanic voter turnout and low Hispanic population growth over the next decade. That allowed Republicans to make the case that the district needed a high number of Hispanics in order to ensure that one would be elected. Under this line of reasoning, Hispanic voters were concentrated in the district not to bleach the surrounding towns and make them more Republican, but to ensure the election of one of their own.

The lawyers, politicians and operatives worked behind the scenes to get conservative Hispanic leaders to support the plans at public hearings. Troupis courted the Mexican American Legal Defense and Education Fund, in hopes, he said in an email, that they would "take the largest legal fund for the Latino community off the table in any later court battle." When Manny Perez and other Hispanic leaders signed on, Troupis couldn't contain his enthusiasm. "Manny is talking right now to MALDEF to coordinate their testimony," he wrote in an email to McLeod, Ottman and Foltz. "Congratulations!"

Andrew Speth, meanwhile, was busy with the congressional lines. Speth had been Paul Ryan's longtime chief of staff and a top political aide. Ryan was less than two years away from becoming Mitt Romney's running mate and five years away from being elected Speaker of the House. Speth had been tight with Reince Preibus, now the chairman of the Republican National Committee, since their college days at the University of Wisconsin–Whitewater. And Preibus became friends with a young Scott Walker as an intern at the state legislature, where Walker first earned a seat at age twenty-five.

Speth's activities remain largely unknown, save a deposition taken in early 2012 for the suit against the Wisconsin Government Accountability Board. Mike Wild—who had an early look at the state maps—played an important coordinating role here as well. Speth testified that his copy of Maptitude came from the Republican National Committee. "Mike Wild loaded it onto the computer," he said.

How did he obtain the census data used to predict performance and draw lines, he was asked in the videotaped deposition?

"I got it from Mike Wild."

Asked if Wild had personally loaded that data onto his computer, Speth testified, "Yes."

When the maps were done, Speth said, "I didn't know how to export the file, so I had . . . to go back to the RNC and ask them to show me how to use the software to export the file. . . . So I had Mike Wild show me how to do that within Maptitude. [Then] I emailed it to Eric McLeod."

The *Journal-Sentinel* laid out the impact:

> Wisconsin's new map helped Republican incumbents generally, including Ryan. But the biggest changes to Wisconsin congressional districts were for [Sean] Duffy, of Ashland, and [Ron] Kind,

of La Crosse. Kind's western Wisconsin seat was reshaped so that it reached into central Wisconsin, gobbling up a Democratic stronghold in Duffy's district. In turn, Duffy's district reached into more Republican turf to the east as well as along Minnesota's border.

Those changes were done for deliberate, partisan reasons, according to a January deposition by Andrew Speth, Ryan's chief of staff who drew the maps.

"Congressman Duffy's primary concern was anything that related to shoring up the district for a political standpoint. . . . His preference was to try and move it from being a strong Democrat district to moving it more toward a Republican district," Speth said in the deposition.

Very little of the coordination and secrecy pleased the panel of three Wisconsin judges. Left with no choice but to enforce the law, and with the law having no clear standard to determine a political gerrymander, they couldn't redraw the lines or strike a blow for competitive elections. They did force the emails to be made public. Beyond that, they were left merely to rail against the lawful undemocraticness of it all in the strongest words they could muster. Their language would be echoed, years later, by the court in Florida.

"Quite frankly the Legislature and the actions of its counsel both give every appearance of [behaving] in a desperate attempt to hide from the court and the public the true nature of exactly what transpired in the redistricting process," they wrote. In a ruling over evidence a month later, the court found that "Without a doubt, the Legislature made a conscious choice to involve private lawyers in what gives every appearance of an attempt—albeit poorly disguised—to cloak the private machinations of Wisconsin's Republican legislators in the shroud of attorney/client privilege. What could have—indeed should have—been accomplished publicly instead took place in private, in an all but shameful attempt to hide the redistricting process from public scrutiny."

The judges insisted that simply moving redistricting meetings across the street from the capitol to the Michael Best offices did not allow Republicans to declare the entire redistricting process protected by attorney–client privilege. "Merely hiding political decisions behind the closed door (and email servers) of a law firm does not make the advice offered any less political."

Meanwhile, in 2015, Republicans in Wisconsin did away with the nonpartisan accountability board, and have pushed for stringent voter ID laws and for unlimited corporate contributions to campaigns. "They don't care what the people think," Jorgensen says. "They don't have to care because of the way they have it set up. They know at the end of the day that they will be OK because of these maps."

Jorgensen vows that if Democrats ever take back the Wisconsin assembly, a nonpartisan redistricting commission modeled after Iowa's nationally respected system will be an immediate priority. He still sounds chilled by the mirth his fellow legislators directed at him after his 2012 reelection. "They could act that way," he tells me, "because they knew they didn't need to talk to Democrats at all." Assembly Speaker Robin Vos, a Republican, did shake hands with all the legislators and asked what they hoped to accomplish in the new session. "Redistricting reform," Jorgensen told him. "He looked me in the eye and said, and this is as cold as I have ever heard anything," Jorgensen remembers, "he said, 'Never going to happen.' That's a handshake I will never forget."

Redistricting need not be this partisan, even in states where the partisan combat is fierce and politics is among the state's favorite pastimes. In Iowa, a handshake over redistricting actually matters, and there's a real example for states that want to make nonpartisan redistricting work.

CHAPTER 10

IOWA

The Redistricting Unicorn

The 127 miles between Waterloo and Des Moines involve just one turn and more corn than the eye can hold. It's a straight shot west across the heart of Iowa, then a 90-degree left through the farmland. The height of the stalks provides the only variance in the view. Every four years, as caucus season returns and would-be leaders of the free world scrap to be photographed with butter sculptures and the world's largest corn dogs, critics say the same thing about Iowa: the state is too homogenous, too corn-fed, too white to maintain its outsized role as the party-starter of presidential politics.

The critics are right about how white Iowa is—more than 91 percent, according to the 2010 census. It was possible, in the summer of 2015, to spend a day in Des Moines and have a "Ben Carson for President" billboard be the first African American face you see. But Iowa can teach the entire country an essential lesson about how to make redistricting work. A state where political passion runs deep has mastered redistricting without rancor.

Here's an example. In 2011, the nonpartisan Legislative Service Agency, which is responsible for drawing the state's legislative and congressional lines, placed the powerful state senate president, Democrat Jack Kibbie, into a district so Republican-leaning that he real-ized he could not win it. Kibbie voted in favor of the plan, then resigned his seat, rather than fight or exert any pressure.

Redistricting here is filled with trust, and no one dares challenge the integrity of the lines. Race certainly matters; Iowa is so white that mapmakers or Republican mischief-makers can't draw all the Demo-cratic vote into one district under the name of minority representa-tion. Nevertheless, for a white, Midwestern state, Iowa—no joke—has long been an ethnic and immigrant melting pot with a communitarian streak; along with people from all religions and all parts of the world has come a sense of civic involvement and a generosity best defined as "Iowa nice." There is a culture of Midwestern fair play. Almost every politician I speak with here makes a similar joke, comparing longtime Republican governor Terry Branstad to the "long-serving" governors of neighboring Illinois; the punch line is that the Illinois leaders are serving their long time in prison for corruption. It also doesn't hurt that the state's 99 counties—leaning Democratic in the eastern part of the state, Republican in the west and south—form a neat rectangular grid which leads to compact lines and a compelling puzzle for those in charge of drawing them.

Imagine this: the Speaker of the Iowa House, Kraig Paulsen, chairs the legislative caucus of the Republican State Leadership Council, which is charged with increasing the number of state chambers under GOP control. His senate counterpart, Mike Gronstal, chairs the Dem-ocratic Legislative Campaign Committee, charged with the same job for his party. They duke it out over redistricting in 49 other states, but neither would dare dream of contesting the lines at home.

Since the year 2000, Iowa has had more competitive congressional races than Texas, California and Florida combined, despite having a fraction of the number of seats. Iowa had five congressmen through-out the 2000s, then lost one of those seats in the 2010 reapportion-ment. Yet only one district has been automatic for either party over that time, with Republicans owning an edge in the rural western cor-ner of the state, where Representative Steve King and the Tea Party have established a heartland base. Every other seat remains in play, or close, every two years.

As the legal counsel for Iowa's Legislative Service Agency, Ed Cook directs the most successful and least controversial redistricting of any state. Iowa's redistricting ease is referred to as a political "miracle," which is not a word attached to redistricting in the forty-nine other states. Cook has a kindly, owlish face that looks like the Iowa district map: long round ears, oblong face, oval glasses. It's a face that inspires trust. You'd buy any car he was selling, free any defendant he represented. The partisans and the people trust Cook and his team to get it right. In turn, Cook and his team treat the process as sacrosanct.

"There's got to be that trust," Cook says. We're in his conference room on the first floor of the capitol, right past the gift shop which sells a color-coded poster of the state legislative map for a dollar, the same price as a Legislative Service Agency lapel pin. "Over the other nine years, I draft legislation for both sides. There's a trust factor with the legislature and our agency; they know that we're not going to work the plan. There's institutional trust that we will be nonpartisan. We've done it enough times that they know, hey, our thumb isn't on the scale."

I have found the redistricting unicorn.

Ed Cook is an Iowa native. He grew up in Des Moines, attended Iowa universities, earned his law degree at the University of Iowa and then spent four years in the Army's Judge Advocate General's corps at Fort Riley in Kansas. When he left the service, Cook landed a position as a screening attorney for the Iowa Supreme Court. He joined what was then called the Legislative Service Bureau in fall 1992; redistricting was a decennial task and just completed, so Cook's first years there were spent drafting official legislative language for proposals by senators and representatives of both parties. By the mid-1990s, he'd been tapped as one of the three LSB staffers to tackle new maps.

Cook looks at me like I am insane when I describe Tom Hofeller's PowerPoint about the need for special security when drawing maps, let alone new locks, always traveling with lawyers and avoiding email. "We do go across the street," he says. "I've got an office in the Miller Building, which used to be the old historic museum. I don't do my usual drafting during that session. We've got a room that I guess we can lock up. But no one's going to break in."

Here's how much trust there is at the Iowa state Capitol. Most government buildings are mini-fortresses. Going to see your legislator is like trying to board a plane: park two miles away and strip to get through security. There is an X-ray machine at the door here, but they don't make me use it. Instead, they use a wooden ramp and a stuffed bear wearing an Iowa State Patrol shirt. You send anything in your pocket down the chute, the bear cushions its fall, and you go on your way.

I'm teasing Cook when I ask him whether the room where they draw the maps is windowless. He laughs at the ridiculousness of the question. "I suppose," he says. "It is an interior room. But no one's gonna . . . I mean, what can they do anyway?"

When you come to the Capitol for lunch, does anyone ever try and work the ref? Anyone waiting outside the door, all, "Hey! Ed! Didn't think I'd see you over here"? Another laugh at a ridiculous question.

"People always ask that. But no. People respect the process. They know what we're doing, they respect the fact that we're going to do our thing, and that they'll get their chance to vote on it."

I'd be sending you a Christmas card that year, I tell him, with my address very clearly stamped on the front. Cook just chuckles. "No. Take all that out of it. I mean, the Des Moines senators, I know they live in Des Moines. But I don't know exactly where. I think it's hard for people to understand. Since the legislature knows they have the final say, I think that's important. If they didn't have the final say, I think they would probably get rid of this; it would be too much of a risk. But they know they have the final say if they really hate it."

Spend a week driving across Iowa and you will see much disagreement on highway billboards about which restaurant has the state's best buffet. Brooklyn's Community of Flags fights Brandon's Big Frying Pan and they both battle multiple coffee-pot-shaped water towers and even a barn modeled after the one in Grant Wood's painting *American Gothic* for Iowa's most oddly wonderful roadside attraction. But there is unanimous pride, from every part of the political spectrum, in the state's partisan-free redistricting process.

"We're proud of the fact that the system we have is perceived as fair by pretty much everybody—and leads to very competitive races," Democratic senate majority leader Mike Gronstal tells me. "The strength of the ideas win elections, not the strength of the people who controlled the map."

Iowa districts had dramatically uneven populations in the decades before the Supreme Court's 1960s decisions on one person, one vote required they be balanced after the 1970 census. Partisan ways died hard. The Legislative Service Bureau consulted the one University of Iowa professor with a powerful enough mainframe to crunch the numbers, and the Republicans who controlled state government that year picked the plan they thought most advantageous.

Just weeks before the 1972 filing deadline, however, the Iowa Supreme Court ruled that the population variance between districts was still too high, and one-person one-vote provisions were being violated. The court drew fresh lines of its own to even things out. This violated the legislators' honor, in addition to taking the lines out of their hands. So in 1980, the Republicans who ran the state—not seeing the Reagan revolution coming, and fearing they'd be swept out of office just in time for the drawing of new lines—passed a comprehensive reform. The nonpartisan Legislative Service Bureau, as it was then called, would draw the lines. The guidelines would be strict: divide the population evenly among districts, don't split counties, don't split cities. No political data could be used. Incumbents would receive no special protection. The legislature would vote it up or down. A down vote, and the Bureau would try again, but this time the population variance would need to improve. A second defeat would send the plans back to the Bureau for a third try, after which the courts would be called upon. Legislators did go all the way to a third plan in 1981, and asked for a second effort in 2001. Other than that, plans have passed with little trouble.

Ed Cook has spread out the poster-sized map of legislative districts on the conference table, and the arrangement of the 99 color-coded districts is pleasing to the eye. "We use Maptitude," he says. But it's not loaded with anything other than population stats. "You're just clicking on the counties and it adds up the population. Unselect, select. Select these three. Unselect those two. Back and forth." Instead of a video game, he sees it as a "big math and geography puzzle."

Since there are only four congressional districts, the Legislative Service Agency tries to knock those out in the first week, leaving the remainder of the forty-five days to be spent on the state assembly and senate lines. "There's judgment calls everywhere, but we're constrained by the criteria," Cook says. If the legislature wants another look, he doesn't mind. "Just means we need to do another plan. The standards don't change. Acceptance or rejection, it's their call. But they really can't steer what the next plan is going to look like."

The map can look so different every ten years, as population shifts and cities grow, that some people have taken to calling redistricting Iowa's form of term limits. But Cook says that competitiveness is not one of the standards he's thinking about. That's not in the statute; it's not allowed to be on his mind.

"No," he says simply. "Because the only way you can figure out competitiveness is to look at the political data. And we basically don't look at anything. So registration data or anything like that, we take it completely off the table."

Kraig Paulsen only has a few pictures behind his desk in the cramped but gorgeous Speaker's chambers. There are his kids. There are his dogs. And there's him and Newt Gingrich—the Speaker who touched off the modern redistricting arms race. When I ask Paulsen about the remarkable faith both sides have in the Legislative Service Agency's integrity, he uses an arms race metaphor, but one that goes back to a different GOP hero, Ronald Reagan.

"I think there is a certain amount of 'trust but verify,' I guess you'd say, in that we believe the maps we're presented by the LSA were not messed with and we trust the parameters in the code," he says. "Of course it could be manipulated some, but I don't believe that occurred in this or any preceding cycles. If it ever did, it would destroy that level of trust and confidence."

Just before the Legislative Service Agency delivered the maps to legislative leaders, Paulsen says, he and Democratic senate leader Mike Gronstal sat down together and agreed they both wanted to be able to see a path to victory. "I'm looking for something where Republicans have a shot at winning both or one of the chambers. He was looking for the same thing. Since I believe Republican ideas will prevail when given an equal chance, and he believes Democrat ideals will prevail given an equal chance, that's all we were looking for."

The Cedar Rapids representative is proud of his work with the Republican State Leadership Committee; he's stepping down as Speaker in a matter of weeks after we talk, and it's easy to imagine him targeting a congressional seat of his own. His goal for the next year is to plot more legislative takeovers for Republicans. They've already got 68 of 98 chambers nationwide. But he seems eager to shoot for more with ideas, not chicanery.

"Other states have to make their own decisions," he says, "but clearly I think the system has worked for Iowa. Iowans are traditionalists. They show up for work, and while they're there they actually work—and they expect nothing less from us. I think that's the mentality that the average legislator shows up with. My members, and I believe his members, expect us to sit down, and actually make a good-faith effort to get something resolved. We're occasionally not successful, but the expectation is the good-faith attempt will be made."

Paulsen is the very strapping picture of a straight-shooting, sirloin-and-potatoes Iowan. Mike Gronstal deploys his Eugene Levy eyebrows in a mischievous manner. We meet on a Sunday in an empty lobby of the downtown Embassy Suites; the senator from across the state in Council Bluffs had a speaking engagement nearby this after-noon. It's rare to hear Democrats and Republicans tell the same story, but the rivals found common ground on redistricting.

"I know the limitations of Kraig's caucus. He knows the limitations of my caucus," Gronstal says. "We're competitive, but both parties need to govern. In 2010 there were five or six very conservative Repub-licans elected. They burned out pretty quick and most of them are no longer here."

Of course, lots of Democrats who held office in 2010 are no longer here, either. REDMAP swept them away. Gronstal chairs the national Democratic Legislative Campaign Committee, and I'm curious about how the Democrats are approaching 2020 differently after being sur-prised and wiped out in 2010.

"I mean, at the DLCC we were trying to make the case during the 2000s that the DNC and the DCCC ought to be paying a lot more atten-tion to this than they were and they kind of treated us like—I don't want to say like the poor stepchild. But you know how the poor step-child feels?

"We're down-ballot," he says. "They patted us on the head and said, 'Yeah, that's a good idea.'"

Will anything change this time? "I believe so," Gronstal says. He sighs and raises those eyebrows. "I hope so."

Outside the Embassy Suites, would-be U.S. senators have parked cars with massive billboards atop advertising their long-shot can-didates. Someone wants to talk to me, earnestly, about Democratic presidential candidate Martin O'Malley. There's a Democratic rally at the amphitheater adjoining the hotel. I follow the muffled P. A. system to the bank of the Des Moines River, and find the Progress Iowa Corn Feed. The creators of Ben & Jerry's ice cream have already stumped for Bernie Sanders. Now a man in a denim shirt and boots is talking about such unlikely issues as a compassionate immigration policy and how this country really needs a thirty-hour work week. The voice is familiar, and sure enough, it's former U.S. Senator Tom Harkin. Seated behind him is Congressman Dave Loebsack. These are the two people I've been trying to hunt down all week. That's Iowa: on any given Sunday, the person you want to talk to might be talking crazy about the labor movement at the Corn Feed.

The beloved Harkin retired in 2015 after serving five terms, but he can still command a crowd. He bounds energetically off stage greeting everyone he sees by their first name, answering questions about retirement, trying to talk others into embracing a new chapter. Everything he says has an exclamation point. "Martin, you should try it! Come down off that tractor!" I push my way through the farmers and the bluegrass music, curious about how Harkin thinks Washington might be different if other states used Iowa's redistricting process.

"It would be wonderful! It would be great! It would be one of the best things we could do nationally! Get rid of this gerrymandering! Let's change it around!" he says. "What you have now is polarization—districts that are basically Democratic, more that are basically Republican, a few swing seats in there but not very many—not very many! What that means is that people can take more extreme positions, knowing that they're going to get elected, and it even promotes more of an extremism in the party because if you have a few activists in the party that are too far right or too far left, they can then tend to pull you that direction because they might decide the primary! Oh my gosh! When I came to Congress we worked with Republicans across the aisle; when I came to the Senate it was Republican, then it was Democrats, then it was Republicans and then Democrats! Back and forth! Boy! That's still true of the Senate, but the House? You've got these locked-in seats now! It's just nuts!"

Harkin grabs my arm and fixes me with an intense gaze. The exclamation points fall away, replaced by sadness. "The whole system now is really bad," he says, and he sounds like a man who has watched his life's work go to pieces. "I don't know what's going to change it. I just don't know what's going to change it. Maybe it will take a calamity. Something big's going to have to happen to get it righted again."

That something might need to be a constitutional amendment, Loebsack tells me. He was a political science professor at Cornell College in tiny Mount Vernon when he stunned moderate Republican and Iowa mainstay Jim Leach in 2006, riding college-town dissatisfaction with George W. Bush and the Iraq war. But he shakes his head when asked if he sees anyone likely to lead that fight.

"Look, everyone's got to do it like Iowa, as far as I'm concerned," he says. "The problem is you have entrenched political interests in every state. Texas got more Republicans, Illinois got more Democrats as a result." But while Loebsack sees both parties taking advantage of the current system, he says his Republican colleagues feel the most pushed to extremes as a result.

"Politicians, generally speaking, find that if there's more competition, then they're more likely to work with one another. Right now there's no question that especially in the Republican Party, in the U.S. House, there are folks on the far right from these districts where the only competition is going to be in a primary. It's a difficult situation. These folks are not easy to rein in. And if we didn't have that many of those folks from that many districts, we wouldn't have the problems that we have today."

The longest-serving governor in American history, Republican Terry Branstad, is a fan of this approach as well. "I credit the Democratic Party and the League of Women Voters for my being governor at thirty-six," Branstad says with a laugh. He was not long out of Drake Law School and working in Des Moines when the coalition of good-government groups prevailed at the Iowa Supreme Court and redrew the maps mere days before the filing deadline for that fall. Way up north, one of the new House districts had 72 miles of Minnesota border and no incumbent. Branstad had grown up on a farm between the district's two major towns, and he seized the opportunity.

After three terms in the House and four years as lieutenant governor, Branstad embarked on the first of six gubernatorial terms: 7,642 days in office later, he broke a record dating back to the Revolutionary War.

"We've been through four cycles with this system," he says. "I think legislators of both parties have come to the conclusion that this is fair. It's worked well—we're a pretty competitive two-party state and most legislative and congressional districts are competitive."

Branstad tells me that he believes 60 to 70 percent of all legislative seats could be won by a member of either party. "You've got seats that are going to change hands. All these other states, where the only thing you have to worry about is the primary? In Iowa, you might have to worry about both. It prevents extremes of either party from having their say. Not that we don't have our differences, but it's not nearly as partisan as it is in Washington, DC, or some of the other states."

It also makes the politicians work together. Branstad notes that over the last four decades, Democrats have controlled both the governor's office and the legislature for four years; Republicans have had it all for only two years. "You don't always get everything you want," he says, a statement which sounds startling coming from a Republican in this climate. "You definitely don't get the excesses you don't want." That's almost more startling.

Branstad concludes that neither party would ever want to mess with the Iowa miracle. "You might be in the majority now, but in this very competitive two-party state? The next election, you might not be."

Ed Cook says he probably has one more set of maps left to do before he retires. This might be the last go-round for the agency's geographer as well. But when I ask Cook if the arrival of two new people is what may finally push Iowa's process into partisanship—if each party conspires to put someone friendly in his chair, or tries to place a Trojan horse in the agency—he peers at me as if this is the nuttiest thing he's ever heard.

"But see," he tells me patiently, "here they don't do that. The statute says we're a nonpartisan agency. And then you've got the standards. You've just really got to focus on the standards."

I feel compelled to tell him I'm not making this up because I'm conspiracy-minded, but because I've just come from Arizona, where both sides pretty much admit they're already thinking about how to covertly influence who will chair that state's supposedly nonpartisan redistricting commission in 2021. A commission without Iowa trust is just partisanship under a different name.

CHAPTER 11

ARIZONA

"You Can't Get Any More Partisan Than This"

If you think an independent commission can remove the politics from redistricting, you haven't watched the nearly three hours of angry public comment that kicked off an afternoon meeting of the Arizona Independent Redistricting Commission in late June 2011.

Furious, sputtering Arizonans, some dressed in brightly striped American flag polo shirts, packed a lecture hall at Tucson's Pima Community College. They unleashed such invective and disdain upon the five beleaguered commissioners that the Democrats, Republicans and independent sat there in agreement on one thing: they had no idea why they'd volunteered to spend months and years, thousands of unpaid hours, crisscrossing Arizona for public hearings before sitting down to redraw the state's congressional and legislative lines, as the second commission empowered under a winning 2000 ballot initiative. It turned out that their summer of hell was only just beginning.

It was 108 degrees outside that afternoon, but collars might have been hotter inside Room 105. Imagine a raucous World Wrestling Federation screamfest filled with every Tea Party know-it-all who dominates Thanksgiving dinner. Many protesters called themselves Citizens for Common-Sense Redistricting, and they hooted, whooped and hollered, gave one another standing ovations, and created such a scene that one frustrated commissioner actually instructed the crowd to stop laughing. That did not improve decorum.

What unleashed this outrage, barely four months into the redistricting process and before a single line had been drawn? It was the selection of a company called Strategic Telemetry as the commission's mapping consultant. The AIRC's two Republican members, Scott Freeman and Richard Stertz, wanted to rehire a company called National Demographics Corporation, the consultants who'd guided the previous commission, the first, which served after the 2000 census. But the commission's chair, independent Colleen Coyle Mathis, and the two Democrats, Linda McNulty and Jose Herrera, found NDC's application sloppy and believed the well-respected firm might lean toward the GOP. Strategic Telemetry's president, however, had done work for Barack Obama's campaign, and also for Michael Bloomberg, the Republican-turned-independent mayor of New York.

Seven mapping consultants had put themselves forward for the job. Four were short-listed and the commission used the state procurement process to judge them. Strategic Telemetry's application was graded highest. Nevertheless, Republicans and the Arizona Tea Party howled that partisanship had infected the redistricting process. The very first speaker on this sweltering summer afternoon called for chairperson Mathis's head.

"It is Ms. Mathis's vote for a heavily and clearly partisan firm and ignoring the compelling evidence and comment that smacks of a highly partisan chair or an incapable chair," stated Kenneth Moyes of Citizens for Common-sense Redistricting. "We call for Ms. Mathis to be served written notice in preparation for removal by the governor." Other speakers jumped to full-blown conspiracy theories. "So slanted have your votes been against Republicans that there is no question what the goal of this Commission is," stated Lynne St. Angelo. "But what can we expect when the Independent is not really an independent." "Cockroaches," someone hollered at the commissioners. Another speaker, herself a political consultant, shook with rage. "I'm not going to use niceties because I am so upset over this situation," said Gini Crawford, also of Marana. "You know, I thought this commission was supposed to be nonpartisan. Dammit, you can't get any more partisan than this," she hollered, "and I hope you got that."

Four summers later, in 2015, this divisive, passionate and not always high-minded debate would come to an elegant end at the pen of Ruth Bader Ginsburg. The Arizona legislature, overwhelmingly Republican since the 1960s, sued the redistricting commission in an effort to regain mapmaking authority, charging that the commission and the maps which it constructed were in violation of the Elections Clause of the U.S. Constitution, which grants that the "times, places and manner of holding elections for Senators and Representatives shall be proscribed to each state by the legislature thereof." The case found its way to the Supreme Court. If the Court found for the legislature, many experts believed it would mean not only the end of the Arizona commission, but that the California redistricting panel would be rendered unconstitutional as well, and other states would be prevented from making similar reforms. The plaintiffs wanted the Court to read the word "legislature" narrowly and specifically, so as to mean only the elected body itself. The redistricting commission's attorneys insisted that the term included all "legislative authority" granted by the state constitution, "including initiatives adapted by the people themselves." The commission took the day, narrowly, prevailing 5–4 in the Supreme Court.

Ginsburg wove together the law, the Federalist Papers, and a rich story of the nation's founding. It would turn the very purpose of the Elections Clause on its head, she argued, to view it in the way the Arizona legislature suggested. It was intended, she wrote, "to act as a safeguard against manipulation of electoral rules by politicians and factions in the States to entrench themselves or place their interests over those of the electorate"—in other words, exactly the behavior Arizona voters had rejected when they backed Proposition 106, which established the independent commission. James Madison insisted on the Clause because he worried legislators would "take care so to mould their regulations as to favor the candidates they wished to succeed." He opposed a delegation from South Carolina that wanted to eliminate the Elections Clause precisely because they had—and wanted to continue—privileging their patrons and party in map-making. "The problem Madison identified," Ginsberg observed, "has hardly lessened over time."

Arizona voters, she wrote, used Proposition 106 to eliminate gerry-mandering as best they could, and to ensure that Congress would have "an habitual recollection of their dependence on the people," quoting Madison once again. Arizonans needed the referendum to restore "the core principle of republican government," she noted, "that the voters should choose their representatives, not the other way around."

In this era of the closely divided 5–4 Court, the decision could easily have gone the other way. "No matter how concerned we may be about partisanship in redistricting," Chief Justice John Roberts wrote in his dissent, "this Court has no power to gerrymander the Constitution." Roberts's dissent was brutally dismissive of Ginsberg's argument and found little value in independent redistricting commissions, suggest-ing they were a "high-minded experiment" that did not accomplish what they promised.

Roberts is wrong about that. Proposition 106 wrested control of redistricting from partisans and established a citizen panel to redraw lines, beginning after that year's census. The first inde-pendent commission proved successful in crafting congressional districts that shifted sides in swing years. Republicans held a 5–1 advantage after 2000, which swelled to 6–2 after the 2002 elections, then evened to 4–4 amid Democratic gains in 2006. Democrats took a 5–3 edge after the Obama win in 2008, and the GOP reversed that in their 2010 wave. So far, so good. Because of population growth, Arizona added a ninth congressional district after the 2010 census, so the second AIRC panel had an additional seat to draw. Their dis-tricts, while mired in controversy and challenged by the state's GOP majority in the legislature and by Arizona's conservative governor Jan Brewer, matched the national waves of 2012 and 2014 as well.

The delegation tipped 5–4 to the Democrats after 2012, and then 5–4 to the Republicans after 2014.

Not long after the Court's decision, with reformers excited that independent commissions remained viable nationwide, I spent a week in Arizona looking for heroes. Powerful political interests had tried to block reform. Individuals and the judiciary had upheld the law. It looked great on paper, but no one draws these maps on paper anymore. Heroes were harder to find than I had imagined.

Jim Pederson brought the first In-N-Out to Arizona, which means he's responsible for bringing the Animal Style burger to the Copper State—and trying to put an end to its infamous animal-style redistricting. The multimillionaire shopping mall developer dotted the Arizona roadsides with Trader Joe's and Buffalo Wild Wings and Nordstrom. Then his three kids went to college and by 2010 he was just an empty-nester tired of yelling at the newspaper every morning about how the legislature was a national embarrassment and the congressional delegation was wildly out of sync with the people.

The problem went deeper than Pederson spitting bitter coffee all over his *Arizona Republic*. The previous three redistricting cycles had played out, as Ruth Bader Ginsburg would later note, against a "background of recurring redistricting turmoil." Every legislative map since the 1970 reapportionment ended up mired in controversy, with many plans either turned down by the courts or refused necessary pre-clearance by the Department of Justice, as required under the Voting Rights Act, because of a state history of bias against Hispanics but also a large and complex Native American population. Republicans tended to control the redistricting apparatus, which meant that maps tilted successively in their favor, driving the state government so far right that in the 1980s and 1990s it refused to recognize the Martin Luther King Jr. national holiday, costing the state a Super Bowl and millions more in lost tourism and business dollars. When the state became a punch line in Jay Leno and David Letterman monologues—and when millions of dollars started going elsewhere—

sections of the state's business community became as concerned as government reformers.

"I'm a developer. I hate competition," Pederson, seventy-three, tells me, as we gaze across downtown Phoenix from his headquarters' penthouse conference room. He's tall, balding, commanding, and dressed in the Arizona August uniform of khakis and a long-sleeve shirt rolled up to mid-arm.

"I'm a big free-enterpriser and I believe in the capitalist system. I go out and build a beautiful shopping center somewhere, a grocery-anchored shopping center, and four months later Walmart's putting one in across the street. I hate that I can't control it, that I can't predict it. It's the same thing for a politician. He hates competition. He wants a safe district and to be reelected with minimal effort every two years."

Arizona's voters are just over a third Republican, a third independent, and a smidgen less Democratic. But Republicans had commanding majorities and just kept moving right. "If you don't have competition, you become insulated. The only thing you have to worry about is being primaried. You drink the Kool-Aid of your base—you run differently, and you govern differently. We as citizens, as voters, have to fight that at every step."

Pederson imagined a system that would remove line-drawing authority from the legislature and hand it to an independent commission. He hoped to end gerrymandering, drive up voter turnout and create fairer, competitive districts in which better candidates would seek office knowing they might have an honest chance to win.

Wealthy developers have a way of ingratiating themselves with politicians of both parties. So when Pederson made it known in the winter of 2000 that he was thinking about underwriting a civic-minded plan to restore competition to the state's politics, he drew quite a crowd, including big city mayors, state attorneys general, even future Obama cabinet secretaries.

Pederson's politico friends pointed him toward the state's constitution if he was serious about change. Arizona gave America conservatives such as Barry Goldwater, liberals such as Mo Udall, and innovations such as the robust state ballot initiative. In 1912, President William Howard Taft threatened to veto Arizona's statehood over progressive elements such as the initiative, referendum and judicial recall; Arizonans bent on judicial recall but insisted on enshrining the citizen initiative.

Almost 100 years later, the initiative provided Pederson with the tool to give Arizona citizens their maps back. He spent in the ballpark of a half-million dollars in support of Proposition 106. It called for an independent commission of five: two Democrats, two Republicans and an independent chair. Arizona's nonpartisan commission on appellate court appointments would collect applications. Legislative leaders could choose the partisans from a vetted list. The four chosen members would choose their own chairperson from a similarly vetted set of names. They'd draw the maps from scratch based on equal population, compactness, compliance with the Voting Rights Act, respect for communities of interest and established boundaries, and competitive districts wherever possible.

Voters backed it 56 percent to 44 percent; half-hearted, underfunded Republican opposition targeted Pederson's wealth rather than defending the legislature's mapmaking prerogatives.

"It was a very easy sell," says Pederson. "All you had to do was put out the message that we shouldn't be letting these politicians draw their own lines. It belongs to the people. It's the people's government. We should have a choice. Easy sell."

After two vicious cycles since Proposition 106 passed, and one battle that has gone all the way to the Supreme Court, Pederson is wary of calling Arizona's commission any kind of silver bullet. He sees it instead as one element in a long-term strategy to bring moderation back to legislatures, and to drive up the number of districts in which both parties have a fighting chance to win. "Compared to what we did have," Pederson says, "that's a radical change."

But when I ask him if the new process has removed politics from redistricting, or simply pushed the politics more front-and-center, he pauses for a long moment. "It's made it more public," he answers carefully. "Now they have to have hearings all over the state. These hearings were raucous. Every possible interest group came out in a very public format trying to influence the commission one way or another. But at least it wasn't in the basement of the state capitol. It was out in front of everyone. A very messy process, but it was very transparent."

By late 2010, Colleen Coyle Mathis had just survived a breast cancer scare. She and her husband Chris, an attorney, had just relocated to the Tucson area. Her health treatments sparked a desire to give back; her new love of the West inspired her to learn more about Arizona history and meet her neighbors. One afternoon, while attending a conference with her husband, Mathis picked up a flier seeking applicants for the Arizona Independent Redistricting Commission. The board needed an independent chair. Mathis was raised a Midwestern Republican in Peoria, Illinois, and her husband had worked for the moderate Republican congressman Bob Michel, who chaired the 1988 Republican convention that nominated George H. W. Bush and Dan Quayle. Though Colleen and Chris attended the New Orleans gathering where Bush gave his famous "no new taxes" pledge, she'd grown frustrated with both parties and uninterested in traditional politics. (Chris later did work for a Democratic lawmaker from Tucson, which launched additional conspiracy theories about his wife's independence.) "I just didn't feel attached to any platform," she told me. "I wasn't a political animal." She didn't know a lot about redistricting, and hadn't lived in Arizona during the Proposition 106 debate. "What got me interested was really the public service component," especially as she began to understand the power of redistricting and the uniqueness of Arizona's independent commission. "I'm postpartisan, so that's what I wanted."

Mathis would steer a process that expanded Arizona's congressional delegation from eight members to nine, enhanced competitiveness, and ultimately be upheld in a challenge before the U.S. Supreme Court which could have put an end to redistricting commissions operating independent of the state legislature. She would also learn just how few

people in Arizona were truly postpartisan. She would be impeached
on a party line vote by Arizona's Republican-led senate and removed
from office for "gross misconduct in office" and "substantial neglect
of duty." (The state Supreme Court reinstated her, unanimously, less
than three hours later.) "Gross misconduct," political scientist Bruce
Cain later wrote in the *Yale Law Journal*, "can apparently mean pro-
posing boundaries the majority party does not like."

Mathis would be called a Trojan horse chairperson, an independent
in name only determined to form a voting bloc with the two Democrats
on the five-person commission and tip Arizona away from the Republicans. She was called every name possible in the press and hollered at
in public meetings. She spent sleepless nights wondering if she needed
to hire security to ensure her safety.

In Arizona, you could take the politicians out of redistricting, but
there was no getting rid of the politics. "There seemed to be no limit
to what we were responsible for if it was bad," Mathis says. It's after
9 P.M. but still over 90 degrees outside as we start dinner at Tucson's
Arizona Inn, a decades-old desert resort of private bungalows and
gardens where there's an unused outdoor croquet court but an active
ice-cream sundae scene by the pool. "You say, 'Wow, I am really at the
bottom of the barrel.' I did get asked by a journalist why I didn't quit.
That's what they were all hoping, that they would put so much pressure on me, I think. People could frog-march me out if they wanted, but
I wasn't quitting."

Mathis still speaks warily and carefully, even a little dispassion-
ately, considering what she has been through. The emotional toll of
being the one independent on the commission, the fulcrum of intense
criticism, is a topic she steers away from as she tries to redraw our conversation's lines back to process and result. Still, frustration remains
over how things turned so nasty, so quickly. Mathis traces the problem to her earliest decisions: to use the state procurement process to
hire outside vendors, then to push for the least partisan legal counsel
to advise the commission. Following the state's procurement process
required holding meetings in executive session to discuss first legal

counsel, and then mapmaking consultants. "I thought that would help us be more transparent," she says, explaining why she chose that procurement path. "Instead, people used it as a cloak, like we were hiding behind closed doors and all this stuff." Mathis would read stories in the press about how secretive she was being. "No," she says. "We were only following the rules." Neither the Democrats nor the Republicans wanted to budge on their preferred legal counsel, but the Democrats ultimately relented, leading to a 3–2 split vote. The procurement office wanted a unanimous decision on the mapmakers, so Mathis pushed harder for a 5–0 vote to hire Strategic Telemetry—the firm led by a former numbers genius for Barack Obama. That wasn't going to happen, even though a majority of the board graded them far and away the highest. "Frankly, the firm that was chosen was the most qualified firm. You can watch this online. You can watch their proposal. They were very transparent. They claimed who they had done work for, whereas not all the other firms did." The only information the company would use would come from public records, the 2010 census and the Arizona secretary of state's office. There would be no data-crunching of voter registration information. None of that mattered. All hell broke loose.

The state's Republican attorney general, Tom Horne, launched an investigation into whether Mathis and the other commissioners had followed the procurement rules as well as the state's open meeting laws. "They're stonewalling," Horne told the *New York Times*, referring to Mathis and the two Democratic commissioners, before raising the stakes to reference the only political scandal to take down a president. "It didn't work in Watergate and it won't work now."

As Horne investigated, the Republican supermajority in the state House and senate pushed the governor to remove Mathis, or even to force a special election to overturn Proposition 106 and return redistricting authority to the legislature. "The gun is loaded," state senator Frank Antenori, a Republican thought to be considering a congressional bid, told an Arizona political tip sheet called the *Yellow Sheet Report*. "It's just figuring out what target to point it at and when to pull the trigger." That statement, coming as it did mere months after

Gabrielle Giffords, a Democratic congresswoman representing Tucson, and seventeen others were shot, with six dying, even caught the attention of the Justice Department.

Mathis endured this months-long nightmare, trapped alone at the center of a political tempest, an independent chairperson negotiating an impossible process for the first time, up against the sharpest political minds in Arizona, the most vocal, angry Tea Partiers, and a determined Republican establishment willing to use every lever at its disposal to retain its statewide advantages. Her first vindication arrived when the Department of Justice granted pre-clearance of the commission's maps, as required under the Voting Rights Act. It was the first time in three decades that a set of Arizona maps was approved by Washington the first time; the Justice Department—each time under a Republican attorney general—had turned down the previous three plans.

Vindication arrives every election day. Mathis took seriously the constitutional directive to draw competitive districts. The commission ended up with four safe GOP seats, two majority-minority seats favoring Democrats, and three that seemed likely to swing either way. Democrats eked out five of the nine seats in 2012. Republicans did earn 180,000 more votes statewide, but also had Libertarian candidates tip two close races they likely would have won without a third-party spoiler. In 2014, the Arizona congressional delegation flipped back 5–4 for the Republicans, when a Democratic incumbent lost one of the competitive districts by just 161 votes. "When an election is decided by 161 votes, you know your vote counts, and you need to show up if you care," Mathis says. "It's one of the important metrics that was mentioned when they drew Proposition 106 up. Those candidates, in turn, need to be able to respond to everybody in the district." Hew too close to a party base, she cautioned, and a candidate will lose a competitive district. "That's why, to me, it's such a great measure of how we should do things."

Well, maybe not so fast. Just when the story of Arizona's independent commission seems clear—a determined partisan effort to hassle and harass commissioners, from the grass roots all the way to the governor's office and the attorney general—lunch with commissioner Scott Freeman complicates things.

Freeman is an affable Republican attorney in Phoenix, a lover of politics and a news junkie, an engaging straight-shooter who tells his story with more bemusement than bitterness. A former engineer, he thought he might be able to play a meaningful role in a democratic process. Instead, he just chuckles at the idea that anyone might think these commissions actually remove any politics from anything. "These independent commissions are being touted to the voters as increasing transparency, removing partisanship, taking the politics out. I think it was the exact opposite," he says as we settle into lunch at Keegan's, a sports bar where the salads have names like the Great Thai Cobb. His commission held hours and hours of public hearings and meetings—an attorney used to billing his time in tenths of an hour, Freeman estimates something close to 2,000 hours—"but the mapping, I think, partially occurred outside the public hearings and in a place that nobody knew until subsequent litigation."

Freeman agrees that the congressional maps created four GOP districts and two majority-minority seats for the Democrats. But he thinks that the commission intentionally overpacked Republicans into those four districts in order to make the other three more competitive, yes, but also friendlier to Democrats. He's right: In 2014, the 161-vote win in the 2nd district, for Martha McSally, was the anomaly. The other Republican wins were by Paul Gosar in the 4th by a 44.2 percent margin, Matt Salmon in the 5th by 39.2 percent, David Schweikert in the 6th by 29.7 percent and Trent Franks in the 8th by a whopping 51.6 percent.

Because these districts are so safe, says Freeman, a Republican himself, they end up being captured by the very far-right candidates that the process was designed to push aside. "That was another purported benefit of these commissions and the competitiveness criteria: more moderate representation," he says. "We got four hyperpartisan, packed Republican congressional districts. You probably don't think of those guys as moderates." Democrats found the perfect way to maximize their votes, he charged. It might look like it's 4–2 with three swing districts. But while the 2nd will always be a nail-biter, the other two swing districts lean decisively Democratic. Representative Kyrsten Sinema, in Phoenix's new 9th district, won by 12.8 percent. "She can probably have that district all ten years," Freeman says. "They all could have been made more competitive. The commission never tried to make those districts more competitive."

Even worse, Freeman says, the 9th district "was essentially drafted in Linda McNulty's living room basically with the aid and help of the interim head of the Arizona Democratic Party." McNulty, according to Freeman, brought a flash drive labeled "CD9" into a meeting and dropped it in a computer. "This is non-negotiable. This will be the district," she said, according to Freeman. "And it was." (McNulty, when we talked, said there had been no coordination with the Democratic Party.)

Redistricting, Freeman has come to believe, is an inherently political game. Last time out, his side got outplayed. "Take your hat off to the Democrats," he says. Come 2020, his side will be smarter. Freeman remains convinced that the Democrats gamed the system, stacking the pool of possible independent chairs with secret allies. In 2020, both sides will try it. "They successfully produced five Manchurian candidates, and this redistricting turned out to be lost at the appellate court nomination level. Next time, it will be game on." He sounds almost admiring. "It was fun, but it was also a waste of time. When people think this is a saintly perfect system?" Freeman laughs. "There's lots of flaws in it. People don't like the maps being drawn in the smoky basements of the legislature. I get that. But at least you know they're being drawn in the legislature and by whom. We don't know who drew these maps."

After election day 2012, celebratory Democrats revealed a little too much about the authorship of the lines. The state's most senior congressmen sounded fully briefed on the most minute details.

The *Arizona Republic* quoted victorious congressman Ed Pastor as saying, "The maps performed like they were designed." And then, the paper noted, he chuckled. "Ann Kirkpatrick winning was a result of the efforts to create a district that leaned Democratic"—northern Arizona's 1st district. Then he explained how the 2nd district generated a 2,000-vote squeaker for Democrat Ron Barber. "We took out many of the Republican-leaning precincts from the old district and inserted more Tucson, Democratic-performing districts that came from [Representative Raúl] Grijalva." Pastor said that Democratic precincts near Phoenix which had been part of his district got added to the new 9th, which was captured handily by Sinema. Pastor just couldn't stop talking. "We thought we'd try to pick up every Hispanic we could in the East Valley, so we went into Mesa and even into Chandler," he told the paper.

Several months later, in March 2013, a three-judge panel in federal court heard *Harris v. Arizona Independent Redistricting Commission*, the Republicans' complaint that the redistricting process had been unfairly rigged for the Democrats and violated the one-person, one-vote standard. While the Republicans lost (the case remains on appeal at the Supreme Court), they managed to recreate a trail of partisan, closed-door maneuvering by Democrats. Lawyers for the Republicans questioned Jose Herrera, one of the two Democratic commissioners, about how well he knew Democratic Party executive director D. J. Quinlan. According to the *Arizona Capitol Times*, he said she was "no more than an acquaintance who offers a friendly hello." He added that he "wasn't sure if the two had each other's telephone numbers." The Republicans' attorneys pulled his phone records and showed that they'd had sixteen conversations between October and December 2011, key map-drawing months. Then the Republican lawyers probed Quinlan's conversations with Linda McNulty. According to the *Capital Times*, Quinlan said he met with her "five or six times at her office and home in Tucson," but any redistricting discussions were "only in general," despite, as the paper noted, "dozens of phone calls between the two."

The question came down to the population included within specific legislative districts. Democrats wanted the 8th district to be as small as possible, so as not to squander votes they could spread into other districts. Republicans argued that the variance was in violation of one person, one vote, and that the Democrats were using the Voting Rights Act as a smokescreen to make other districts more competitive. In other words, they'd use as few of their voters as possible to create the mandated majority-minority seats, and spread as many Democrats as they could elsewhere. The court found merit in both sides. "The evidence clearly shows that partisanship played some role in [the 8th district's] creation," the court found, arguing that "McNulty's competitiveness proposal was neither applied consistently nor in a nondiscriminatory fashion. It was applied to approve Democratic prospects in one single district." However, the court allowed the district to stand, finding that the Republican plaintiffs had discovered partisanship but had not proven that partisanship trumped legitimate purposes, such as aiming for Justice Department pre-clearance. Judge Wake, in a separate opinion, condemned the commission's "systematic overpopulation of Republican plurality districts and underpopulation of Democratic plurality districts" as "old-fashioned partisan malapportionment." And Supreme Court Chief Justice Roberts was clearly disturbed by this case when he dissented in the Arizona legislature case. "A finding that the partisanship in the redistricting plan did not violate the Constitution hardly proves that the Commission is operating free of partisan influence—and certainly not that it complies with the Elections Clause," he wrote.

The partisan influence was not limited to one side. The Republicans may have been less effective on the committee, but allied groups appear to have spent more money. One of the murkiest groups involved was called FAIR Trust, which hired the lawyers who sued the commission. FAIR Trust, in turn, was funded by $150,000 from a group called the Center to Protect Patient Rights. They, in turn, received millions from the Koch brothers and allied donors. Sean Noble, who ran the Center and was a former aide to an Arizona congressman, distributed a reported $137 million in 2012 to back right-wing activism, according to *ProPublica*. Thanks to *Citizens United*, very little is known about where that money came from or how it was spent.

FAIR Trust lawyers—the acronym stood for "Fair Arizona Independent Redistrict"—were in attendance at commission meetings, and would argue the case for districts that were friendliest to the Republican incumbents. "They clearly were doing somebody's bidding," McNulty told *ProPublica*, "but they wouldn't say whose it was."

As the *Arizona Capitol Times* noted, the attorneys would not admit they were representing the incumbent Republicans, even though "the recommendations they've made would create safe districts for the four Republican members of Congress who will seek reelection in 2012: U.S. Reps. Trent Franks, Paul Gosar, Ben Quayle and David Schweikert. . . . And if they have it their way, the group's financial backers will remain a secret."

More traditional pressure was also exerted. A congressman's mom—who also happened to be the wife of the former vice president of the United States—reportedly called Governor Brewer to complain about how the new lines would affect her son's district, exerting pressure on her to remove chairperson Mathis. Ben Quayle, then a first-term Republican congressman, would have seen his Phoenix district become more competitive. Marilyn Quayle, in an oddly worded denial to the *Arizona Capitol Times*, said that she "never placed a phone call" to Brewer and "nor have I spoken with her about redistricting at any time." The *Huffington Post*, however, quoted a Tucson state representative who said that three Republican state senators had told him that Quayle made the call. The chairman of the state Democratic Party went on Chris Matthews's MSNBC show *Hardball* and repeated the charge. If the Quayle family was concerned, they had good reason: redistricting pushed him into the same district as a fellow young freshman conservative, David Schweikert. Schweikert won a bruising, bitter primary 53 percent to 47 percent in the summer of 2012.

The closer one looks, the less independent the Arizona Independent Redistricting Commission appears, and the more it looks like a similar partisan fight, moved to an arena with slightly fancier strategies. Perhaps the joke is on anyone who thought it would be otherwise. After all, even while Arizona lawmakers protested all the way to the Supreme Court that the legislature could not be cut out of the redistricting process, the truth is, they weren't. The legislative leadership named four of the five members of the committee. That partisans landed on the commission, that politics would still infuse the process, that gamesmanship would ensue—well, maybe it shouldn't be so surprising that every perceived loophole would be poked and prodded.

As Republicans dialed up the pressure on Colleen Mathis and the commission during the summer of 2011, two respected Arizona politicians coauthored an op-ed in the *Arizona Republic*, the state's largest newspaper. Terry Goddard, a Democrat who served as mayor of Phoenix in the 1980s and also state attorney general, and another former Phoenix mayor, independent (and former Democrat) Paul Johnson, defended the commission from politicians afraid that they "might lose some of their power if the commission creates districts that are fair and competitive." Unwilling to take that risk, the former leaders wrote, "they are trying to blow up the commission before it can do its job."

Goddard, the son of an Arizona governor, played as important a role as anyone in making Phoenix's elections more inclusive and competitive when he led the fight during the 1980s to end at-large council seats and replace them with neighborhood districts. The city's politics instantly became more diverse. He's a calm, kindly presence, both preppy and priestly, and I'm not surprised later to learn he's a Unitarian. You get the sense he's always looking to compromise toward a better common ground. We meet at Hob Nob's in downtown Phoenix for coffee; the 1980s hair-metal band Def Leppard makes for an incongruous soundtrack to the café's artsy, cozy charm. As Goddard explains the Democratic perspective and offers valuable state history, the hopelessness of an independent result from a five-person panel with four partisans comes into focus.

Democrats embraced nonpartisan redistricting after decades on the outs in Arizona, especially in the state legislature, which had been controlled by Republicans since the 1960s. But after the first go-around with an independent commission after the 2000 census, "Sure enough, it got worse!" he says. This time, the problem was not wily Republicans. It was an ambitious Democrat. A legislative leader with the power to appoint one of the two Democrats to the AIRC dreamed of a congressional run, Goddard says, and tapped a nominee whose only interest was drawing the best possible seat for his political mentor. "This candidate ultimately didn't run, ironically, but was willing to trade anything to get that one district," he says. The commissioner "teamed up with two very smart Republicans, and they screwed us."

The problem, he says, is that the backers of the referendum—and the voters—wanted more competitive districts. The Voting Rights Act is what gets in the way, he argued. "It's voting rights with an unusual twist," he says. "Pack all the minority voters into a majority-minority district—and wipe out the chance for competitive districts in any of the others." The two Latino districts make those congressmen "bulletproof," he says—but at a price in terms of competitiveness that is "horrendous."

The partisanship on the committee, he concedes, "put the chairman into a very difficult situation. Then he makes a small confession: "McNulty's great, and there's no question she's a partisan advocate, and a good one. I had to talk her into it. A number of us did." The backroom activity, then, preceded even the selection of commissioners. This would mean that the Democrats convinced partisans to apply for the committee, fed their names through the appellate court review process, and had legislators primed and ready to pick the pre-chosen candidates. "You can't say it's an overwhelming success," he says, while praising the newly competitive congressional districts, "but I prefer that to the backroom deals and the amazing gerrymandering that took place the last time the legislature did it." And yet in the end, it sounds like Arizona partisans simply moved the backroom someplace new.

James Huntwork is the sharp Republican lawyer Goddard mentioned, and I make him my next visit. Huntwork has the quiet confidence that comes when everyone around you knows exactly how smart you are, freeing you up to do your job really well. He's an election law expert and even helped organize the Ukrainian independence referendum in 1990 based on Soviet Union election law. He was the very first person, naturally, appointed to the very first independent commission in 2001, by the Republican Speaker of the House.

As any good lawyer would, Huntwork believes in knowing the rules, then following them scrupulously. Without rules to follow—in public, with complete transparency—this goes from "an interesting experiment in democracy to an absolutely terrible idea," he says. Huntwork believes in intellectual transparency as well. He is that rare honest partisan who believes that redistricting is the reason why a state almost evenly divided between Democrats, Republicans and independents has so many polarized districts and a legislature that tends toward extremism.

Like Goddard, Huntwork pins some of the blame on the Voting Rights Act. The state senate, he notes, has 30 electoral districts. The federal government wants to be sure that nine are majority-minority seats. "It packs Democrats," he says. And it makes competitiveness impossible in the other districts. The 21 remaining districts are the only ones left to design, and they are loaded with Republicans and independents. When you try and make as many of those as you can competitive, it packs the remaining Democrats in even tighter. "We start with 21 noncompetitive districts," he says, "try and make five or six competitive and equal—and we now have 15 or 16 that are absolutely, completely noncompetitive." The only voters these politicians care about are in the Republican Party. "And the dialogue in the primary is, 'I am completely crazy!' The next guy says, 'I am even crazier than you!' That's what's in control of our legislature right now."

Huntwork wonders if the answer is *more* gerrymandering: fill as many districts as you can with enough independents so as to give Democrats a chance to win, but also to exert a moderating force on Republicans. His argument: Democrats are not going to control the legislature in Arizona, because of the Voting Rights Act. The best strategy they can employ—and the best strategy for reasonable government in the state—would be to try and place the brakes on the far-right, Tea Party wing. Create 21 districts that are a quarter Democrats and more than a third independent, he says, "then a Republican who wants to secede from the union—I'm being a little facetious but not so much—would have no chance of getting elected in 16 or 17 of those districts." If the legislature is going to be dominated by Republicans either way, try and force a different kind of Republican. "They're applying competitiveness 180 degrees wrong," he says, "if you want to prevent the state from being controlled by highly radical, extreme representatives of the Republican spectrum."

Huntwork does not believe the state is better off than it was before the commission passed in 2000. But perhaps what matters most in Arizona is merely that the commission survived. If its legacy, so far, is to prove the constitutionality of citizens reclaiming their lines from the politicians, and to encourage other states to attempt a difficult process—ideally one less messy and more transparent—then that's a solid achievement. Arizona's post-2010 redistricting was a mess, and one gets the sense that the machinations on both sides remain buried on email servers and in cell phone records, perhaps never to be made fully public. Its chairman was placed in an impossible position by both Democratic partisans and a Republican legislature and governor. That she was rescued and reinstated by the state's highest court is a positive for judicial independence, but that she could be—and was—removed at all shows the fierceness with which politicians will fight to defend their ability to choose their own constituents.

Democrats came away with the best maps they could hope for; in a good year for the party, they can win 5 of the 9 congressional seats. They carry the two Voting Rights Act districts almost automatically. Then they pretend those seats are off the table, and play a three-card monte game to convince Republicans they should be happy with four of the remaining seven. Republicans, meanwhile, would prefer a stronger hand in all seven remaining districts, rather than being packed into four and forced to accept that competitiveness means making as many of the non-Voting Rights Act districts as competitive as possible.

Given the chicanery nationwide in 2011, if the Arizona redistricting process had been under GOP control Republicans would probably control 7 of the 9 seats and create a partisan imbalance. One can argue that Arizona's politics are slightly fairer after the Democrats' hardball, that a 5–4 outcome either way hews closer to the state's partisan breakdown than a guaranteed 7–2 or 6–3 for the GOP. We should, however, be able to aim for a higher standard than "slightly fairer," or at least be able to define that legally. That may be the next redistricting reform test for courts to determine.

CHAPTER 12

A THEOREM TO DETECT RATFUCKING

S am Wang is a neuroscientist, and when the Princeton professor hears how Steve Israel and David Price and others explain 2010—that the Democrats got caught unaware and just didn't think to dominate redistricting and exploit it for partisan advantage—his circuits appear to blow.

"See, that's freaky," Wang says. It's a glorious spring day outside Princeton's Small World Coffee. Wang is sitting with his beautiful dog, Betty, alongside one of those blocks of centuries-old homes and busy outdoor cafés that you only find in college towns. "The general strategy actually does go back over 200 years."

Wang moonlights as a political scientist and builds sophisticated computer models to predict election results when he's not using neural imagery of the cerebellum to search for the causes of autism. His book *Welcome to Your Child's Brain: How the Mind Grows from Conception to College* has been translated into fifteen languages; an earlier version for kids called *Welcome to Your Brain* was named Young Adult Science Book of the Year.

What does a man of the cerebellum know about gerrymandering? He is one of three leading redistricting reformers, all of whom approach the topic differently, but with thoughtful solutions involving complicated math, judicial and constitutional challenges, ideas for channeling citizen anger into statewide ballot initiatives, and even promoting entirely new systems of voting. All of them would reinvigorate democracy.

Wang has sleuthed out the impact of gerrymandering as well as anyone. His real passion is good government. When George W. Bush defeated John Kerry for the White House in 2004, Wang's models—among the earliest and most advanced poll aggregators—nailed the Electoral College result of 286–252. In 2012, he called 49 of 50 states, but more impressively, predicted the exact two-candidate percentages for Barack Obama and Mitt Romney, 51.1 to 48.9. For that, the *Washington Post*'s Wonkblog named Wang the best election modeler of the year, ahead of even the amazing Nate Silver, then with the *New York Times*. (The difference between the two genius prognosticators: Wang predicted Heidi Heitkamp's 3,000-vote upset win in a North Dakota Senate race, while Silver had it going to the Republicans.)

Accolades or not, Wang, wasn't impressed with his own work. He had argued throughout the fall that Democrats had a shot to take back the House in 2012 if they carried the aggregate popular vote, as seemed likely given Democratic turnout in a presidential election year. Many experts told Wang that his models missed the impact of redistricting after 2010, but Wang kept arguing that Democrats had a shot. He underestimated the influence of the new maps. Democrats earned 1.4 million more votes than Republicans in congressional races nationwide, but captured just eight additional House seats. Republicans maintained control, John Boehner retained his Speaker's gavel. Wang had gotten the numbers right but the politics wrong.

"The election happened and I was proved wrong," he says. You don't graduate from Caltech with a physics degree at nineteen by being wrong very often. The error—more embarrassing, in that he hadn't seen the influence of gerrymandering—made Wang dig deeper into what he'd missed. How was it possible that he predicted the numbers correctly but got the results so wrong? The post-2010 gerrymander, his analysis revealed, was historic and different from others in the modern era. "It appeared to be the case that there was something about the districts that did not allow the Democrats a chance to retake the House. I wanted to know what that was."

That difference, of course, was REDMAP. "Through artful drawing of district boundaries, it is possible to put large groups of voters on the losing side of every election," Wang explained, sharing his research in a *New York Times* op-ed piece called "The Great Gerrymander of 2012." Then he applied his background in neuroscience and statistical research to try to understand his error and the historic aberration that, for only the second time since World War II, had prevented the party with the most overall votes from capturing the House. Wang wanted to determine, as scientifically as possible, whether the artful line-drawing was the reason Republicans had kept control. He started with the idea that a party that wins more than half the votes ought to win at least half the seats. That low bar of basic representative fairness, he observed—in which the partisan interests of the state's voters are reflected by the officials sent to Washington—was not cleared in five states: Arizona, Michigan, North Carolina, Pennsylvania and Wisconsin. Percentages won't ever match exactly, of course, but the ideal is what happened in Colorado, where 51.4 percent of the 2012 congressional vote went to Republicans, electing a delegation that favored the GOP 4–3.

Then Wang broke out the math. He wanted to calculate something he called the appropriate seat breakdown of each state—what the delegation would like if the lines were not twisted. He set up a control group: random combinations of districts from around the country that added up to the same statewide vote totals. These districts, he argued, represented what would have happened if that state had districts that looked like others across the country. Keep in mind: these control districts are still the post-census, GOP-dominated lines. But Wang's model revealed the big con.

Start with Pennsylvania. Wang had his computer run 1,000 simulations for outcomes with a 50.7 Democratic/49.3 Republican vote. The median result? 9.7 GOP seats, 8.3 Democratic seats. The actual result in Pennsylvania? 13–5 to the Republicans. The 13–5 result came up once in the 1,000 simulations. The 5 Democrats won with an average of 76 percent of the vote, the 13 Republicans with 59 percent. That outcome, Wang found, would arise by chance far less than 1 percent of the time. "In other words," he wrote, "gerrymandering's contribution to Pennsylvania's partisan outcome was about five times as large as the effect of overall structural advantages." Even simpler: the odds against Pennsylvania voters sending 13 Republicans and 5 Democrats to Congress were nearly 1,000 to one.

The numbers suggested to Wang that something had happened to skew the delegation. "This math doesn't tell you what that something is," he tells me. "That's for somebody else to prove. People who are aware of the political process can say, 'There was a partisan process of drawing boundaries. There was partisan intent.' All I'm providing is a forensic standard that says, 'Look! Something happened! Why don't you go take a look.'"

Wang kept looking, and found troublingly skewed results from the nine most egregious states: Arizona, Michigan, North Carolina, Pennsylvania and Wisconsin, along with Texas, Ohio, Illinois, and Indiana. Six of those states had been redistricted by Republicans, one by Democrats, one by an independent commission and one by Republicans with input from the Justice Department.

Wang concluded in his *Times* piece, first, that Republican-controlled redistricting led to a swing in margin of at least 26 seats, almost as large as the 31-seat majority of the new Congress. Second, that in those nine states, the net effect of both parties' redistricting combined was a swing of 11.5 seats toward the GOP. If all of the lines had been drawn by nonpartisan commissions, Wang argued, it would have led to a swing of at least 23 seats toward the Democrats—or 222 for the GOP and 213 for the Democrats in 2012. "It is possible that in the absence of partisan gerrymandering," he argued, "control would have been within reach for the Democrats."

That would have created a very different Congress. If Speaker Boehner had held such a narrow majority, he would likely have been forced to govern in the spirit of compromise. "I actually think they still would have gotten the majority. But it would have been a much more closely divided House, which would have changed the flavor of politics in the ensuing year. Those were 15 votes Boehner needed. If he had 15 fewer? It became fairly apparent that partisan redistricting paid off for the Republicans."

Perhaps because one of Wang's specialties is autism, he recognized the patterns that political scientists and journalists missed. He doesn't seem particularly motivated by which party runs Congress, so long as it is the one which earns the most votes.

"I think politics is very important," he says. "I can't contribute in the domain of writing speeches, but given these really imperfect mechanisms in democracy, it's good to try to find ways to make them move toward a better ideal case. Think of our democracy as basically Democracy 1.0. We are great because we are first. But the problem is now we've got centuries of precedent that have been accumulated, so the challenge is how to get what we have to work well. I think that a technical person could maybe make a contribution there."

A technical precedent is actually exactly what Wang has in mind. If he can pull it off, Wang might be able to do nothing less than return the people's House to the people. Here's his thinking. The Supreme Court has refused, time and again, to get in the way of a partisan gerrymander. In *Davis v. Bandemer*, in 1986, the Supreme Court found that a partisan gerrymander was justiciable, but said they had no standard by which to strike one down. Eighteen years later, in *Vieth v. Jubelirer*, Justice Scalia tried to call time, arguing, in his majority opinion, that proponents of reform had had nearly two decades to determine a standard and, none having emerged, it was time to conclude that drawing lines was simply a political process, and the courts should move out of the way.

Not so fast, wrote Justice Kennedy. Kennedy did not believe the *Vieth* plantiffs had found a partisan gerrymander. But he welcomed future efforts to determine what one was. He wrote:

> The rapid evolution of technologies in the apportionment field suggests yet unexplored possibilities. Computer assisted

districting has become so routine and sophisticated that legislatures, experts, and courts can use databases to map electoral
districts in a matter of hours, not months. . . . Technology is both
a threat and a promise. On the one hand, if courts refuse to enter-
tain any claims of partisan gerrymandering, the temptation to
use partisan favoritism in districting in an unconstitutional
manner will grow. On the other hand, these new technologies
may produce new methods of analysis that make more evident
the precise nature of the burdens gerrymanders impose on the
representational rights of voters and parties. That would facili-
tate court efforts to identify and remedy the burdens, with judicial intervention limited by the derived standards

Wang read an invitation in those words. "He appears to be saying
here, basically, that a technological approach is making this situation
worse, but could also be the source of a judicial standard that he could
sign on to," he says. "He's saying it is justiciable, and I'm waiting for
some nerd to tell me what the standards are. I think Kennedy's position here could be interpreted as being the Democrats' best route to
getting a level playing field."

"I have a feeling," he says with a slight smile, "that it can be solved
mathematically. I'm sort of surprised nobody's come up with it yet."

That's right: he's attempting to write a theorem to detect ratfucking. Wang grabs a napkin and begins to sketch a graph. Along one axis,
the proportion of the vote. Along the other, the number of seats a party
wins. Political scientists call this the seats–votes curve. Win 30 percent of the national vote, you won't win many seats. Win 70 percent,
as Democrats did in the 1930s and 1940s, you'll carry a huge majority. His argument is revelatory. For too long, the courts and the media
have tried to find gerrymandering by studying the boundaries and the
shapes of districts. They've been looking in the wrong place. If a court
wants to judge partisan asymmetry, he says, they need to compare the
results from every district in the state.

Wang draws two curvy lines, which form a bowtie of sorts. Results that land within the bowtie pass muster. Outside the bowtie, there's a problem. "The national standard is this zone I've drawn right here. If you're in the zone, that's good. If you're outside of it, you're moving away from proportionality. If Democrats win 51 percent of the vote and they only get 30 percent of the representation, as per Pennsylvania, that's a problem. I have to come up with the statistical criterion for how far away from the line is a foul. What I'm trying to do is cook up a forensic tool where a judge could figure out what happened and draw a bright line saying, 'Don't do that.' My view is that's another way to achieve an outcome that's good for democracy. More votes, more seats. Changes in votes leads to changes in seats. Responsiveness, competitiveness."

What other options do we have, Wang asks sincerely, other than putting faith in math and courts? I explain what seems to be the Democratic strategy heading into 2020: raise millions, copy what the Republicans did in 2010, keep their fingers crossed. A bank shot.

"So the strategy here is, raise a lot of money? It's 'they did it, we didn't think of it, now we're going to do it'? That doesn't sound like a winning strategy," he says, looking back to his napkin graph. "That strikes me as something that could have worked in 2006, but not now. The horse has left the barn. And not to be too thumb-sucking about it, but it's not actually a step in the direction of good government."

Sam Wang is a professor very committed to this issue, but not in the same way as Lawrence Lessig is. Sam Wang is not about to launch a bid for the presidency grounded in gerrymandering. Perhaps that's why Lawrence Lessig seems distracted by his phone. The mild-mannered Harvard Law professor renowned for his work on cyberspace, copyright and campaign finance realized the evils of money in politics and became a valuable and outspoken crusader. After TED talks and efforts to mount a new Constitutional Convention, he decided he would run an unconventional race for the 2016 Democratic nomination. If enough small donors helped him raise $1 million before Labor Day 2015, he'd jump in the race and run a single-issue campaign around electoral reform: an end to partisan gerrymandering, automatic voter registration, an overhaul of campaign finance laws. He'd enact these reforms, then resign and become Professor Lessig again.

It was late Friday afternoon before Labor Day when we talked, and Lessig was still about $60,000 shy of the goal. The Sunday political talk shows wanted him on if he crossed the goal. He could be Don Quixote for the next few months, or he could be back in Cambridge on Tuesday teaching copyright law to the next generation's 1 percent. He was checking his donations like a teenager watching Snapchat, and talking with me in the lobby of New York's Tribeca Grand Hotel. His shirt had a couple more buttons undone than that of the average presidential candidate.

Lessig's politics are not easy to pin down—he clerked for both provocative, prolific and unpredictable judge Richard Posner and conservative Supreme Court icon Antonin Scalia—but his frustration is. What we have, he argued, is a crisis of equality, a representative democracy that has become so coopted and corrupted by special interests and partisan interests that it is neither representative nor democratic. Campaign finance has long been his focus. But the more closely Lessig examined our electoral system, the more he realized that politicians choosing their voters—and parties drawing unequal and noncompetitive district lines—was just as central to our democratic decay.

"I came to recognize the obvious point," he says, "that political corruption denies a basic equality: the equality of citizens. Once you see equality as the flaw, then it's obvious what the bugs are. In a world where half the money in the election cycle has come from 400 families, that's a world of radical inequality. The way we district is the most obvious. When you've got 435 seats in Congress, and only a handful of them are competitive, that means all the rest are not competitive! That means the minority in hundreds and hundreds of districts basically has no representation. And there's no reason for it."

Lessig holds the idealistic notion that Congress might fix this, though he's smart enough to know they won't fix it on their own. He also thinks he knows politicians. If you can rally the country behind political reform and make it the kind of issue that can elect an outsider president, then other elected officials will get on board with change rather than get run over by it themselves. "They're just politicians," he says. "If you make it more costly to resist it than to embrace it, you know, they'll just do it."

Redistricting takes place at the state level, but Congress could step in and ensure that districts are drawn in a way that mandates equality, Lessig argues. He likes the plan advanced by a group called FairVote, which calls for fewer districts represented by multiple members, and proportional voting that would allow people to rank their top choices. Under such a system, calculated partisan chicanery of the Ohio and Florida variety would no longer be effective, and the Republicans of Massachusetts and the Democrats of Montana would have a better chance of sending someone to Washington who represents their views.

If we don't want a country in which a political party can raise millions in dark money, dump it into legislative races in swing states, tilt chambers, take control, redraw the lines and build themselves a decades-long firewall, well, that's why Lessig was watching his iPhone for that last $40,000. He wanted an election that would also be a referendum on voter equality.

"'Do you believe in a system where we draw lines to disenfranchise voters?' Ask that question of the American people and the answer would be overwhelmingly no," Lessig says. "This is not a theoretical problem! If you're in one of these districts and you're in the minority, you have no reason to be part of this democracy. Why would you? The democracy just doesn't work. We have a country where there are ten states that are competitive in presidential elections. There are a few dozen seats where Congress is competitive. We have all these structures for making the voter irrelevant in the vast majority of America. Why would we do that?"

It's hard to argue with a rhetorical question so true, especially when it comes from a renowned law professor. Any response is bound to make you feel a little like an underprepared and overeager student in *The Paper Chase,* the classic 1970s film in which John Houseman played

Professor Kingsfield, the brilliant, bullying Harvard Law scholar. But it would take a "Schoolhouse Rock" video to turn gerrymandering and campaign finance into front-burner national issues; no matter their fundamental importance, they're seen as just process issues. Presidential campaigns get fought along the usual tired partisan lines. Lessig peered back at me through oval, gold-wire-rimmed glasses. He paused. It is excruciating to wait so long merely to be told off.

"I don't know where the word 'just' comes in that sentence," he says finally. "When Martin Luther King was pushing the Voting Rights Act, one could have said, 'Why are you doing that?' it's just process. Obviously you recognize that it's process, but that is the core process which makes it possible for African Americans to have some say in their democracy and actually get the return and the equity that they're entitled to.

"So I don't actually think that it's hard to get people—if you talk about it—to see the connection. I think it's true that people have a sense that money calls the shots, and they have a belief that that's just not right. They don't have a clear sense about what you can do about it. Why don't we try a representative democracy? For 230 years we have not had it. Let's just try it for once."

Lessig's critique drives political writers who believe in the basic goodness of our politicians and political institutions crazy—especially those analysts who focus on the big differences between the parties on social issues and among their bases, and not on the similarities in their stances on foreign policy and the donor classes on Wall Street. When Lessig started contemplating his run, the usually astute analyst Thomas Mann actually compared him to Donald Trump.

"Big and important issues divide the two parties today and the stakes of public action or inaction are huge. We don't have the luxury of using the election to try to build a mandate for a set of political reforms that would have no chance of passing in the face of GOP opposition and would be of only incremental utility if they did," Mann wrote. "Both Lessig and Trump, despite their differences in visibility and importance in the election, will have contributed to the dumbing down of American politics, a reality that will bring tears to the eyes of civics teachers and political science professors across the country."

That's a remarkable critique: inside Washington's elite media circles, gerrymandering is a settled issue. Both sides do it, goes the conventional thinking, and always have. That's politics as the game is played. Articulating the idea that something different happened in 2010, or that something is fundamentally broken, is enough to get even a Harvard Law professor compared to a populist demagogue.

Mann might argue that Lessig is dumbing things down, but the trend in journalism these days is to argue that the opposite of what's right in front of our nose is true. Careers are made by taking the counterintuitive position that's sexy, has a greater intellectual degree of difficulty and stands out from the crowd. That's the guiding principle behind, for example, the *New York Times*'s "Upshot" columns on redistricting which try to show that it's not the lines, that we've sorted ourselves, liberals and minorities in cities, conservatives in suburbs and rural areas. (Just forget about redlining or years of racial inequality. We all chose to live where we live, and the history behind it doesn't much matter!) In reality, the lines have been drawn so artfully and intentionally that to undersell or deny the significance of this is also to deny the reality of the multimillion-dollar industry that has grown up around it.

"Especially with the money issue and gerrymandering, people are unwilling to acknowledge it," Lessig says. "Like, sometimes people have these huge deformities on their face, but they don't notice them, right? They just learn not to see them. And it's kind of that with this. We have this huge bulbous growth in our democracy, like the most obvious thing. Anybody else would look at this and say, 'What is that on your face?' And yet we have this studied refusal to even acknowledge it."

Lessig made his fundraising goal and announced his candidacy for president. He was not, however, invited to appear in the first Democratic debate, sponsored by CNN. The Democrats did give a podium to Lincoln Chafee, a former Republican senator from Rhode Island dancing with 0 percent in the polls. During the debate, Chafee explained his vote in favor of repealing the Depression-era Glass–Steagall Act—an essential step in allowing big banks to become "too big to fail" and among the causes of the 2008 Great Recession—by telling Anderson Cooper that he didn't really understand the bill. His dad had just died, he offered, and that was his first vote in office. The Democrats also gave a podium to former Virginia senator Jim Webb, who, like Chafee, in a poll with a 3 percent margin of error might be at minus 3. Webb, a Vietnam veteran, was asked by Cooper to name an enemy he'd made. Webb replied, "I would have to say the enemy soldier that threw the grenade that wounded me, but he's not around right now to talk to."

Lessig soon dropped out of the race. A search of the complete transcripts for the first three Democratic debates revealed not a single mention of the word "gerrymandering." Hillary Clinton, Bernie Sanders and Martin O'Malley debated tiny, nuanced differences between their proposals on climate change, gun control, capping the growth of college tuition fees and other important issues. Not once, however, did any of them raise the real reason why all of their ideas were dead on arrival—that a Republican Congress was a nearly unsurmountable reality until an election was fought on new maps. The first Congress after new maps will be sworn into office in January 2023. That would be the third year of President Clinton, Sanders or O'Malley's second term. That's the impact gerrymandering has on policy, and it's beyond curious why Democrats appear unwilling to make the argument or even allow a single candidate to make it during a presidential debate.

A solution to gerrymandering is unlikely to come from either of the two parties. The Republicans may have perfected it in 2010, but both sides have had a long, successful history of manipulating redistricting for their own advantage. A political party is built to win elections, after all—as well as to raise money and employ consultants and operatives. Their leaders always believe they can win the next one, and that reformers will stop howling once their side regains power. Too often, sadly, that's true.

If this problem is going to be solved without Wang's judicial theorem, it will require creative state and local solutions, inventive uses of the referendum and initiative process, and new alliances of frustrated citizens which defy party boundaries, rooted in the belief that fair elections which reflect an honest majority are as important as which side wins. It will take people to stand up and say that our democratic values matter too deeply to ratfuck.

The hopeful news is that there are states where this is happening. In 2010, in Florida, the nonpartisan Fair Districts Now coalition sponsored two statewide ballot amendments that demanded an impartial approach to redistricting. Florida amendments require a 60 percent supermajority at the ballot box, so any winning coalition must have broad appeal; these two amendments won with 62 percent support, and in a year when Republicans swept into office in waves—a sign that conservatives and liberals alike are fed up with a partisan process of drawing lines. Politicians did not relinquish control easily, as the judicial challenges revealed, but the courts ultimately put a spotlight on the GOP's backroom machinations, tossed out the tainted maps, and in December 2015, the state Supreme Court finally signed off on what appeared to be fairer, less partisan, and more compact congressional districts.

In 2015 in Ohio, voters overwhelmingly approved—with 71 percent— a ballot issue to expand the state's apportionment board from five members to seven, and to give the minority party a larger role in the process of drawing state legislative districts. Under the new plan, if at least two members of the minority party approve the new maps, the lines go into effect for a full ten years. If not, the panel returns to the table in four years. The plan is limited in its scope, does not remove politics from line-drawing, and some redistricting reform advocates were frustrated that it did not include new provisions for drawing congressional lines as well. It is, however, a step forward in a state where the House lines have been so skewed that Republicans hold a supermajority of seats despite often receiving a minority of total votes cast. And when a referendum passes with the support of more than 70 percent of voters, the minds of reasonable politicians begin to change. Indeed, just weeks after the resounding victory for a less partisan process, Ohio governor John Kasich—who signed into law those maps designed by GOP partisans in the Bunker—sounded a very different tune. "I support redistricting reform dramatically," said Kasich in a speech in Columbus, Ohio. "This will be something I'm going to do, whether I'm elected president or whether I'm here.... I think we need to eliminate gerrymandering. We've got to figure out a way to do it. We've got to be aggressive on it. We've got to have more competitive districts."

In Maine, a state with a long history of electing third-party candidates and independents, such as former governor and current U.S. Senator Angus King, an even more revolutionary plan began in 2014. That's when two lawmakers—a Democratic state representative and a (now former) independent state senator—began a signature drive with the goal of changing the state's winner-take-all elections to a ranked-choice/instant-runoff system for state officials and members of Congress. It took them well over a year to generate the necessary 70,000 signatures and have them certified by the state, but the ballot question will officially appear before voters on election day 2016. If it passes, Maine would become the first state to experiment with an instant runoff. Dick Woodbury, the former state senator, argued that allowing voters to rank candidates would civilize, transform and open up our politics, without anyone having to worry about wasted votes, spoilers, or having a vote for a preferred candidate help elect someone that voter opposes.

"Elected candidates can serve with a credibility and mandate that can only be delivered by a majority," he wrote in the *Bangor Daily News*, noting that in forty years, only two of Maine's governors have won with a majority vote. "Most importantly, campaigns will be more civil and respectful, as candidates avoid alienating their opponents' supporters. Rather than appealing to loyal supporters alone, a winning candidate needs to appeal to a genuine majority of all voters, including those whose first choice may be somebody else."

Maine is a small state with quirky, independent-minded politics. Nevertheless, any move from winner-takes-all voting to an instant runoff would be an immediate step in the direction of more robust democracy, and a dramatic move away from a closed system that can be manipulated by one or both major parties. If that happens—and the big wins in Ohio and Florida are a sign that redistricting reform is an issue that resonates with voters, no matter what Steve Israel and other Democratic leaders may say—much of the credit will belong to the tireless idealists of FairVote. The DC-based activists have pushed for both instant runoffs and multiple-member congressional districts for years, only to have insiders dismiss their ideas as too radical or impractical a change for Americans to accept. Perhaps the insiders underestimated the potential ratfucking backlash.

For FairVote executive director Rob Richie and senior staff attorney Drew Spencer, gerrymandering is only part of the problem. Unlike Lessig, they don't see a pure Constitutional fix, and unlike Wang, they don't have a silver-bullet theorem in mind. In their minds, even independent commissions of the sort John Tanner proposed, or Arizona-style bipartisan free-for-alls, aren't the way to address the problem. They see both parties as being at fault, and trust neither with the solution. It's the voting system itself which needs to be fundamentally overhauled. The group does not have a preferential partisan outcome, beyond wanting to see the House reflect the people in the clearest and most exact way possible. After all, pure political saints could draw the districts, Richie argued, and you still wouldn't be fairly represented in Congress if you're a Republican in Massachusetts or certain parts of California, let alone if you're a Democrat in Wyoming, or support a third party and feel relegated to permanent spoiler status and ceaseless debates about Ralph Nader.

Their solution—multi-member districts and ranked-choice voting—would work like this. Instead of a state with 12 districts, for example,

imagine that state divided into 4 districts which each elect 3 representatives. That would end winner-takes-all politics and, since you
would not need 50 percent to get elected, it would also open the door
to more innovative thinkers, bridge-builders, and people outside the
two-party mind-set. It would wipe out gerrymandering and make it
possible for everyone to feel represented, no matter where they live.
Most importantly, a majority of votes would translate into a majority
of seats.

"Aren't these gerrymanders terrible and don't they make things
worse? Yes," Spencer tells me. We're in FairVote's crowded office in a
Takoma Park, Maryland, professional building, filled with interns and
boxes of position papers. Located several Metro stops outside Washington, this is not one of those glamorous K Street buildings where
former congressmen play golf in their offices and wait for cars to take
them to lunch. There is, however, a Thai place nearby that will deliver.
The only former congressman I see here is a photograph of John
Anderson, the Illinois Republican who ran a third-party presidential
race in 1980 and serves on FairVote's board. (As does Krist Novoselic,
the bassist of the iconic 1990s rock band Nirvana.) A framed letter
from Pete Seeger hangs on the wall.

"But the key point is, if you took the gerrymander away completely,
how would people feel about what's being done after that?" Spencer
asks. "All of the things that people hate about gerrymandering would
still be there. The question of whether things were worse with these
crazy lines and sophisticated techniques isn't necessarily the right
question."

FairVote knows as well as anyone how noncompetitive congressional elections are. Two days after the 2014 elections, FairVote
released a study predicting every single congressional race in 2016.
You might call that crazy, except that when they did the same thing
for 2014 in the days after the 2012 election, they got 99.7 percent of
them right. That's a winning percentage that might make a predictor
as good as Nate Silver or Sam Wang jealous. FairVote identified 373
safe seats out of the 435 congressional districts, or 85 percent. They

found only 14 pure tossups. And they identified 212 seats as automatic Republican districts, meaning the GOP needs to win only six seats to run the House.

We have been sorted into red districts and blue districts. But under the FairVote model, every district looks purple. "We have these multi-seat districts for every state, and we basically say what would be the partisan implementations. Lo and behold, it's pretty easy color-coding, because every single one is purple," says Richie. "In the whole country. In every single district, we believe the numbers are there that *both* parties would win seats, and overall it would be a much more balanced thing."

As Richie sees it, Newt Gingrich shifted the nature of congressional elections in 1994. By nationalizing congressional elections with his Contract with America, they became more partisan—on both sides. "Back in 1993, there were 113 crossover representatives," he says, meaning members who won in a district where registration numbers favored the other party, "and after 2013 it's 26. Now it's down to 18." Politics became more partisan, he says, and so did voters. It will take a big new idea to defeat the us-versus-them mentality which pervades the news media, our social media silos and, yes, Congress itself.

In spring 2015, the day before I visited their offices, FairVote sponsored what it called a National Democracy Slam at American University in Washington, DC, where leading scholars and thinkers gathered to talk about fair representation voting, top-two primaries, right to vote amendments. I recalled how Steve Israel and David Price, two reform-minded liberals, shook their heads dismissively at the idea of enacting multi-member districts, and worried that I was watching the best cult band in the world play a set of just its Japanese B-sides before an adoring audience which knows every note.

After watching Richie over parts of two days keep his spirits high and keep fighting for electoral reform that makes so much sense yet also seems such an uphill battle in a country that still uses an Electoral

College, it seems natural to wonder how he keeps going. I want to know if he ever simply despairs at the state of our democracy.

"I guess from a reformer's perspective," he says, "we kind of need things to get pretty bad to see change. From our perspective, we're talking about a statute. It's not changing the Constitution. It's just the political will to pass a law. If things are so bad, can't we pass a law and deal with it?"

Richie's not a partisan, but we lay out the two most likely possibilities: Hillary Clinton wins in 2016 with about the same margin as Obama's reelection, and Congress stays with the Republicans. They won't cooperate; they run the same obstruction playbook as they did with Obama. "The House will have every incentive to have her fail, because they want to set up the midterm, and you can almost see that coming."

The only way out of the cycle? Clinton loses. Republicans and their appointees control all three branches.

"Then the 2018 midterms are the Democratic midterms," he postulates. "They actually bump up to this number, and they probably don't take the House back, but it gets people even more pissed off. Republicans probably keep the House, and they of course have the White House—so you can imagine the reaction to a year of losing the vote and actually keeping everything. *That* would be interesting. Then maybe people will say this has to change."

What Richie describes is the opposite of a democracy. It is an unaccountable minority. At the beginning of the 2012 presidential campaign, the keen conservative strategist Grover Norquist, the head of Americans for Tax Reform and one of the most masterful grass-roots Republican leaders in decades, spoke at the Conservative Political Action Conference to a packed hall of activists who found Mitt Romney's conservative bona fides uninspiring. So what, he told them. "We are not auditioning for fearless leader. We don't need a president to tell us in what direction to go. We know what direction to go. We just need a president to sign this stuff. Pick a Republican with enough working digits to handle a pen to become president of the United States."

Solid majorities of Americans would like to see gun control laws become more strict (55 percent, according to Gallup in October 2015), define themselves as pro-choice (50 percent to 44 percent, Gallup, May 2015), support same-sex marriage (55 percent, Pew Research Center, May 2015). Fifty-nine percent of Americans believe we need to continue making changes to ensure blacks are on an equal footing with whites (Pew, July 2015). Sixty percent would like to see funding for Planned Parenthood continue (Pew, September 2015). Sixty percent would like to see an increase in the minimum wage and mandatory paid sick leave (Associated Press/GfK, February 2015). Also, 72 percent of Americans told Pew pollsters that undocumented immigrants living in the U.S. should be able to stay, if they meet certain requirements. Only 17 percent backed a "national law enforcement effort to deport" all immigrants living in America illegally. On climate change, a December 2015 Quinnipiac poll found 66 percent of Americans either very or somewhat concerned about climate change, and 34 percent not so concerned or not concerned at all. Asked whether they would like to see the next president support or oppose action on climate change, the Quinnipiac results were even more striking: 69 percent support, just 23 percent oppose.

Congress's job approval rating, meanwhile, sat at 14 percent in a December 2015 CNN poll, and at 13 percent in a Gallup poll and 15 percent in a CBS/*New York Times* poll that same month.

Harvard political science professor Theda Skocpol has tracked what she calls "the Koch effect" pushing House Republicans to the right, especially since 2010. How far to the right? The House elected in 2010, she wrote, "took the biggest leap to the far right in recorded quantitative measurements of the kind that political scientists use to track legislators' positions."

At CPAC, Norquist told the GOP's most fervent activists not to worry about which Republican is in the White House. "The leadership now for the modern conservative movement for the next twenty years will be coming out of the House," he said. They're one election—and a pen— away from achieving an unimaginable goal in a country which sees itself as a beacon of democracy: a veto-proof supermajority operating without majority support. Such an outcome would have been almost impossible a decade ago, when moderate Republicans could still get elected, before members of Congress inhabited districts where their only challenge was from a more extreme part of their party's base. Now this has become the strategy for governing from the minority: If you can't beat 'em, ratfuck 'em.

CODA

Some seven years after that exuberant late-night speech in Grant Park, a no longer jubilant Barack Obama—wearier, grayer, even enervated—began the last year of his second term with a speech in the East Room of the White House, announcing executive action on gun-control measures which he had been unable to get through Congress. The red tie was long gone, along with Obama's postpartisan dreams. Shedding tears as he discussed the young victims of gun violence and school shootings in Newtown, Connecticut, and Knoxville, Tennessee, the president set out steps to close the gun show loophole and mandate background checks for every gun purchase, to deny guns to individuals on the no-fly list, and to improve funding for mental health. It was, if anything, a largely symbolic move, whose efficacy was questioned even by liberal columnists and supporters. Obama despaired that a similar package of reforms had failed to move through Congress after twenty elementary school students were massacred at Sandy Hook in December 2012. He wondered aloud why Republicans had become so intransigent on any gun control, why even the basic background checks supported by Ronald Reagan, George W. Bush, John McCain and once even by the NRA were now met with cries that the government wanted to take away citizens' guns. "Yes, the gun lobby is loud," Obama said. "The rest of us, we all have to be just as passionate." Congress blocks laws, the president argued, "because they want to win elections." Make it hard for Republicans to win elections, he suggested, and "they'll change course. I promise you."

Obama's frustration and tears were real, despite the peanut-gallery suggestions from conservatives in the media that they were generated by an onion stashed somewhere behind the podium. His analysis, however, missed the root cause of congressional inaction. In 2012, Democratic candidates for Congress received more votes than Republican candidates. For the first time in forty years, the party that received the most votes failed to take control of the House. The people did vote for candidates who believed in gun-control reforms. Obama had it backward: it's the Republican mapmakers who have made it hard for the *voters* to affect elections. If the 2012 election had been fought without the REDMAP firewall, some form of the gun-control reform which failed to make it through Congress after Sandy Hook likely would have been enacted. On issue after issue—climate change, immigration, reproductive rights, guns, the minimum wage—public-opinion polling shows broad support for the president's proposals. They have been stymied not because they are unpopular but because our politics have become paralyzed, held hostage by the most extreme wing of a minority party which figured out how to rig the game in its favor.

The strategists behind this plan may not even have realized how effective it would be—or how hard it would be to control. Throughout the spring, summer and fall of 2011, Republican consultants and mapmakers cashed in the gains from their successful REDMAP strategy. Flush from victories that gave them control of almost 70 legislative chambers nationwide just in time for the crucial decennial redistricting, they set to work transforming the nation's political map. It started in cities such as Columbus, Madison, Raleigh, Lansing and Tallahassee, as well as in other purple-state capitals that tilted decisively toward the GOP. But as John Boehner's political team helped influence Ohio's new congressional lines, he probably never imagined that his party's aggressive redistricting maneuvers would contribute to his being toppled as Speaker of the House just four years later. Ratfucking had blowback, and there would be unintended consequences—for the Republican Party and the entire U.S. government.

On September 25, 2015, Boehner announced that he would step down as Speaker and also resign from Congress. In a twist worthy of Shakespearean tragedy, or at least a plot twist on *House of Cards*, the powerful Republican second in line to the presidency was destroyed by uncontrollable renegades from his own party, most of them new members of Congress elected during the 2010 Tea Party wave or with the friendlier REDMAP lines in 2012 or 2014. These Republicans, fueled by *Fox News* and conservative talk radio, and protected by gerrymandered districts, cared for compromise as little as they liked Obamacare.

Boehner found himself stuck. He was trapped by the demands of governance, specifically by his responsibility to negotiate with a Democratic president on things as important passing a federal budget and avoiding a default on the national debt. Meeting those responsibilities, and meeting the president somewhere in the middle, only inflamed the House Freedom Caucus—the "suicide caucus," as they were dubbed by conservative commentator Charles Krauthammer. The renegades preferred to force a government shutdown, or at least a showdown, over Tea Party principles rather than hammer out agreement. They viewed even as staunch a conservative as Boehner, once a newcomer revolutionary like themselves, as just another suspect, dealmaking Washington insider. With a 247–188 GOP majority, Boehner held the largest Republican House advantage since 1947. Yet he could no longer command it.

The majority may have been built with a gerrymandered mirage, but no one told that to the new congressmen representing these carefully designed and overly insulated districts. All but two of the 45 House Freedom Caucus rebels who deposed Boehner were "guaranteed" reelection with only the most token opposition, wrote Hedrick Smith, a former Washington bureau chief of the *New York Times*, in an op-ed in the *Los Angeles Times*. Those 45 members won by an average of 38 points in 2014, he noted. Only two had faced a legitimate challenger.

Three had faced no opposition at all. More than 30 of them had arrived thanks to the 2010 Tea Party wave, or the REDMAP maps that followed. "With protected political monopolies back home, the rebels take little or no political risk and pay no political price for opposing their speaker and adopting extremist positions that bring Congress to a halt," Smith wrote.

For the rebels, the GOP majority was real. They wanted to use the party's edge, aggressively and decisively, to roll back Obamacare, derogate and defund Planned Parenthood, battle over the debt limit, and enforce a hard line on immigration. They did not care if the Speaker and other party leaders weren't up for the same fight. The huge GOP congressional majorities, meanwhile, created outsized expectations of conservative victories, especially among the base and within conservative media, firing up a virulently angry GOP electorate just as the 2016 presidential race began and fueling the rise of outsiders like tough-talker Donald Trump and trusted true believers like Ted Cruz and Ben Carson. Veteran conservative leaders including Jeb Bush, John Kasich and Chris Christie struggled to find traction as the legislative hydra unleashed by gerrymandering took over the GOP. Talk about ratfucked.

For Boehner, however, the end was almost poetic. It came at the hands of Mark Meadows, the former owner of Aunt D's sandwich shop in Sylva, North Carolina. Meadows found his way to Washington after the 2011 North Carolina gerrymander transformed the 11th congressional district, represented at the time by three-term Democratic incumbent Heath Shuler, into one of the most conservative in the state. Shuler took one look at the new lines and knew he was finished. The rural mountain towns of North Carolina have never been particularly friendly to Democrats; this is the terrain where Eric Rudolph hid for years after being identified as the 1996 Olympics bomber.

Before 2011, the heart of the 11th had been the funky college city of Asheville, home to art galleries and vegan cafés and feminist bookstores. The GOP mapmakers cracked the city. They split Asheville in two, scattering the Democratic votes. (This is another example of why the Big Sort redistricting theory fails; the like-minded Democrats may have sorted themselves by moving to Asheville, but their political influence was diluted intentionally by how the boundaries were drawn.) Shuler was a classic Blue Dog Democrat, a moderate-to-conservative religious Southerner who supported gun rights and opposed abortion. He was no fan of Obamacare or Nancy Pelosi; he stood against her for minority leader. But his nuanced approach fit the district; even in the 2010 cycle that had proven so challenging for Democrats, Shuler was reelected by 21,000 votes and a 54.3 to 45.7 margin.

The new 11th established a safe Republican district for a very different kind of conservative. Meadows campaigned as a Tea Partier and repeatedly questioned President Obama's citizenship. "2012 is the time we're going to send Mr. Obama home to Kenya or wherever it is," he said at one rally. He won with 57 percent of the vote, and increased his numbers to 63 percent in 2014. Gerrymandering had replaced a complicated, nervy Democrat, one who knew how to work with the other side and was regularly rated as one of the least partisan House members, with an intractable, obdurate Republican.

But Meadows did have a savvy understanding of parliamentary procedure, especially for a newcomer from the mountains of western North Carolina. In late July 2015, Meadows offered what's called a motion to vacate the chair, essentially a vote of no confidence in Boehner, to the surprise of both House leadership and even Meadows's band of revolutionaries. It hadn't been tried in the House in more than 100 years, but this move ultimately forced the split within the caucus to a head, and pried the gavel from Boehner's hands. "The displeasure and difficulty this decision created with some of my colleagues is hard to hear," Meadows later told the *Daily Signal*, a news site run by the conservative Heritage Foundation. "People who disagree with me don't know the support I have back home."

This parliamentary move may have been what broke Boehner's back, but it was not Meadows's first aggressive play. In August 2013, after being in Congress for only eight months, Meadows collected the signatures of 80 conservative House members on a letter to Boehner calling for the Speaker to link defunding Obamacare to a possible government shutdown. Boehner had already decided against this course. Even Karl Rove thought it was a horrible idea. The Democrats at this point, after all, still controlled the Senate, so there was no chance it would actually work. But when Boehner caved to the insurgents' strategy, the *New Yorker*'s Ryan Lizza and David Wasserman, the leading voice on the demographics of House districts, wanted to know more about who these 80 members were and where they lived. They ran some numbers and discovered, shockingly, that Republican districts in 2012, after redistricting, had been drawn more white, even as national trends marched toward greater diversity. The average district won by a Republican in 2012 was 2 percent more white than it had been in 2010. Those 80 conservatives were elected from districts, on average, that were 75 percent white, compared to the national average of 63. In the 2012 presidential election, Obama defeated Romney by 4 percentage points. In the 80 districts held by the insurgent conservatives, Romney won by an average of 23 points. The congressmen—and 76 of the 80 were men—managed even larger victory margins, an average of 34 points.

These are the numbers that led to a government shutdown. These are the numbers that explain why twenty elementary school children can be gunned down in Newtown, Connecticut, and yet a horrified nation demanding gun control can't find a majority in Congress. These are the numbers that led two of the wisest nonpartisan analysts in Washington, Thomas Mann and Norman Ornstein, to ring the alarm bells for democracy. "The Republican Party continues to demonstrate that it is an insurgent force in our politics," they wrote in their essential book *It's Even Worse Than It Looks: How the American Constitutional System Collided with the New Politics of Extremism.* "The old conservative GOP has been transformed into a party beholden to ideological zealots," they added, without "respect for facts, evidence, science, [or] a willingness to compromise."

The Republicans built themselves an unbreakable majority. They turned Democrats like Heath Shuler into a caucus of firebrands like

Meadows. The party's control was complete. Except, of course, that they were no longer in control at all. No one was.

My search for the last open-minded Republican congressman brought me to Iowa City and lunch with Jim Leach. The two largest employers in Leach's hometown of Davenport, Iowa, are the Rock Island Arsenal—the most massive government-owned weapons depot in the country—and John Deere. When an eighth-grade assignment required an essay on what he wanted to do when he grew up, Leach's father knew he had to broaden his son's horizons. He suggested the teenager find a book on the foreign service at the Davenport library, and from that moment Leach determined that he'd leap from the Quad Cities to the State Department.

He made himself into a Russian expert through studies at Princeton, then graduate work at Johns Hopkins' School of Advanced International Studies and the London School of Economics. Sure enough, he arrived on the Soviet desk and was about to be assigned to Moscow when he resigned abruptly in protest in fall 1973. Foreign service officers are presidential appointees, and after Richard Nixon demanded the dismissal of Watergate prosecutor Archibald Cox, prompting the resignation of the U.S. attorney general and his deputy in what became known as the Saturday Night Massacre, Leach decided he could not have any dotted line back to a president so corrupt as to put himself above the law. He sent a telegram with his resignation, returned to Davenport and joined his dad's propane gas business.

His public service dreams seemed finished, but when no one would run against a popular congressman in 1974, a local Republican county chairman talked Leach into being the sacrificial lamb. He lost—something else for which to thank Richard Nixon—but won the following outing and served in Congress for the next thirty years, rising to chair the banking committee and to become a senior member of the committee on international relations.

Jim Leach became the kind of congressman it is impossible to imagine now—of either party.

He was a fierce *Republican* critic of Ronald Reagan's Iran-Contra arms-for-hostages dealings. He supported abortion rights up until the third trimester, and when his party got wiped out in the off-year governor's races in 1989, and some Republican elders feared that too strong a stance on social issues would doom them in the 1990 midterms, Leach took the House floor and blasted the GOP's "rigid, narrow views on one of the most difficult and divisive issues." When Newt Gingrich faced questions over his ethics, Leach refused to support him for House Speaker. He voted against the majority of impeachment charges against Bill Clinton, with the exception of the charge for lying under oath, which the steadfast Leach viewed as an "absolute breach of an absolute standard." After September 11, he was one of seven House Republicans to vote against the Iraq War, convinced that Saddam Hussein had neither weapons of mass destruction nor any connection to al-Qaeda.

Iowans reelected Leach fourteen times, until 2006. By then, the Iraq War had gone as poorly as Leach had predicted. Leach's district was centered around the university town of Iowa City, and the Bush presidency convinced the electorate that they wanted a liberal Democrat, not an erudite moderate Republican, to represent them. Twenty-two GOP incumbents went down for the party's extremism, one of them Leach, a victim of what he'd been warning against for three decades. He owed his first defeat to Nixon and his last to W. He went down with his principles intact: the Republican National Committee tried to send out a mailer attacking his opponent for supporting same-sex marriage, and Leach insisted they stop or else he would not caucus with Republicans if reelected. When he lost, he spent a year directing the Institute of Politics at Harvard's Kennedy School before Barack Obama asked him to lead the National Endowment for the Humanities. Finally, a law professorship at the University of Iowa beckoned him back to his beloved Iowa City.

Leach walks with a slight hunch and a giddy shuffle; he wears a navy sweater over a white button-down with khakis a touch too big. It's clear why colleagues found him priestly and sometimes thought Latin

might be his native language. Downtown Iowa City's sidewalks double
as a walk of fame for the writers and poets associated with the university's renowned writing workshop; Leach is the rare congressman of
either party who name-checks Wallace Stegner, Raymond Carver and
John Cheever as we walk. One of his proudest moments at NEH was
finally seeing through the publication of the *Autobiography of Mark
Twain.*

Redistricting contributed to Leach's loss; the 2000 cycle drew him
and a very conservative congressman, Jim Nussle, into the same district. The liberal Republican knew there was no surviving a GOP primary against a conservative favorite and moved his family to Iowa
City. He's clearly a favorite regular here at Basta, an Italian restaurant not far from campus, where he tucks into the special of lobster
and shrimp fettuccine, with an Arnold Palmer to wash it down. Win
or lose, he praises the Iowa system as "wonderful" and "the best in the
country." Leach takes notes on the margins of the morning's *New York
Times* as I lay out my argument and ask how Congress might be different and more functional if the entire country followed Iowa's model.

"Many people know that redistricting is a problem. The reason that
it isn't central to reform initiatives is very simple. I make an analogy
to genealogy. Genealogy is really helpful and interesting to a family,
but nobody cares about somebody else's genealogy. Redistricting is
the genealogy of politics: incredibly important, and yet nobody cares.
Those that recognize its importance can get a great deal done with
surprisingly little effort. There's probably no part of politics that less
money has bought more. It's a factor, and a big factor."

Leach lost in 2006 before the Tea Party arrived in force, but he
watched in slow, sad horror as the moderates on both sides got hol-
lowed out. The combination of *Citizens United* and redistricting, he
says, turned independent thought into partisan heresy, and made
working across the aisle impossible.

"It used to be that compromise was the art of politics," he says.
"Now intransigence is the art of survival. It's very simple. Redistricting makes the races between the parties uncompetitive. The only

competition is within a party, so if a Republican chooses to vote moderately or chooses to work with a Democrat on an issue, that precipitates a primary challenge that will be well-funded."

Leach is a lifelong Republican, but he's honest about the asymmetry. "A Democrat could try," he says. "I always want to be balanced, but it's more severe on the Republican side. What's at issue is the nature of democracy. It's this nexus of *Citizens United* nationalizing elections, with the redistricting process, and it's created a nefarious and dangerous approach to politics which is out of step with what the Founders envisioned. It takes the competition out, and it plugs the ears of people in the legislative process. That doesn't mean legislators might not hear the other side, but they don't hear it deeply."

Safe districts only amplify the echo chamber. "My view is, decent people run for office, but the low road ends up being the most traveled because it's the principal way to getting elected. The lower the road, the less ability there is to work together after an election, and the less respect there is from the public toward those elected. We have a systemic problem. We need a new approach to financing elections and a new approach to how districts are established. The complicating factor is what has been made constitutionally impossible based upon five voices on the Supreme Court. We've given the big edge to sophisticates with money."

It's the governing side of the problem that really offends Leach. He looks at the annual hostage scene over raising the debt ceiling and can't believe, first, that America is the one country that requires such a ridiculous vote. Then he shakes his head over how this vote went from something mischievous but harmless to the threat of a shutdown and default every twelve months.

"It leads to dysfunctionality," he says, pointing out that there may be only two dozen districts left in America capable of electing a representative with an open mind and extended hand. "Over my time in the Congress, if you take the Republican Party, conservatives were always in the majority but there was a healthy group of moderates. Today moderate Republicans are extinct. On the Democratic side there were also so-called moderate Democrats in not trivial numbers. Many Southern Democrats would even call themselves conservatives. Now they don't exist."

Leach is describing the way a bridge-builder like Heath Shuler becomes a bomb-thrower like Mark Meadows. It's not a mushy middle, or a bland split-the-baby centrism he mourns; it's people looking to get a job done, while recognizing there's a constructive give-and-take to the process.

"I make the distinction between constructive legislators and obstructionists," he says. "Governing is all about constructive decision-making, and much of it is a matter of parsing subtleties and then parsing small distinctions. These true conservatives now think they have the only value structure—and someone who doesn't agree with them has no values."

We finish our cappuccinos and head for the door. What's the title of your book going to be? Leach asks. "All I can tell you is that it's a necessity to have a title that doesn't have the word redistricting in it. That might be in the subtitle, after a colon." There is no title yet, I tell him, so he throws one out. Call it *Democracy in Peril*," the longtime Republican lawmaker suggested. "That's not bad. It's catchy, and it's true."

Leach is right about "democracy in peril," but that title is too passive and doesn't assign responsibility for how our most sacred civic values became so debased. We have been ratfucked. A deep dysfunction and electoral disconnect has settled into our politics, and it will not be easily defeated or removed. As the political scientists Jacob Hacker and Paul Pierson observed, "Republicans are gaining more influence even though Americans seem less satisfied with the outcomes of increased Republican influence. Poll after poll shows that major GOP positions are not all that popular. Among swing voters, there has been nothing like the party's right turn." The House Republican caucus simply continues its four-decade march to the right. Defeat in presidential years is rationalized away with the argument that the nominee was not sufficiently conservative.

Meanwhile, thanks to redistricting, there are no electoral consequences for extremism; indeed, back home, it may even be rewarded. Ignored are the large majorities who would like to see sensible gun-control laws, or the same consideration for debt-burdened homeowners and students that the big banks and Wall Street receive. A 2013 *National Journal* analysis by the veteran reporter Ronald Brownstein showed just how insulated House Republicans are: "Back in 1995, 79 House Republicans represented districts that backed Clinton in the previous presidential election; just 17 House Republicans now represent districts that Obama won."

In the *New York Times*, the top-notch national politics writer Thomas B. Edsall observed that while Washington is gridlocked, conservatives have made significant policy gains in the states. Republicans, he wrote, have full control of the government in twenty-four states, with 47.8 percent of the population. Democrats? They control just seven states, with 15.8 percent of the population. (In the other seventeen states, control is divided between the parties.)

But as we've seen, the GOP has often retained this control with less than 50 percent support, due, in part, to the way district lines are drawn. This has serious policy implications. Take a state like Michigan, where the state House lines drawn by Jeff Timmer in 2011 proved durable enough to give Republicans a 59–51 majority in 2012, despite losing the overall popular vote. Voters favored Democratic House candidates 54.7 percent to 45.3 percent. Republicans passed a new "emergency manager" law allowing the state to take control of cash-strapped cities. Voters repealed the law in a 2012 referendum, but state legislators voted to reenact it weeks later. One of the cities which received an emergency manager was Flint. It was the emergency managers who pushed the move to tainted water as a money-saving move.

What is happening here, and how can we fix it? Redistricting is an essential part of the strategy, but it is not the entire plan. As Ari Berman explored in his influential work *Give Us the Ballot*, and Jim Rutenberg has masterfully documented in a *New York Times Magazine* series, gerrymandered Republican majorities in state Houses have also tried to cement the GOP's edge through increasingly restrictive voting laws. Republicans argued that new voter ID laws, cutbacks in early voting days, and more complicated registration processes were necessary to cut back on voter fraud. Of course, it also worked to the Republicans' advantage that these new laws most squarely affected minorities, the working poor, and other constituencies that tend to vote overwhelmingly Democratic. Redistricting plus restrictive voter registration laws are a strategy designed to stave off GOP demographic oblivion in a country becoming more diverse each year. A failure to recognize and combat this strategy will lead to electoral apartheid.

The most comprehensive study yet of voters, non-voters and presidential-year-only voters shows how crucial turnout is to any effort to defeat the gerrymander. The report, by Harvard political scientist Stephen Ansolabehere and the University of Massachusetts's Brian Schaffner, sampled millions of voting records from 2006, 2008, 2010 and 2012. What they found was shocking: only a quarter of all Americans voted in each of those elections. That quarter of the population was disproportionately whiter, wealthier and older than those who stayed home. The professors then broke the results down into three groups—non-voters, presidential-year-only voters and core voters—and conducted additional interviews. In 2010, the non-voters would have broken to the Democrats 34 percent to 31, while the presidential-year-only voters backed Democrats by a slightly wider margin, 43 percent to 37. The core voters who turned out regularly? They went for the GOP, 50 percent to 46.

The genius Republican strategist who imagined REDMAP has to pick up his daughters from school. Chris Jankowski has spent several hours answering every question honestly from someone he knows has a different political orientation. Knowing our time is winding down, I pose a very simple question: Is this fair? Take Pennsylvania, where more voters cast ballots for Democratic candidates than Republican ones, but the delegation tilts 13–5 GOP. Is that democratic?

He pauses for a moment. He's a deeply likable and soft-spoken guy, and in the pause I can't quite tell if he's disappointed that I'd frame his crowning achievement in such naive terms, or if he just hasn't thought of it in this way.

"I sleep well at night knowing that I have a job and there's people who play on the other team who should do their job," he finally answers. "But to answer the question directly, if it's not fair, there's a method of changing it in America. Elections. In my opinion, part of the spoils of an election is someone's got to draw the lines. I don't believe you can do it without impacting one party or the other, and the winner of the previous election gets to do it. I feel comfortable telling my kids what I do for a living. The other side is perfectly welcome to get in. Unfortunately"— and here a small smile returns—"given the circumstances, it's going to be very hard for them to turn it back."

If Democrats tried a BLUEMAP, they'd have to win in 2020 on these GOP-drawn maps. There also would be no element of surprise. Republicans designed this play and will be ready for the Democrats to try one of their own.

"We're not going to be outspent," he says, and returns from boastful operative to savvy analyst to explain why it won't matter what the Democrats do to try and untilt the table.

"History suggests it is too much to overcome. In a great year, they will get a seat at the table that will be helpful to them. It will take further Democratic trends in the *next* decade to make that seat at the table result in real congressional gains that stabilize this thing back to 'fairness.'

"Look, if you get the Ohio House back—which is feasible; I don't think you're going to get the Ohio senate back, ever—you'd still have to make a deal there. It was the sweeping nature of 2010. If North Carolina Republicans have truly overreached, [voters] will most likely take it out on the House. You'll still have a North Carolina Republican senate and the governor doesn't get a say [in redistricting]. We flipped both chambers and that changed the congressional map.

"So is it fair? I will let others decide that. Do I feel like I'm doing something unfair? No. We did what our team is supposed to do."

Sometime during the 2020s, he suggests, the demographic shift that

Democrats always claim is around the corner might actually arrive. "I think it would be an oversell beyond that," he says. "If the Republican Party continues to underperform, we will be a minority party regardless of redistricting."

Still, it will be 2031—a generation from now—before lines might reflect that. "I guess it is, when you think about it," he says. "We used to fight cycle by cycle for control of the House after 1994. It looked like, 'This back and forth will go on forever.'" Jankowski issues a small chuckle. "No."

"I read [the Democrats'] clips. I see some of their target states. Even if they are successful in gradually getting some gains back—if you only get one chamber, all you've bought yourself is a seat at the table. You don't have control. So what do you do with a seat at the table when you have an overwhelming congressional delegation of Republicans? Well, you're not shifting it to overwhelmingly Democratic. You might knock off one Republican.

"It's really hard for me to see their path forward. If Hillary gets elected, it seals their fate." Historically, a first-term president almost always sees losses in Congress in the midterm elections. Democrats would then have too much to reverse in 2020. "There's the Supreme Court, and the Obama agency overreach continues, but it doesn't do a damn thing for Congress. It seals their fate."

His worst-case scenario for the GOP is a president getting elected who is in way over his head. "Another Jimmy Carter," he says. "A really unpopular Republican president. But that's not enough. [Democrats] would have to set another historic record in 2018, and then 2020 would have to be another big one."

The one thing that gives Jankowski pause is the "Washingtonization" of it all. This is the guy, remember, who didn't want to leave South Carolina for DC because he disliked the political culture so much. He is perhaps the brainiest and most successful Republican strategist of his generation, responsible for locking in decades of congressional control at Dollar General prices, yet he works in Richmond by choice, sharing a small office.

"All the things that make DC so detestable to me may, arguably, be part of the tactics that we're now taking down to state capitals," he admits, but then his mood brightens. "If you go back and look at the press clips [from after 2010], you can see the outrage. 'This is wrong! I spent $10,000 on my last election. They spent $50,000 in one week!' Yeah, sorry. This has an arms-race quality feel to it. I don't feel good about that, but we don't tend to lose."

He rises from the table. "I'd rather be us than them."

Listen carefully to Jankowski, and you can see a plan for how to counter the revolutionary extremism that has captured the House and so many state capitals. The theorem to detect and destroy ratfucking would have to look something like this:

1. First, it is impossible to remove all the politics from something so inherently political. The political scientist Charles S. Bullock III calls redistricting "the most political activity in America," and he may well be right. The Democrats, traditionally, have not been as cut-throat as Republicans became in 2010; they used redistricting as an incumbency protection racket rather than as a tool to gain a major-ity they wouldn't otherwise obtain. But Democrats in Maryland and Illinois did manage egregious partisan gerrymanders, and the 1980s California gerrymander and the 1990s Texas redistricting were con-sequential and undemocratic as well. There's a reason, however, why REDMAP worked as well as it did: Republicans shrewdly targeted states where they could dominate the entire redistricting process. State or federal reforms which blocked one party from having exclu-sive control over line-drawing would, at the least, provide a check on the worst partisan excesses and prevent congressional delegations from becoming as lopsided and unrepresentative as those of Pennsyl-vania, Ohio, Florida and North Carolina.

Brian Beutler, the astute *New Republic* analyst, has suggested that Democrats—under the big "if," that the party can flip enough chambers in 2020 to play a bigger role in redistricting—should offer a permanent gerrymandering disarmament plan. "Neither party would be allowed to draw districts that structurally favor one party over the other for the sole purpose of partisan gain," he wrote, adding an alternate suggestion that Democrats could propose a national, nonpartisan redistricting plan that kicked in after a "critical number" of states passed it. It's a good idea, even if it first requires big wins in 2020 and then a willingness by Democratic leaders to embrace reforms they ignored after regaining control in 2006. But perhaps the decade of the 2010s has provided the wake-up call Democratic leaders need; the solution cannot be a decennial arms race which makes even local state House races too costly for anyone except wealthy candidates.

2. Independent commissions, whether bipartisan or nonpartisan, do not always work, and are not a one-size-fits-all solution. While reformers cheered the 2015 Supreme Court decision that upheld the constitutionality of the Arizona commission, it's clear that politics both infiltrated and pressured its work, and that both parties worked aggressively to game the system. Iowa's approach, meanwhile, requires more political trust than most states have, and is made easier by Iowa's rare racial homogeneity. Other states, such as New Jersey, have had success with a commission of politicians or other partisans chaired by an independent outsider or academic.

Many reformers have also admired California's independent commission, which was established through a ballot initiative in 2010. Democrats had long wired the state's congressional delegation; indeed, Nancy Pelosi and other Democrats and Democratic-aligned groups spent millions trying to defeat the initiative. Nevertheless, it passed with more than 61 percent support. It brought immediate results: In the previous decade, from 2002 through 2010, spanning some 500 elections, only one incumbent was defeated. Districts drawn by an independent commission—14 citizens without ties to any politician or party, chosen through an elaborate interview and essay process—

introduced more competition. Fourteen California congressmen decided not to run for reelection or lost in 2012, which meant that just over a quarter of the delegation were new faces.

Democrats did try to influence the process behind the scenes. As the *Eureka Times-Standard* noted, following up on a *ProPublica* investigation, "Democrats met behind closed doors at the party's Washington, DC, headquarters, hired consultants, drew their ideal districts and presented maps to the panel through proxies who never disclosed their party ties or 'public interest' groups created specifically for the purpose." This sounds similar to what Republican operatives did in Florida. Nevertheless, Republicans seem to think they fared better with an independent commission than they would have if Democratic lawmakers had drawn the lines. "I thought the commission did a so-so job, but they did ten times better than Republicans would have done under the Democrats," Allan Hoffenblum, a former Republican consultant in California, told *Politico*.

3. Redistricting reform and anti-gerrymandering measures are politically popular. When they hit the ballot, as they have this decade in Arizona, California, Florida and Ohio, they win with bipartisan support and double-digit margins in red, blue and purple states alike. Not every state allows the referendum or citizen initiative, but in states where it is available, one way to take the legislative process back from unaccountable majorities is for voters to push the issue to the ballot themselves, with the help of nonpartisan groups like the League of Women Voters. In Florida, of course, the Fair Districts amendment smothered the redistricting process under new forms of insider subterfuge, but it did allow for an ultimately successful court challenge that not only required new, fair maps, but also revealed the lengths to which partisan operatives will go to retain their advantages and the technological weapons at their disposal. Perhaps those email trails and secret meetings will also help convince political scientists and the media of just how carefully voters are being sorted. Every big win also demonstrates to politicians that voters care about what might

otherwise seem like a dull process issue; a 20-point victory for Ohio's anti-gerrymandering measure, for example, convinced Governor John Kasich, a Republican who approved the GOP-tilted districts in his state in 2011, that redistricting had become a problem in need of a solution. At the least, the threat of a referendum—and the prospect of having redistricting removed from control of either party—could scare legislators into finding acceptable reforms themselves.

4. Not only do voters in states as different as Arizona and Ohio, California and Florida, agree on gerrymandering, but it's something that conservative Supreme Court justice Antonin Scalia and liberal John Paul Stevens have agreed on, in principle. Scalia wrote in *Vieth v. Jubilirer* that "severe partisan gerrymanders" are incompatible with democracy. The unsettled debate in the courts, Stevens wrote, is whether the judiciary can say when a gerrymander goes too far and what is to be done about it. Courts can and do recognize and remedy racial gerrymanders, and could do the same for partisan ones, he wrote, imagining an (admittedly unlikely) constitutional amendment requiring districts that are contiguous, designed neutrally, and in which "the interest in enhancing or preserving the political power of the party in control of the state government is not such a neutral criterion."

5. This is already an ambitious set of reforms. But to truly solve the problem of partisan districting, FairVote's proposals for multi-member districts should be examined. Bipartisan or nonpartisan commissions might draw fairer lines, but that doesn't help a Republican in Connecticut or a Democrat in Louisiana earn representation in Congress. It would take only one state to give it a try for voters elsewhere to see how easy and effective—if different—this would be.

6. Finally, voters need to get angry, and voters need to turn out. Fair representation is a civil rights issue and a democratic rights issue. The vote is being rigged to favor a limited partisan interest and a shrinking older, whiter and more conservative demographic. Anyone

opposed to this use of corrosive assault on our most basic and valuable democratic right, the vote itself, must fight this deception and fraud as aggressively and strategically as those who would tilt things in their favor.

7. Finally, Democrats need to vote in midterm elections and not just in presidential years. Republicans built their current advantage with a 40-year effort to create their own media ecosystem, think tanks and political action groups. They have fought a battle of ideas and influence in Washington, but also in state legislatures and local school boards and county commissions. Democrats, in contrast, yearn for a charismatic hero every four years, have ignored the hard work of party building—and the harder work of knowing what they stand for.

Democrats announced their 2020 redistricting play to great fanfare in 2015. It did not, however, include these strategies. Instead, the DLCC launched something called Advantage 2020 and announced plans to spend in the ballpark of $70 million "trying to chip away at GOP majorities." Virginia governor Terry McAuliffe later signed on to run Unrig the Map, an effort through the Democratic Governors Association. "We're late to the game, but we don't have to come up with a new strategy," a leading Democratic fundraiser told the *New York Times*. "We just have to adapt to their strategy."

That won't be easy, even if they succeed in raising that much money. Indeed, Democrats are losing already. During the summer of 2015, the RSLC launched REDMAP 2020, a $125 million project to lock in and expand their gains.

"REDMAP 2020 will work to maintain the historic highs we hold today, including those in Obama-blue states, while working to pick up additional majorities in states like Kentucky, Maine and New Mexico where the legislatures play a vital role in crafting district boundaries, and Republicans currently control only one of the two state chambers," the RSLC proclaimed. "It's exciting for the future of the Republican Party."

The Republicans are strategizing in plain sight once again. Perhaps most troublingly, they may not have learned any lessons from 2010 about how hard it is to keep control of the base after taking control of a state.

In December 1988, not long before he left the presidency, Ronald Reagan sat for a long interview with veteran journalist David Brinkley, who was then at ABC. He used the presidential bully pulpit this last time to campaign for redistricting reform, and to call attention to the dangers of allowing politicians to draw their own lines and pick their own voters. Reagan prefaced his comments by calling them "sheer dynamite," and cautioning that "some people are going to erupt when I say it, but I think maybe our Founding Fathers made something of a mistake in the method of reapportionment." Reagan had to work with a House of Representatives weighted in the Democrats' favor; perhaps that's why he saw the problem so clearly. "I think that this is a great conflict of interest," he said, before promoting a plan for a bipartisan citizens' committee of top-ranking citizens to handle redistricting in each state.

In his final State of the Union address in 2016, wearing a black and gray striped tie perhaps chosen to avoid a color associated with either party, Barack Obama, like Reagan, clearly identified the problem right at the end of his presidency. "There are a whole lot of folks in this chamber, good people who would like to see more cooperation, would like to see a more elevated debate in Washington, but feel trapped by the imperatives of getting elected, by the noise coming out of your base," the president said. "But that means if we want a better politics— and I'm addressing the American people now—it's not enough just to change a congressman or change a senator or even change a president. We have to change the system to reflect our better selves. I think we've got to end the practice of drawing our congressional districts so that politicians can pick their voters, and not the other way around. Let a bipartisan group do it."

Maybe, as a first step toward compromise, both parties could admit that Ronald Reagan *and* Barack Obama are right. The House of Representatives was designed to be the chamber most responsive to the will of the people. Instead, it has become impervious and insulated from it. More money flows into politics with each cycle. Mapmaking technology will only improve. We allow partisans of either side to continue controlling this hidden but essential function at our own peril.

NOTES

INTRODUCTION

xii   **"The question now becomes":** Dante J. Scala quoted in Abby Goodnough, "Democratic Gains by Lawmakers in Northeast," *New York Times*, November 5, 2008.

xiii   **"2010 is not just any election year":** Adam Nagourney, "Governors' Races Offer Republicans an Opening," *New York Times*, July 21, 2009.

xvi   **"*Ratfucking?*' The word struck":** Carl Bernstein and Bob Woodward, *All the President's Men* (New York: Simon and Schuster, 1974), 128.

xvi   **Project Ratfuck:** Michael Kelly, "Segregation Anxiety," *New Yorker*, November 20, 1995.

xvii   **"Some of the most important contests this fall":** Karl Rove, "The GOP Targets State Legislatures: He Who Controls Redistricting Can Control Congress," *Wall Street Journal*, March 4, 2010.

xviii   **the anti-Federalist Patrick Henry used his powerful persuasive tools:** Robert Draper, "The League of Dangerous Mapmakers," *Atlantic*, October 2012.

xviii   **the Federalists won 51,766 votes:** John Paul Stevens, *Six Amendments: How and Why We Should Change the Constitution* (New York: Little Brown, 2014).

xviii   **"Partisan gerrymandering has always been a weapon":** Jacob S. Hacker and Paul Pierson, *Off Center: The Republican Revolution and the Erosion of American Democracy* (New Haven, CT: Yale University Press, 2006).

xix   **Here's what the Republicans spent:** Republican State Leadership Committee, final REDMAP report, 2010, available online at http://www.redistrictingmajority project.com/?p=638.

xx   **the biggest rout in modern history:** Louis Jacobson, "GOP Chalks Up Historic Gains," *Governing*, November 3, 2010.

xx   **Republicans ended election day 2010 with majorities:** RSLC, final REDMAP report, 2010.

xx   **during the 1991 redistricting, Democrats controlled:** Ibid.

xx   **After election day 2010, the transformation was complete:** Ibid.

xxi   **Republican Linda McMahon would spend $100 million:** Peter Applebome, "Personal Cost for 2 Senate Bids: $100 Million," *New York Times*, November 2, 2012.

xxi   **"Democrats would need to win the national popular vote by between six and**

seven points": David Wasserman, "October House Overview," *The Cook Political Report*, October 2013.

xxi **that would require "100 Democratic voters":** Tim Dickinson, "How Republicans Rig the Game," *Rolling Stone*, November 11, 2013.

xxi **GOP lawmakers would admit in court filings:** Ian Millhiser, "Virginia Republicans Admit They Rigged the State's Congressional Districts to Elect GOP Lawmakers," *ThinkProgress*, October 1, 2015.

xxiii **The most influential book:** Bill Bishop, *The Big Sort: Why the Clustering of Like-Minded America is Tearing Us Apart* (Boston/New York: Mariner, 2009). The discussion of gerrymandering is on 28–31.

xxiii **"Democrats often blame gerrymandering":** Nate Cohn, "Why Democrats Can't Win the House," *New York Times*, September 6, 2014. Cohn's piece earned a response from *Slate*'s expert, David Weigel: "Gerrymandering and the 'Big Sort' Fallacy," September 8, 2014.

xxv **Chaka Fattah:** Rhodes Cook, "Republicans Win Fewer Votes, but More Seats than Democrats," CQ Voting and Elections Collection, 2013, http://library.cqpress.com/elections/rcookltr-1527–84193–2523552.

CHAPTER 1: THE MASTERMIND

1 **Republicans swept to modern record gains:** The Republicans grabbed 680 new seats in state legislatures. Tim Storey, on his blog *The Thicket*, for the National Council of State Legislatures, and Louis Jacobson at *Governing* magazine were quick to recognize the historic implication. The NCSL gave the figure of 680 in a November 3, 2010, press release titled "Republicans exceed expectations in 2010 state legislature elections." *Politico*'s Darren Samuelsohn listed the state-by-state details in "GOP Poised to Take Redistricting Prize," November 2, 2010.

1 **"shellacking":** Lucy Madison, "Obama's 2010 'Shellacking' Is Like Bush's 2006 'Thumping,'" *CBS News*, November 3, 2010.

1 **"the Democrats will not soon recover":** Mike Baker, "Besides Seats, GOP Wins Sway in 2010 Redistricting," Associated Press, November 7, 2010. Jankowski made similar remarks to Darren Samuelsohn of *Politico*; see "GOP Poised to Take Redistricting Prize."

2 **Justin Levitt's redistricting website:** Titled "All About Redistricting," Levitt's site is perhaps the most essential web resource for maps, court cases, redistricting law and reform efforts. It is located at http://redistricting.lls.edu/.

2 **"The rationale was straightforward":** Republican State Leadership Committee, "2010 State Elections: REDMAP's Execution," available on the RSLC's website, www.redistrictingmajorityproject.com.

3 **a *Rolling Stone* hit piece:** Tim Dickinson's article was among the first to piece together the legacy of 2010; "How Republicans Rig the Game," *Rolling Stone*, November 11, 2013.

4 **Gillespie and Jankowski took a PowerPoint presentation on the road:** Nicho-

las Confessore followed the money brilliantly in "A National Strategy Funds State Political Monopolies," *New York Times*, January 11, 2014.

4 **their fundraising haul:** Numbers from ibid. and collected from the RSLC's FEC filings.

5 **"pass-through for controversial Indian tribe donations":** Alexander Burns, "GOP Group Snared in Money Scheme," *Politico*, August 4, 2014.

5 **"GOP relied on opaque nonprofits":** "How Dark Money Helped Republicans Hold the House and Hurt Voters," *ProPublica*, December 21, 2012.

5 **The Republican Governors Association was active as well:** Fredreka Schouten, "Big Cash Edge for GOP in State Bids: Stakes Are High in Voting 'Super Bowl,'" *USA Today*, September 24, 2010.

7 **"I believe in Jesus Christ as my personal savior":** David Grann, "Ghosts: Can Lee Atwater's Legacy save George W.?", *New Republic*, February 21, 2000.

7 **setting a goal for Republicans to retake Southern legislative seats, and then Congress:** "I began working at the RNC in 1989, and Lee Atwater's first words to me were 'Do something about redistricting,'" Ginsberg told Michael Kelly in "Segregation Anxiety."

9 ***BMW v. Gore*:** The Supreme Court rulings in the case are collected by the Legal Information Institute at Cornell University Law School, www.law.cornell.edu/supct/html/94–896.ZO.html.

12 **the headlines were apocalyptic:** Brad Knickerbocker, "Election 2010: How Bad Is It for Democrats?", *Christian Science Monitor*, September 5, 2010.

13 **"It appears that the best type of candidate to be":** Jeffrey Jones, "Americans Most Likely to Favor GOP Newcomers for Congress," Gallup Poll, September 3, 2010.

13 **"Conditions have deteriorated badly":** Larry Sabato, "Sixty Days to Go: The Crystal Ball's Labor Day Predictions," September 2, 2010, www.centerforpolitics.org/crystalball/articles/ljs2010090201/.

CHAPTER 2: PENNSYLVANIA

23 **"The gerrymander of the decade":** "In Pennsylvania, the Gerrymander of the Decade?" asked Sean Trende in a prescient and far-reaching analysis in *Real Clear Politics*, December 14, 2011. It's a terrific district-by-district analysis of how the maps evolved between 2000 and 2010 and how the new districts were likely to perform throughout the 2010s, and provides much of the statistics and background here.

23 **"The most gerrymandered map I've seen":** Charles Thompson, "Congressional Redistricting Puts Pa. Congressmen at a Distance," *Harrisburg Patriot-News*, December 18, 2011.

23 **Republicans reversed it to 12–7:** Statistics from Harry C. "Neil" Strine IV, "Raw Political Power. Gerrymandering, and the Illusion of Fairness: The Pennsylvania Redistricting Process, 2001 and 2011," in William J. Miller and Jeremy D. Walling,

eds., *The Political Battle Over Congressional Redistricting* (Lanham, MD: Lexington, 2013).

23 **more Republican *than the country as a whole*:** Trende, "The Gerrymander of the Decade."

23 **"Pennsylvania is arguably the most distorted map in the country":** Timothy McNulty, "How Gerrymandering Helped GOP Keep Control of the House," *Pittsburgh Post-Gazette*, November 26, 2012.

24 **All of this starts:** Trende, "The Gerrymander of the Decade."

24 **five Democrats who won in 2012:** Ibid.

24 **"The basic idea that guided Republicans":** Ibid.

24 **"They were so greedy":** McNulty, "How Gerrymandering Helped GOP Keep Control of the House."

24 **That meant fortifying the lines:** Specifics of new districts are drawn from ibid.; Trende, "The Gerrymander of the Decade"; Strine, "Raw Political Power"; and Heidi Przybyla, "Road to Democratic House Majority Bypasses Pennsylvania," *Bloomberg Business*, April 13, 2012.

25 **Meehan added almost 40,000 rural, Republican-leaning voters:** Przybyla, "Road to Democratic House Majority Bypasses Pennsylvania."

25 **"It's a pretty amazing redraw":** Ibid.

25 **A Philadelphia firm called Azavea:** Azavea's analysis of the Pennsylvania maps and their compactness, "Pennyslvania Congressional Redistricting: We Have a Plan," is available at http://www.azavea.com/blogs/atlas/2011/12/pennsylvania-congressional-redistricting-we-have-a-plan/.

31 **Dominic Pileggi:** Pileggi's 2011 suggestions for Electoral College reforms are discussed in Katharine Q. Seelye, "Pennyslvania GOP Weighs Electoral Vote Changes for 2012," *New York Times*, September 19, 2011. His 2012 efforts were chronicled in, among other places, Angela Couloumbis, "Pileggi to Reintroduce Plan to Change Pennsylvania Electoral-Vote System," *Philadelphia Inquirer*, December 5, 2012. His ouster by conservative Senate caucus members was analyzed by Dan McQuade in "Chester's Dominic Pileggi Ousted as Pennsylvania Senate Leader," *Philadelphia*, November 12, 2014. Mike Turzai's admission about GOP hopes of electing a Republican president through voter ID laws were reported in Kelly Cernetich, "Turzai: Voter ID Law Means Romney Can Win PA," *Politics PA*, June 25, 2012. Judge Bernard McGinley's ruling against that voter ID law was covered by, among others, Ari Berman, in "Pennsylvania Ruling Shows the Problem with Voter ID Laws," *The Nation*, January 17, 2014.

CHAPTER 3: NORTH CAROLINA

33 **"last prominent unabashed white racist politician":** David Broder, "Jesse Helms, White Racist," *Washington Post*, August 29, 2001.

34 **last white Democrat:** Deirdre Walsh, "Last White Democrat from Deep South Loses Congressional Seat," CNN.com, November 5, 2014.

34 **Cook Partisan Voting Index:** available at www.cookpolitical.com.

35 *Thornburg v. Gingles:* Decisions available at www.supreme.justia.com/cases/federal/us/478/30/case.html.

35 **"Do something about redistricting":** Kelly, "Segregation Anxiety."

36 **"I guess you could call it an unholy alliance":** Paul Taylor, "GOP Will Aid Civil Rights Groups in Redistricting," *Washington Post*, April 1, 1990.

36 **brought redistricting into the courts:** Ari Berman's masterful *Give Us the Ballot: The Modern Struggle for Voting Rights in America* (New York: Farrar Straus & Giroux, 2015) recreates the thinking behind the Southern strategy, especially in North Carolina.

36 **"truly space-age" software:** Taylor, "GOP Will Aid Civil Rights Groups in Redistricting."

36 **"get the living hell beat out of me":** Richard L. Berke, "GOP Tries a Gambit with Voting Rights," *New York Times*, April 14, 1991.

36 **"The fact is that minorities remain grossly underrepresented":** Ben Ginsberg's September 28, 1990, comments before the Congressional Black Caucus are available at http://library.cqpress.com/cqresearcher/document.php?id=cqresrre1991021506.

37 **argued with the CBCF for patience:** Jeffrey Wice's comments are available at http://library.cqpress.com/cqresearcher/document.php?id=cqresrre1991021506.

38 **the largest black caucus in Congress since the days of Reconstruction:** Berman, *Give Us the Ballot.*

38 **Racial gerrymandering:** George Will, "The Voting Rights Act at 30," *Newsweek*, July 10, 1995.

38 **"Just Dreamin' A Bit Too Much Plan":** Berman, *Give Us the Ballot.*

38 **"If it helped Republicans, so be it":** Ibid.

39 **found themselves in a Howard Johnson's off I-95:** Jon Meacham, "Voting Wrongs," *Washington Monthly*, March 1993.

39 **"district respects no county lines":** Ibid.

39 **"unexplainable on grounds other than race":** *Shaw v. Reno* decisions are available at https://supreme.justia.com/cases/federal/us/509/630/case.html.

40 **Watt's response was outrage:** Berman, *Give Us the Ballot.*

42 **Some $1.25 million was shoveled to Real Jobs NC:** Olga Pierce, Justin Elliott and Theodoric Meyer, "How Dark Money Helped Republicans Hold the House and Hurt Voters," *ProPublica*, December 21, 2012; Jane Mayer, "State for Sale," *New Yorker*, October 10, 2011.

42 **"Steve Goss . . . nice guy":** Pierce, Elliott and Meyer, "How Dark Money Helped Republicans."

42 **John Snow had dozens of mailers sent:** Mayer, "State for Sale."

42 **"the hooker ad":** Ibid.

43 **"We know the ongoing redistricting process":** Chris Jankowski, letter, n.d., quoted in Pierce, Elliott and Meyer, "How Dark Money Helped Republicans." Available online at http://www.propublica.org/documents/item/537408-hofeller-sglf-rslc-letter.

43 **Jankowski wasn't kidding:** Pierce, Elliott and Meyer, "How Dark Money Helped Republicans," and Draper, "The League of Dangerous Mapmakers."

44 **"What I've Learned About Redistricting—The Hard Way":** Tom Hofeller's PowerPoint presentation is available at http://www.ncsl.org/documents/legismgt/ The_Hard_Way.pdf.

45 **"incorporate all the significant concentrations":** Tom Hofeller, email, quoted in Pierce, Elliott and Meyer, "How Dark Money Helped Republicans."

45 **"segregate African American voters in three districts":** Ibid.

46 **an email trail which lays out the subterfuge:** Ibid.

46 **"When Nathan and I counted earlier":** Brent Woodcox, email, available as part of discovery in *North Carolina NAACP v. Governor Pat McCrory*, at http:// s3.documentcloud.org/documents/537529/naacp-460.txt.

46 **To knock out Representative Heath Shuler:** Draper, "The League of Dangerous Mapmakers," and Tracy Jan, "Turning the Political Map into a Partisan Weapon," *Boston Globe*, June 23, 2013.

47 **to challenge the artistry or the reality on election day 2012:** Statistics and quotes from Pierce, Elliott and Meyer, "How Dark Money Helped Republicans"; Adam Serwer, Jaeah Lee and Zaineb Mohammed, "Now That's What I Call Gerrymandering," *Mother Jones*, November 14, 2012; and Draper, "The League of Dangerous Mapmakers."

47 **"That is huge":** Richard E. Cohen, "Race Politics Hit N.C. Redistricting," *Politico*, May 4, 2011.

48 **Justice Paul Newby was badly trailing:** Lou Dubose, "Redistricting in Raleigh," *Washington Spectator*, April 1, 2014.

CHAPTER 4: MAPTITUDE

54 **our voting preferences almost shamefully easy to predict:** A June 2014 Pew Research Center study on Political Polarization in the American Public found that Republicans and Democrats are "more divided along ideological lines—and partisan antipathy is deeper and more extensive—than at any point in the last two decades" (www.people-press.org/2014/06/12/political-polarization-in-the-american-public/). Americans' voting preferences are easier to predict because they have become increasingly tied to partisan preference, and more of us are down-the-line partisans. Pew found that the percentage of Americans who "express consistently conservative or consistently liberal opinions has doubled over the past two decades," from 10 percent to 21 percent. At the same time, 38 percent of "politically engaged Democrats" are consistent liberals. Only 8 percent said that in 1994. It's similar on the Republican side: 33 percent maintain "consistently conservative views," a jump from 23 percent in 1994.

55 **Every ten years, a magazine or website will show the strangest-looking new districts:** The *Washington Post*'s list, by Christopher Ingraham, was published on May 15, 2014, and is available at https://www.washingtonpost.com/news/wonk/

wp/2014/05/15/americas-most-gerrymandered-congressional-districts/.
The mapmaking firm Azavea's report "Redistricting the Nation," available at
https://s3.amazonaws.com/s3.azavea.com/com.redistrictingthenation/pdfs/
Redistricting_The_Nation_Addendum.pdf, was the source for *Buzzfeed*'s list of the
most contorted districts, available at http://www.buzzfeed.com/qsahmed/the-10-
most-gerrymandered-districts-in-america-dh45.

56 **Caliper Corporation:** Caliper's history and quotes from Howard Slavin come from
Ivan Levingston, "The Software that Redraws the Political Landscape," *Roll Call*,
July 29, 2015.

CHAPTER 5: MICHIGAN

61 **The 14th was drawn:** The history of the new 14th district is told in Michael K.
Romano, Todd A. Curry and John A. Clark, "Michigan: Republican Domination During a Population Exodus," in Miller and Walling, eds., *The Political Battle Over Congressional Redistricting*, and Chris Christoff and Greg Giroux, "Republicans Foil
What Majority Wants by Gerrymandering," *Bloomberg Business*, March 18, 2013.
Jeff Wattrick of *Deadline Detroit* and Marisa Schultz of the *Detroit News*'s tours of
the district were also a tremendous help.

62 **There was once a town in the heart of America:** Details about Detroit are drawn
from David Maraniss, *Once in a Great City: A Detroit Story* (New York: Simon and
Schuster, 2015).

62 **This is the hellscape of Delray:** Delray details are drawn from Matt Gomez
and Aaron Haithcock, "The Delray Project," Global Change Program, University of Michigan, http://www.globalchange.umich.edu/globalchange2/current/
workspace/sect006/S6G6/delray%20pres.ppt; Tim Lougheed, "Arising from the
Ashes? Environmental Health in Detroit," *Environmental Health Perspectives*
122, no. 12 (December 2014); Tom Henry, "Detroit River: The Good, the Bad, the
Ugly," *Toledo Blade*, November 17, 2014; John McArdle, "Health Worries Stalk
Neighborhoods in Detroit's 'Sacrifice Zone,'" Greenwire/ *New York Times*, September 12, 2011; Tina Lam's series "48217: Life in Michigan's Most Polluted ZIP
Code," *Detroit Free Press*, June 2010; and Suki Gershenhorn, "What About Delray?
The Past and Future of Detroit's Forgotten Neighborhood," *Huffington Post*, Octo-
ber 9, 2012.

63 **"true monstrosity," "Eight Mile Mess":** Romano, Curry and Clark, "Michigan:
Republican Domination During A Population Exodus."

66 **Hamtramck:** Monica Davey, "Michigan Town Is Left Pleading for Bankruptcy,"
New York Times, December 27, 2010.

66 **the 27th best place to live in America:** *Money*'s "Best Places to Live 2013" list is
available at http://time.com/money/collection/best-places-to-live-2013/.

69 **Pontiac Silverdome:** Candice Williams and Mark Hicks, "Demolition of Pontiac
Silverdome to Begin Spring '16," *Detroit News*, October 29, 2015; "Pontiac Silver-

dome to Meet Wrecking Ball," *Detroit Free Press*, October 29, 2015; and Wikipedia, "Silverdome," https://en.wikipedia.org/wiki/Silverdome.

73 **He fell into the headlines not long after redistricting:** Rachel Maddow provided some of the most detailed reporting on this issue, including "Michigan Running in Very Small Circles," *The Rachel Maddow Show*, MSNBC, April 10, 2012; "Michigan, This Is Your Democracy," April 26, 2012; and "Michigan Republican, Very Funny, Ha Ha," June 27, 2012. Michigan Public Radio, in an April 10, 2012, report by Lindsey Smith and Rick Pluta, asked, "Who's Behind the Group Citizens for Fiscal Responsibility?" Rick Haglund tracked how "Special-Interest Money Floods Ballot Measures," *Bridge*, July 31, 2012. The Detroit daily papers also provided valuable context.

73 **unsung genius of the Super PAC age:** Bob LaBrant's autobiography, *PAC MAN: A Memoir: A personal political history of the campaign finance, redistricting, ballot question, recall and judicial election battles in Michigan 1977–2014,* may be self-published but it is an essential and honest guide to the rise of PACs, the growing role of the U.S. Chamber of Commerce, and the sophisticated GOP efforts to fight Democrats in state capitals.

76 **Powell wanted the business community to offer a counternarrative to that of Ralph Nader's consumer coalition:** The political scientists Jacob Hacker and Paul Pierson explain why the Powell memorandum is so important in *Winner-Takes-All Politics: How Washington Made the Rich Richer—and Turned Its Back on the Middle Class* (New York: Simon and Schuster, 2011), excerpted on Bill Moyers's website at http://billmoyers.com/content/the-powell-memo-a-call-to-arms-for-corporations/.

76 **Tom Donohue took over the national organization:** Donohue's terrific influence is captured in Sheryl Gay Stolberg, "Pugnacious Builder of the Business Lobby," *New York Times*, June 1, 2013.

76 **the national Chamber became one of the most reliable financial supporters of the Republican State Leadership Committee:** Andy Kroll followed the corporate–business money with great success in "Meet the Fortune 500 Companies Funding the Political Resegregation of America," *Mother Jones*, November 21, 2014.

77 ***Austin v. Michigan Chamber of Commerce:*** The *Ann Arbor News* and the other papers in Michigan's MLive chain carried the *Austin* story; see Jim Harper, "U.S. Supreme Court Could Overturn Landmark Austin v. Michigan Chamber of Commerce Case," January 10, 2010.

81 **director of the Michigan office of Americans for Prosperity:** Lund's appointment was covered in Paul Egan, "Former GOP Lawmaker Lund to Head Anti-Tax Group," *Detroit Free Press*, May 20, 2015.

CHAPTER 6: OHIO

The emails and secret GOP strategies discussed in this chapter were revealed by Jim Slagle, the manager of the Ohio Campaign for Accountable Redistricting, a project of the League of Women Voters of Ohio and Ohio Citizen Action. The group published "The

Elephant in the Room: How Power Was Used in the Political Backrooms to Manipulate Districts to Benefit the Political Insiders," a 22-page Ohio Redistricting Transparency Report (plus three lengthy appendixes loaded with documents, timelines, invoices, email exchanges, and more) on December 12, 2011. Further details can be found at www .lwvohio.org.

84 **"maintaining and expanding our new House majority":** Richard E. Cohen, "Boehner Expands Political Machine," *Politico*, January 28, 2011.

85 **Renacci had been the recipient of almost $210,000:** Aaron Marshall, "Public Records Show Speaker Boehner's Aide Called Shots on Secret Redistricting Process," *Cleveland Plain Dealer*, December 12, 2011.

86 **REDMAP allocated nearly $1 million":** Final REDMAP report, 2010.

86 **"a margin so huge as to overwhelm other explanations":** Steve Hoffman, "Boehner Says He's Got a Mandate?", *Akron Beacon-Journal*, December 5, 2012.

86 **REDMAP's 2012 summary report concluded:** Republican State Leadership Committee, REDMAP Summary Report, 2012, available online at http://www .redistrictingmajorityproject.com/?p=646.

88 **"All restraints went by the boards":** Hoffman, "Boehner Says He's Got a Mandate?"

96 **"The problem is":** Eric Cantor interviewed on *HARDtalk*, BBC, October 15, 2015.

97 **Tom Whatman, meanwhile:** Philip Rucker and Robert Costa, "In Ohio, Portman Tries to Shield Himself from Trump Shrapnel," *Washington Post*, December 17, 2015.

CHAPTER 7: DEMOCRATS

98 **Republicans controlled 32 of the nation's 50 governorships:** Matt Yglesias at *Vox* has been at the forefront of political writers pointing out the Democrats' problems down-ballot and at the state level; see "Democrats in Deep Trouble," *Vox*, October 19, 2015. Sheryl Gay Stolberg, Michael D. Shear and Alan Blinder dove deep into the party's ills after the 2015 election in "In Obama Era, GOP Bolsters Grip in States," *New York Times*, November 13, 2015. Chris Cillizza, who runs "The Fix" for the *Washington Post*, ran the numbers in "The 2015 Election Tightened the Republican Stranglehold on State Government," November 4, 2015. The *New York Times*'s Thomas Sowell, the *Washington Post*'s Greg Sargent and *National Journal*'s Ronald Brownstein have also written thoughtfully on these topics. Other numbers and insights come from Tim Storey at the National Conference on State Legislatures and from the United States Election Project, run by Michael McDonald of the University of Florida, at www.electproject.org.

105 **John Tanner:** Tanner's redistricting efforts were covered wisely over the years by *Politico* (Victoria McGrane, "Tanner Pushes Redistricting Reform," July 24, 2009), *The Hill* (Josephine Hearn, "Tanner Redistricting Bill Gains Senate Sponsor," March 1, 2006) and *Roll Call* (Morton M. Kondracke, "To Tame Polarization of Politics, Fix Our Redistricting System," October 27, 2005), among other publica-

tions. Robert Draper spoke extensively with Tanner for his magisterial "The League of Dangerous Mapmakers" in the October 2012 issue of the *Atlantic*.

108 **a 2014 Pew Center poll:** "Political Polarization in the American Public: How increasing ideological uniformity and partisan antipathy affect politics, compromise and everyday life," available at http://www.people-press.org/2014/06/12/political-polarization-in-the-american-public/.

111 **The importance of redistricting hit home:** Martin Frost discusses his history with redistricting in his book *The Partisan Divide: Congress in Crisis*, written with former congressman Tom Davis and Richard Cohen (Campbell, CA: Premiere, 2014). The discussion of Texas redistricting during the 1990s and 2000s is drawn from Jeffrey Toobin's definitive "Drawing the Line: Will Tom DeLay's Redistricting in Texas Cost Him His Seat," *New Yorker*, March 6, 2006.

117 **Its director, Mark Schauer:** Schauer's appointment to run Advantage 2020 was covered by Benjy Sarlin ("Democrats Launch New Super PAC to Combat GOP Gerrymanders," MSNBC, February 18, 2015), among other writers. Schauer discussed his plans in a *Huffington Post* op-ed, "Drawing the Line: Taking the Lead in the Fight for Redistricting," March 17, 2015). The approximately $10 million raised by the Democrats in 2010 for redistricting was reported by *ProPublica* (Pierce, Elliott and Meyer, "How Dark Money Helped Republicans") and the *Washington Post* (Amber Phillips, "The 2020 Redistricting War Is (Already) On," July 16, 2015). The Republican State Leadership Committee's statement on REDMAP 2020's plans can be found on the RSLC's website, http://rslc.gop/blog/2015/07/16/rslc-launches-redmap-2020-sets-125-million-investment-goal/.

CHAPTER 8: FLORIDA

121 **"Legislative districts or districting plans may not be drawn":** The history and constitutional language can be found at www.fairdistrictsnow.org.

121 **When Jeb Bush was elected governor in 1998:** Aubrey Jewett, "'Fair' Districts in Florida: New Congressional Seats, New Constitutional Standards, Same Old Republican Advantage," in Miller and Walling, eds., *The Political Battle Over Congressional Redistricting*.

121 **brilliantly designed the two new districts:** Ibid.

121 **Obama outpolled John McCain:** Ibid.

122 **the smartest Republican strategists gathered at party headquarters:** Final judgment by Judge Terry Lewis, *Romo v. Detzner*, 2012 CA 412 (2014), 23.

123 **Frank Terraferma:** Mary Ellen Klas, "Terraferma, Genius Map Drawer, Is Called to Testify Again with New RNC Docs," *Miami Herald*, May 30, 2014.

123 **"Does he age?":** Peter Schorsch, "Brightest Minds in Florida Politics," www.saintpetersblog.com, May 22, 2014.

123 **Rich Heffley:** Matt Dixon, "Former Senate President Ally Got $10,000 Monthly to Help with Redistricting," *Naples Daily News*, May 16, 2014; "Brightest Minds in Florida Politics," www.saintpetersblog.com, May 21, 2014.

123   **Pat Bainter:** Matt Dixon, "The Most Influential Man in Florida GOP Politics You Don't Know," *Naples Daily News*, November 29, 2014.

123   **Another participant, according to testimony:** Ben Ginsberg quoted in Mary Ellen Klas, "Emails Show Legislative Leaders Talked with Party over Redistricting Maps," *Miami Herald*, February 4, 2013.

124   **"This group of Republican consultants or operatives":** Final judgment, *Romo v. Detzner*.

125   **"An extreme statistical outlier":** The report is available as part of the trial record, at http://redistricting.lls.edu/cases-FL.php#FL.

125   **thousands of pages of exhibits, depositions, testimony and private emails:** See Marc Caputo, Kathleen McGrory and Michael Van Sickler, "Emails Show GOP Consultants 'Almost Paranoid' Mission to Circumvent Fla's Gerrymandering Ban," *Miami Herald*, November 23, 2014. The documents are also available at http://redistricting.lls.edu/cases-FL.php#FL.

125   **Posada testified:** The video is available at https://www.flsenate.gov/Session/Redistricting/Hearings.

126   **submitted a set of congressional maps:** Details of the alexposada22@gmail.com submission come from Mary Ellen Klas, "Surprise Witness Emerges in Redistricting Trial," *Miami Herald*, May 29, 2014, and "Alex Posada, Redistricting Mystery Man," *Miami Herald*, May 30, 2014.

126   **Alex Posada:** Details about the real Alex Posada come from Klas, "Surprise Witness" and "Alex Posada."

126   **"Got it—we'll let you know if we have any questions":** A jpeg of the email is available at http://miamiherald.typepad.com/.a/6a00d83451b26169e201a73dcec7a4970d-pi.

127   **perfectly matched the seven districts:** Ibid.

127   **Terraferma readily conceded:** Mary Ellen Klas, "GOP Official Can't Explain How His Maps Match Public Submission, Final Plan," *Tampa Bay Times*, May 23, 2014.

127   **Vince Falcone:** The story emerges in Posada's deposition, available at http://miamiherald.typepad.com/files/posada-alejandro-e.-05-29-14.pdf.

128   **"I won't say what my mom taught me":** Rich Heffley's testimony is available at http://redistricting.lls.edu/files/FL%20romo%2020140721%20pls%20app.pdf.

128   **The massive paper trail and Judge Lewis's ruling tell a different story:** Judge Terry Lewis wrote: "What is clear to me from the evidence, as described in more detail below, is that this group of Republican political consultants or operatives did in fact conspire to manipulate and influence the redistricting process. They accomplished this by writing scripts for and organizing groups of people to attend the public hearings to advocate for adoption of certain components or characteristics in the maps, and by submitting maps and partial maps through the public process, all with the intention of obtaining enacted maps for the State House and Senate and for Congress that would favor the Republican Party. They made a mockery of the Legislature's proclaimed transparent and open process of redistricting by doing all of this in the shadow of that process, utilizing the access it gave them

to the decision makers, but going to great lengths to conceal from the public their plan and their participation in it." Available at http://www.floridaredistricting.org/documents/2015B/Filed_07-09-2015_Opinion.pdf.

129 **a five-page list of names:** Bainter's emails are available at http://www.florida supremecourt.org/pub_info/summaries/briefs/14/14-1200/Filed_11-25-2014_Unsealed_Document_F.pdf#search=Randolph Skip.

129 **"Why were you drawing maps?":** Caputo, McGrory and Van Sickler, "Emails Show GOP Consultants' 'Almost Paranoid' Mission."

130 **"We will NOT exactly copy this map":** Bainter's emails, at http://www .floridasupremecourt.org/pub_info/summaries/briefs/14/14-1200/Filed_11-25-2014_Unsealed_Document_F.pdf#search=Randolph Skip.

131 **Tampa was far from perfect:** Judge Lewis' opinion, quoting the email, is available at http://www.floridaredistricting.org/documents/2015B/Filed_07-09-2015_Opinion.pdf.

132 **"Please get with me":** Ibid.

132 **"Stafford is getting me 10 more people":** Caputo, McGrory and Van Sickler, "Emails Show GOP Consultants' 'Almost Paranoid' Mission."

132 **replied with a state senate map:** Bainter's emails, at http://www.florida supremecourt.org/pub_info/summaries/briefs/14/14-1200/Filed_11-25-2014_Unsealed_Document_F.pdf#search=Randolph Skip.

132 **the legislature said that it had used not only the Posada maps:** Brandon Larrabee, "Florida Redistricting Records Unsealed; Revealing Apparent Scheme to Funnel Maps Through Members of the Public to Conceal the Origins," *Florida Times-Union*, November 25, 2014.

132 **"Well, we certainly had":** Bainter's previously sealed testimony is available at http://redistricting.lls.edu/files/FL%20romo%2020140721%20pls%20app.pdf.

132 **"Again, I—the mischaracterization":** Ibid.

133 **the emails show how hard the consultants worked:** All Bainter's emails, scripts, and talking points referenced in this section are available at http://www .floridasupremecourt.org/pub_info/summaries/briefs/14/14-1200/Filed_11-25-2014_Unsealed_Document_F.pdf#search=Randolph Skip.

135 **"Drawing maps is kind of like doing a Rubik's Cube":** Mary Ellen Klas, "GOP Consultant Got Sneak Peek at State Redistricting Maps," *Miami Herald*, May 19, 2014.

135 **"The fact that they're on my computer":** Ibid.

CHAPTER 9: WISCONSIN

Background for this chapter was provided by Brendan Fischer, "Wisconsin's 'Shameful' Gerrymander of 2012," Center for Media and Democracy, February 4, 2013; Bill Lueders and Kate Golden, "Redistricting Credited for GOP Success in Wisconsin Congressional Races," Center for Public Integrity, November 20, 2012; Pierce, Elliott and Meyer, "How Dark Money Helped Republicans"; and Nicholas Kusnetz, "Redistricting:

GOP and Dems Alike Have Cloaked the Process in Secrecy," Center for Public Integrity, November 1, 2012.

137 **one of the worst blizzards in 130 years:** Blizzard details from Doug Erickson and Sandy Cullen, "Snowstorm Drifts Away: Blizzard Rages Overnight, Gives Way to Immense Cleanup Effort," *Wisconsin State Journal*, February 3, 2011; and Meg Jones, "Wisconsin Is Closed for Business," *Milwaukee Journal Sentinel*, February 2, 2011.

137 **"I will likely make it in later this morning":** Hundreds of pages of emails detailing redistricting plans were made public through court challenges and by Democrats when they briefly took back the Wisconsin senate, and are available at media .jsonline.com/documents/redist-021712-emails.pdf. This email, with the subject line "Good meeting," includes among its recipients Jim Troupis, Sarah Troupis, Eric McLeod, Todd Ottman and Michael Foltz.

137 **McLeod was among three Michael Best attorneys:** Patrick Marley, "Justice Gableman Not Charged Legal Fees in Ethics Case: Justice's arrangement with firm raises questions about cases, ethics rules," *Milwaukee Journal Sentinel*, December 15, 2011.

138 **"Justice Gableman Rules Against Michael Best":** Patrick Marley, "Justice Gableman Rules Against Michael Best: Judge goes against firm that gave him free legal advice for two years," *Milwaukee Journal Sentinel*, March 27, 2012.

138 **a conference room in Michael Best's modern glass building:** Patrick Marley, "Two Legislative Aides Working out of Law Firm Office Instead of Capitol," *Milwaukee Journal Sentinel*, February 9, 2012.

138 **The legislature also hired Joe Handrick:** Patrick Marley, "Republican National Committee Got Preview of Legislative Maps," *Milwaukee Journal Sentinel*, December 28, 2011.

138 **The federal lines were in the hands of Andrew Speth:** Patrick Marley and Jason Stein, "Kind Says Ryan's Redistricting Plan Lacked Consultation," *Milwaukee Journal Sentinel*, August 13, 2012.

138 **spent $1.1 million:** Republican State Leadership Committee, "How a Strategy of Targeting State Legislative Races in 2010 Led to a Republican U.S. House Majority in 2013," 2012, available at www.redistrictingmajorityproject.com.

138 **"We'll be providing air cover":** Keith Johnson and Brody Mullins, "Redistricting Battles Spur Wave of Cash," *Wall Street Journal*, October 12, 2010.

140 **"There is no question—none":** Bill Lueders and Kate Golden, "Wisconsin Vote Split Was Closer than Results: Redistricting credited for GOP's success in congressional and legislative races," Wisconsin Center for Investigative Journalism, November 18, 2012.

140 **filed suit in July:** Mayer and the plaintiffs base their argument on a new standard called the efficiency gap, developed by University of Chicago law professor Nicholas Stephanopoulos and Eric McGhee, a research fellow at the Public Policy Institute of California. They posit that between "cracking" and "packing" districts—dividing voters of one party across a number of districts, or cramming them into a small

handful—you can measure the number of wasted votes. See Nicholas Stephanopoulos and Eric McGhee, "Partisan Gerrymandering and the Efficiency Gap," *University of Chicago Law Review*, October 1, 2014.

140 **"We're particularly frustrated":** Patrick Marley, Andrew Hahn and Meg Jones, "Democrats Sue State Election Officials over 2011 Redistricting," *Milwaukee Journal Sentinel*, July 8, 2015.

140 **"I myself am guilty":** Ibid.

141 **"There is close to a zero percent chance":** Ed Treleven, "Democrats Sue State over Redistricting, Call It 'One of the Worst' Gerrymanders Ever," *Wisconsin State Journal*, July 9, 2015.

141 **"Now, off to the races":** In the email thread "Good meeting," January 31, 2011, available at media.jsonline.com/documents/redist-021712-emails.pdf.

141 **clear $400,000:** Patrick Marley, "Republican Leader OKs Payments for Redistricting Work: Law firm helped draw legislative map favorable to GOP," *Milwaukee Journal Sentinel*, July 13, 2012. "In all," Marley wrote, "taxpayers have spent more than $1.5 million to draw the maps, defend them in court and pay a group that successfully sued over how the lines were drawn."

141 **"Four decades in office":** Patrick Marley, Daniel Bice and Jason Stein, "Lawmakers Were Made to Pledge Secrecy over Redistricting," *Milwaukee Journal Sentinel*, February 6, 2012.

142 **"Legislators will be allowed into the office":** Ibid.

142 **The agreement the legislators signed:** Ibid.

142 **"charade," "cover up a process":** "Federal Judges Scorch Wisconsin," Courthouse News Service, January 5, 2012.

142 **"Public comments on this map":** Marley, Bice and Stein, "Lawmakers Were Made to Pledge Secrecy."

142 **"I honestly don't know":** Ibid.

143 **lawyers at Michael Best had told him to share the maps:** Patrick Marley, "Republican National Committee Got Preview of Legislative Maps," *Milwaukee Journal Sentinel*, December 28, 2011.

143 **"We find those statements to be almost laughable":** The court's ruling is available at https://www.doj.state.wi.us/sites/default/files/2012-news/opinion-order-03222012_0.pdf.

143 **identical word-for-word declarations by Ottman and Foltz:** Foltz and Ottman declarations, *Baldus v. Brennan*, No. 2:11-cv-00562 (E.D. Wis.). Civil Action File No. 11-CV-562. Three-judge panel 28 U.S.C. § 2284.

143 **Fortunately, a cache of emails:** The entire collection of emails is available at http://media.jsonline.com/documents/redist-021712-emails.pdf.

143 **Wisconsin Republicans wanted to pack as many Hispanic voters:** Ibid.

143 **"areas we will be most interested in":** Ibid.

144 **"By wildly gerrymandering the 7th Assembly District":** Ibid.

144 **Gaddie provided complex algorithms:** Ibid.

144 **to get conservative Hispanic leaders to support the plans:** Ibid.

145 **"Manny is talking right now to MALDEF":** Ibid.

145 **"Mike Wild loaded it onto the computer . . . e-mailed it to Eric McLeod":** Speth's deposition is available at https://assets.documentcloud.org/documents/539678/dep-of-andrew-speth-dkt-143–11cv562.pdf.

146 **"Quite frankly the Legislature . . . any less political":** The judge's ruling is available at http://wispolitics.com/1006/20311976122.pdf.

CHAPTER 10: IOWA

148 **91 percent:** Iowa census details are available at http://quickfacts.census.gov/qfd/states/19000.html.

149 **Kibbie voted in favor of the plan, then resigned:** James Q. Lynch, "Five Senators Tender Resignations: Recent redistricting activated quirk in state law," *Cedar Rapids Gazette*, February 1, 2012.

149 **Redistricting here is filled with trust:** The entire process is spelled out in Legislative Service Agency, "Legislative Guide to Redistricting in Iowa," available at https://www.legis.iowa.gov/docs/Central/Guides/redist.pdf.

149 **an ethnic and immigrant melting pot with a communitarian streak:** Colin Woodard's discussion of Iowa's ethnic and religious history and how it shaped the state's unique politics is a fascinating read: "Yes, Iowa Still Matters," *Politico*, December 2, 2005.

149 **more competitive congressional races:** Ronald Brownstein, "Iowa Puts Politicians Through the Paces," *Los Angeles Times*, October 15, 2002.

152 **Iowa districts had dramatically uneven populations:** NPR's *Weekend Edition* with Linda Wertheimer did a terrific history of Iowa redistricting on April 21, 2007, available at http://www.npr.org/templates/story/story.php?storyId=9750943.

152 **they be balanced after the 1970 census:** Public Interest Institute, "Malapportionment and the 'Miracle' of Iowa," June 2013.

152 **Just weeks before the 1972 filing deadline:** The entire history is given in Legislative Services Agency, "Legislative Guide to Redistricting in Iowa."

CHAPTER 11: ARIZONA

160 **Furious, sputtering Arizonans:** Video and transcripts of the Arizona redistricting commission meetings are available on its website, www.azredistricting.org.

161 **the selection of a company called Strategic Telemetry:** Frederic I. Solop and Ajang A. Salkhi, "Redistricting in Arizona: An Independent Process Challenged by Partisan Politics," in Miller and Walling, eds., *The Political Battle Over Congressional Redistricting*, is a detailed guide to the demographics of Arizona and the ins and outs of the 2000 and 2010 processes. Evan Wyloge, "Redistricting Panel Hires D.C.-Based, Democratically Connected Mapping Firm," *Arizona Capitol Times*, June 29, 2011, and an Associated Press story by Paul Davenport, "Redistricting Embroiled in Politics Early," July 9, 2011, tracked the commission's progress.

162 **the pen of Ruth Bader Ginsburg:** The Supreme Court's ruling in the AIRC case is available at http://www.supremecourt.gov/opinions/14pdf/13–1314_kjfl.pdf.

162 **the California redistricting panel would be rendered unconstitutional:** Phil Willon and Christine Mai-Duc, "Why the Supreme Court's Redistricting Decision Matters for California," *Los Angeles Times*, June 29, 2015.

163 **"No matter how concerned we may be":** The Supreme Court's ruling in *Arizona State Legislature v. Arizona Independent Redistricting Commission* is available at http://www.supremecourt.gov/opinions/14pdf/13–1314_kjfl.pdf.

164 **an empty-nester:** The best piece on Pederson and the referendum push is Amy Silverman, "What's My Line?", *Phoenix New Times*, October 5, 2000.

164 **Every legislative map since the 1970 reapportionment:** Solop and Salkhi, "Redistricting in Arizona."

166 **an independent commission of five:** Solop and Salkhi, "Redistricting in Arizona."

166 **Voters backed it 56 percent to 44 percent:** Silverman, "What's My Line?"

166 **half-hearted, underfunded Republican opposition targeted Pederson's wealth:** Ibid.

167 **additional conspiracy theories about his wife's independence:** Stephen Lemons, "Arizona's Redistricting Commission Should Regard the Tea Party as Disruptive Loons," *Phoenix New Times*, July 28, 2011.

168 **impeached on a party line vote:** Mary Jo Pitzi, "Arizona Redistricting Chief Ousted," *Arizona Republic*, November 2, 2011.

168 **"Gross misconduct . . . does not like":** Bruce Cain, "Redistricting Commissions: A Better Political Buffer?", *Yale Law Journal*, April 10, 2012.

169 **"They're stonewalling":** Marc Lacey, "Arizona Redistricting Commission Is under Attack, Even Before its Work Is Done," *New York Times*, September 3, 2011.

169 **"The gun is loaded":** "Brewer Not Champing at the Bit, Either," Yellow Sheet Report, *Arizona Capitol Times*, July 14, 2001.

172 **"The maps performed like they were designed":** Rebekah L. Sanders, "Arizona Election Adds to Debate over Redistricting," *Arizona Republic*, November 23, 2012.

173 **"We thought we'd try to pick up every Hispanic":** Ibid.

173 *Harris v. Arizona Independent Redistricting Commission:* Evan Wyloge and Gary Grado, "Democrats Deny Republican Allegations that Redistricting Process Was Rigged," *Arizona Capitol Times*, March 29, 2013. Also, ADI News Services, "'Interesting' IRC Suit to Be Heard This Week," *Arizona Daily Independent*, March 24, 2013. The judges' rulings are available at https://casetext.com/case/harris-v-ariz-indep-redistricting-commn.

174 **"A finding that the partisanship":** Justice John Roberts, in 576 U.S. ___ (2015) [sic], available at http://www.supremecourt.gov/opinions/14pdf/13–1314_kjfl.pdf.

174 **FAIR Trust:** Kim Barker and Theodoric Meyer, "The Dark Money Man: How Sean Noble moved the Koch's cash into politics and made millions," *ProPublica*, February 14, 2014.

175 **"They clearly were doing somebody's bidding":** Ibid.

175 **"the recommendations they've made":** Evan Wyloge, "FAIR game? How GOP Politicians Are Trying to Secretly Influence the IRC," *Arizona Capitol Times*, October 31, 2011.

175 **"never placed a phone call," "nor have I spoken":** Jeremy Duda, "Marilyn Quayle Refutes Rumors that She Called Brewer on Redistricting," *Arizona Capitol Times*, November 7, 2011.

175 **three Republican state senators had told him that Quayle made the call:** John Celock, "Marilyn Quayle, Dan Quayle's Wife, Said to Have Called Jan Brewer about Arizona Redistricting," *Huffington Post*, November 6, 2011.

176 **"might lose some of their power":** Terry Goddard and Paul Johnson, "Stop Attacking Redistricting Commission," *Arizona Republic*, August 27, 2011.

CHAPTER 12: A THEOREM TO DETECT RATFUCKING

183 **Wang explained:** Sam Wang, "The Great Gerrymander of 2012," *New York Times*, February 3, 2013.

185 **In *Davis v. Bandemer*:** Available at https://supreme.justia.com/cases/federal/us/478/109/.

185 **in *Vieth v. Jubelirer*:** Available at http://caselaw.findlaw.com/us-supreme-court/541/267.html.

190 **"We don't have the luxury":** Thomas Mann, "Election 2016: Dumbing Down American Politics, Lawrence Lessig and the Presidency," Brookings Institute, August 27, 2015.

193 **the state Supreme Court finally signed off:** Jeremy Wallace and Mary Ellen Klas, "Legislature Won't Appeal Redistricting Ruling," *Miami Herald*, January 20, 2016.

194 **"I support redistricting reform dramatically":** Jim Siegel, "End Gerrymandering, Kasich Says," *Columbus Dispatch*, December 26, 2015.

194 **"Elected candidates can serve with a credibility and mandate":** Dick Woodberry, "No More Spoilers, a Focus on the Issues: Six Reasons It's Time for Ranked Choice Voting in Maine," *Bangor Daily News*, January 26, 2015.

195 **multi-member districts and ranked-choice voting:** FairVote's reports on ranked-choice voting are available at http://www.fairvote.org/rankedchoicevoting#research_rcvamericanexperience. Their reports on redistricting are available at http://www.fairvote.org/redistricting#research_redistrictingoverview.

196 **a study predicting every single congressional race in 2016:** Available at www.fairvote.org/monopolypolitics.

198 **"We are not auditioning for fearless leader":** David Frum, "Norquist: Romney Will Do as Told," *Daily Beast*, February 13, 2012.

CODA

204 **The rebels take little or no political risk:** Hedrick Smith, "Gerrymandering May Prove a Pyrrhic Victory for the GOP," *Los Angeles Times*, October 7, 2015.

204 **Shuler took one look at the new lines:** Shuler's struggle, and Asheville's, is told in a great article by Tracy Jan, "Turning the Political Map into a Partisan Weapon," *Boston Globe*, June 23, 2013.

205 **"2012 is the time":** Joshua Miller, "Candidate Appears to Flirt with Birtherism," *Roll Call*, June 26, 2012.

205 **"People who disagree with me":** Josh Siegel, "Home in North Carolina, Mark Meadows Reflects on Move to Oust John Boehner with 'No Regrets,'" *Daily Signal*, August 24, 2015.

206 **But when Boehner caved:** Ryan Lizza, "Where the GOP's Suicide Caucus Lives," *New Yorker*, September 25, 2013.

206 **"The Republican Party continues to demonstrate":** Thomas E. Mann and Norman J. Ornstein, *It's Even Worse Than It Looks* (New York: Basic Books, 2013).

211 **"Republicans are gaining more influence":** Jacob Hacker and Paul Pierson, "No Cost for Extremism," *American Prospect*, Spring 2015.

212 **"Back in 1995, 79 House Republicans":** Ronald Brownstein, "Republicans More Insulated Against Backlash," *National Journal*, October 1, 2013.

213 **The most comprehensive study yet of voters, non-voters and presidential-year-only voters:** Available at http://people.umass.edu/schaffne/ansolabehere_schaffner_core_periphery.pdf. Sean McElwee broke it down in "The GOP's Stunning Election Advantage," *Salon*, December 5, 2015.

217 **In the previous decade, from 2002 through 2010:** A study sponsored by the League of Women Voters, "When the People Draw the Lines" by Raphael J. Sonenshein, declared it a success (available at www.cavotes.org/redistrictingreport). A FairVote analysis was less convinced that the success was meaningful; see http://www.fairvote.org/did-the-california-citizens-redistricting-commission-really-create-more-competitive-districts.

218 **"Democrats met behind closed doors":** Lisa Vorderbrueggen, "California Democrats Secretly Influenced Drawing of New Political District Boundaries," *Contra Costa Times*, December 21, 2011.

218 **"I thought the commission did a so-so job":** Todd Purdum, "California's Redistricting Success in Jeopardy?", *Politico*, March 1, 2015.

219 **convinced Governor John Kasich:** Kasich's change of mind is chronicled in Caitlin Yilek, "Kasich Wants an End to Gerrymandering in Ohio," *The Hill*, December 26, 2015.

219 **"the interest in enhancing":** Stevens, *Six Amendments*.

219 **FairVote's proposals for multi-member districts:** Fairvote.org is a treasure trove of research, interactive models, and smart, forward-looking ideas.

220 **"We're late to the game":** Jonathan Martin, "Democrats Unveil a Plan to Fight Gerrymandering," *New York Times*, August 3, 2015.

220 **"REDMAP 2020 will work to maintain":** Republican State Leadership Committee, "RSLC Launches REDMAP 2020, Sets $125 Million Investment Goal," press release, July 16, 2015.

221 **Ronald Reagan sat for a long interview:** The interview can be seen at https://www.youtube.com/watch?v=EfTb_pKiEoY.

ACKNOWLEDGMENTS

This book owes so much to so many. I want to start with Chris Jankowski, who generously cleared a day and spoke with candor and intelligence about REDMAP, with a writer whom he knew had a different set of politics, and at a time before this book had taken shape. His political acumen may be unrivalled among his generation of strategists; he is a true gentleman as well.

Many others gave freely of their time and insights, both on and off the record. I'd especially like to thank two other brilliant GOP minds in Michigan, Bob LaBrant and Jeff Timmer. In Iowa, Ed Cook, Governor Terry Branstad, House Speaker Kraig Paulsen, Senate Majority Leader Mike Gronstal and Congressman Jim Leach were kind and thoughtful hosts.

Past and present members of the Arizona Independent Redistricting Commission opened up about their experiences, including Colleen Mathis, Linda McNulty, Scott Freeman, Steven Lynn, Daniel Elder and James Huntwork. Willie Desmond had me to his home to explain the inner workings of Maptitude. Thanks also to Jim Pederson and Terry Goddard.

In Pennsylvania, David Levdansky spent an entire Sunday with me poring through his records and reliving his difficult 2010 defeat. Mary Ellen Balchunis and Bill Thomas drove me across Pennsylvania's wildly sprawling 7th district, and showed me just how hard it is—and how dedicated you must be—to seek office in a district that looks like Donald Duck kicking Goofy.

The passionate reformers at FairVote made me their guest at the National Democracy Slam and spent the busy morning after that with me in their offices; my deep appreciation to Rob Richie, Drew Spencer and the entire team for the important work they do. Also in Washington, DC, my thanks to congressmen David Price, Steve Israel and their staffs, as well as NBC's Chuck Todd and former congressmen Martin Frost and John Tanner.

I am also indebted to Michael Li at the Brennan Center for Justice, Sam Wang at Princeton University and Tim Storey of the National Council of State Legislators. Also my appreciation and thanks to, among many others, Kathleen Clyde, Mark Salling, Norman Ornstein, David Kessler, Margaret Dickson, Gerry Hebert, Jeff Danielson, Gary Kroeger, Paul Johnson, former congressman Christopher Shays, Jeff Wattrick, Jon Hoadley and Jeremy Moss.

My thanks, as well, to the redistricting scholars who either shared their time and research, or whose work this book stands on: Nate Persily of Stanford, Jacob Hacker of Yale, Paul Pierson at the University of California Berkeley, Michael McDonald of the University of Florida and his essential United States Election Project website (electproject. org/redistricting), Justin Levitt at Loyola Law School and his magnificent resource All About Redistricting (redistricting.lls.edu), Theda Skocpol of Harvard University, and everyone at Ohio State's Moritz College of Law and their terrific site at moritzlaw.osu.edu/election-law. As a political science student, I was lucky enough to study with inspiring professors including Marc Landy and William Schneider at Boston College, and Thad Beyle at the University of North Carolina at Chapel Hill.

This book also stands on work done by many terrific scholars and journalists. Ari Berman's *Give Us the Ballot* is a peerless look at the Voting Rights Act and helped me assemble parts of the North Carolina history. The Institute for Southern Studies did essential work on the 2010 campaign and its aftermath in North Carolina, as did Jane

Mayer in the *New Yorker*. My thanks to them all. The contributors to *The Political Battle Over Congressional Redistricting*, edited by William J. Miller and Jeremy D. Walling, provided helpful background for several states. Jim Slagle of the Ohio Campaign for Accountable Redistricting almost single-handedly revealed the backroom dealings in that state, and his Freedom of Information Act requests and reports laid out the story. Robert Draper's study of Thomas Hofeller in the *Atlantic* is magazine writing at its very best.

Justin Elliott, Olga Pierce, Kim Barker and Theodoric Meyer at *ProPublica* did perhaps more than any other reporters to uncover the dark money connections behind REDMAP and the redistricting that followed. Their work was an amazing resource, and Justin, a passionate and tenacious reporter, generously shared documents he and his colleagues uncovered.

I'm indebted to, among many others, the work of Jeffrey Toobin and Michael Kelly in the *New Yorker,* David Wasserman of the *Cook Political Report,* David Weigel now of the *Washington Post,* Nicholas Confessore of the *New York Times,* Ronald Brownstein of *National Journal,* Stephen Ohlemacher of the Associated Press and Tim Dickinson of *Rolling Stone.*

I'm also deeply appreciative of the brilliant work done by state capital reporters in states where redistricting spilled into the courts. I'd particularly like to thank Patrick Marley of the *Milwaukee Journal-Sentinel*, Mary Ellen Klas of the *Miami Herald*, Mary Jo Pitzi of the *Arizona Republic*, and Jeremy Duda and Evan Wyloge of the *Arizona Capitol Times*. Their work was heroic and indispensable. At a time when state capital reporting has been undervalued and dramatically reduced by newspapers, they stand as journalistic beacons.

Maps by the University of Sheffield urban studies and planning professor Alasdair Rae made the effects of gerrymandering transparent and easy to understand. Timothy Hodler's fact-checking saved me time and again. Brendan Gauthier, Katie Yee, Jessica Mendenhall and Jacqueline Welsh provided valuable transcription work.

Thomas Frank was there at the beginning with kind words and inspiration.

There's no better job in journalism than working with the talented and devoted team at *Salon*. My thanks to our CEO Cindy Jeffers and everyone on the brilliant editorial team, past and present, whose dedication is an around-the-clock marvel.

The opportunities I have had in journalism have been made possible by Chris Morrill, Gary Duchane, Kyrie O'Connor, Bernie Davidow, Brian Toolan, Mary Dolan, Bennie Ivory, Arnold Garson and Kerry Lauerman, and my deep appreciation to all of them for their faith, kindness and mentorship.

My thanks as well to Bill Curry, Bertis Downs, Brian Weinberg, Tom Navin, Mike O'Neill and Scott Timberg, who read early versions, offered valuable and thoughtful advice, and kept me on the right path. Thank you to Paul Specht for the jacket photo. Thank you, Jack McFadden, Melissa Geoffroy, Kristen Fabiszewski, Molly Ringwald and Panio Gianopoulos.

No writer—especially with a first book—could be luckier than to land with the dynamic and brilliant team at W. W. Norton and Liveright. My boundless thanks to Phil Marino, Peter Miller, Cordelia Calvert, Will Menaker, Katie Adams, Allegra Houston, and Bill Rusin. Thanks as well to Peter Hildick-Smith of Codex. Elizabeth Riley of Norton made this book possible in countless ways, both big and small.

My agent, Alice Martell, brought this all to life. Her enthusiasm and high spirits for this project kept me aloft at numerous times. She believed in the importance of this book and guided me through the process with patience, kindness and tremendous care. Thank you for everything.

I'd long been told that there's no finer book editor in all of publishing than Bob Weil, and what amazing fortune to learn up-close exactly how true that is. Bob's passion for this project has been its soul from the very beginning. His careful and attentive edits turned court transcripts and reporting into narrative storytelling. His high standards pushed me to go deeper than I'd imagined. This book emerged from our shared belief, discovered over a first lunch, that much of our country's political dysfunction stems from gerrymandering. His faith that I could explain this big picture, and his friendship and generosity throughout this time, was a sustaining force.

We lost my dad, Donald Daley, suddenly and unexpectedly while I was reporting in Iowa. I've always been blessed with family generous beyond belief, but my aunt and uncle, Benson and Cathy Treadow, my cousin Julie and her husband Matt Brennan outdid themselves to hold us all together during the days and weeks that followed. It's something I can never repay and will never forget. I'm equally blessed by sensational in-laws, Sarah and George Smedes, my sister-in-law Kate Smedes and her partner Kristen Murray. Endless love to you all.

My mom, Toby Daley, has been a tower of strength and unconditional support for forty-five years. I have lacked for nothing thanks to her love and sacrifices. Somehow, she's an even better grandmother.

My amazing wife, Jennifer Smedes, lived every word of this book with me. She's my best friend, my best editor and sounding board, and makes me better every day. Her patience and thoughtfulness and love pushed this over the finish line. I am extraordinarily lucky to have her by my side. Wyatt Hudson is an everyday wonder and the best thing we've ever done. Here's hoping we've solved this gerrymandering problem by the time you cast your first congressional vote in 2032.

I miss you every day, Dad, and wish you were here for this. This book is for you.

INDEX

ABOUT THE AUTHOR

David Daley is the editor in chief of *Salon* and the Digital Media Fellow for the Wilson School of Humanities and the Arts and the Grady School of Journalism at the University of Georgia. His work has also appeared in *National Journal, Rolling Stone, New York* magazine, *Interview, USA Today, Details* and many other publications. He is a graduate of Boston College and attended journalism school at the University of North Carolina at Chapel Hill. He lives in Brooklyn, New York, with his wife and son.

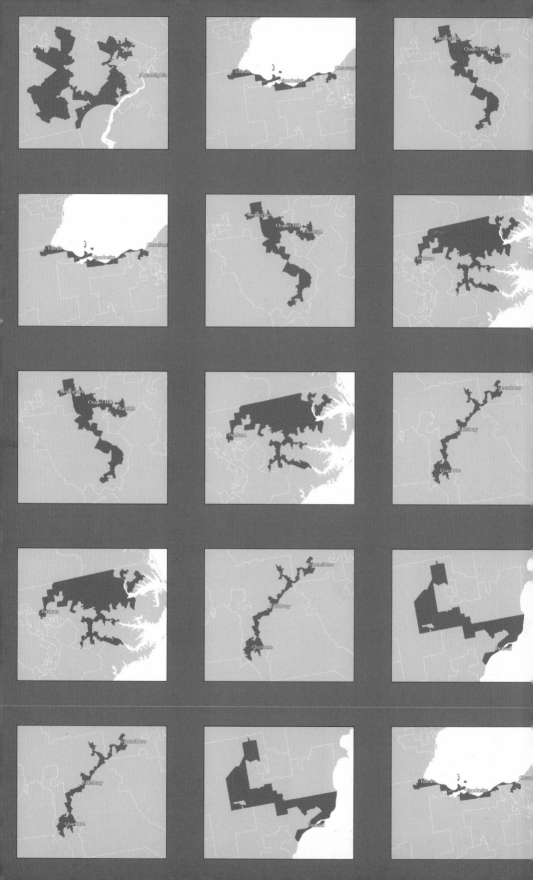